Scouting Around The Mendips 1909-2007

The history of Scouting in and around Weston-super-Mare

Duncan K Siddall

Scouting Around The Mendips 1909-2007

The history of Scouting in and around Weston-super-Mare

By D. R. Biddulph

Published by D. R. Biddulph

ISBN – 978-0-9559970-0-6

Printed and bound in Great Britain by:
Limited Editions, Remus House, Coltsfoot Drive
Woodston, Peterborough PE2 9JX

Contributors

1st Weston-Super-Mare (YMCA)	Mr D Andrews, Mr C Copp, Mr D Tottle, Mr C Norman, Mr E F Redman, Mr M White, Mrs M Haynes, Mr R Johns, Mr T Dunstone
2nd Weston (Clarence Park)	Mr R Faraghar
3rd Weston-Super-Mare (St Paul's)	Mr R Ivens, Mr D Perriman, Mr I Thomas Mrs D Dexter, Mr P Neathway, Mr M Timms
4th Weston-Super-Mare (St Saviour's)	Mr A Marshall, Mr C Hart, Mr P Holley, Mr P Robinson
7th Weston-Super-Mare (1st Uphill)	Mr C Hart, Mrs A Hodgin, Mr R Lay, Mr P Austin, Mr D Perriman
8th Weston (Hill Road)	Mr A J Glass
9th Weston-Super-Mare (Emmanuel)	Mr R Faraghar
17th Weston-S-Mare (Broadoak)	Mr J Anderson, Mr P Austin, Mr Spillane, Mr R Ivens, Mr P Robinson, Mr K Tucker, Mrs Court, Mrs Goold, Mr D Whittington, Rev'd Piper
19th Weston-S-Mare (Milton & Worle)	Mr D Perriman, Mr S Gambling, Mr A Slingsby Mr S Coombs, Mr R Cooke, Mr D Poole
20th Weston-S-Mare (Upper Milton)(Upper Milton)	Mr K Blake, Mr K Trego
24th Weston-S-Mare (Hill Road)	Mr S Coombs, Mr A J Glass, Mr P Harris, Mr C Hart, Mr J Codrington, Mr C Raymond, Mr T Gilbert, Mr P Hoskins, Mr Eastman, Mrs J Bird, Mr R Spindler, Mr T Brown, Mr P Robinson
29th Weston-S-Mare (St Peter's)	Mrs B Atherton, Mrs J Dunstone, Mrs N Sparkes, Mrs Ayliffe, Mr D Cox, Mr J Underhay,

	Rev. D Taylor, Mr K Dudley, Mrs E Nock, Mr D L Biddulph
32nd Weston-S-Mare (Oldmixon)	Mrs A Coombs
33rd Weston-S-Mare (1st Worle)	Mrs J Kattana, Mrs P Langley, Mrs E Nock
1st North Worle	Mr P Elliot, Mr K Kattana
2nd Worle (Meadvale)	Mr K Peters, Mrs A Coombs
1st Ashcombe	Mr R Spindler, Mr K Dudley, Mr & Mrs M & J White, Mr T Brown, Mrs D Biddulph, Mr D R Biddulph
1st Axbridge	Mr M Bass, Mr K Peters
1st Banwell	Mr & Mrs K & J Kattana, Mrs K Edwards
1st Blagdon	Mrs P Riley
1st Bleadon	Mr H Boyce, Mr D S Biddulph
1st Burrington & Wrington	Mr P Endicott, Mr M Parsons, Mr P Badman
1st Cheddar	Mrs E Mills, Mr G Burnell, Mr T Dyer
1st Congresbury	Mr K Hill, Mrs A Ballard
1st Kewstoke	Mrs P Langley, Mr M White
1st East Harptree	Mr D Lions, Mr W Beer
1st Hutton	Mr D Sutton
1st Redhill	Mr M Parsons, Mr J Ashman
1st Sandford	Mr D Perriman
1st Shipham	Mr & Mrs D Rogers, Mrs S Ovenden, Mrs P Hoyland
1st Wedmore	Mr & Mrs A & V Banwell, Mr & Mrs W & N Belshaw
1st Winscombe	Mr & Mrs M Turner, Mr K Peters, Mr R Faraghar, Mrs P Evans
2nd Winscombe (Sidcot School)	Ms C Gladwin, Mr R Hinton

District, County and Beyond

Mrs Ann Coombs, (District Secretary) Mr B Taylor, (former DC), Mr R Ivens, (Avon Scout County Archivist) Mr P Bourner (Somerset Scout County Archives), Mrs P Styles & Mr P Molyeux (Gilwell HQ Archives), Mr & Mrs Nock (Axe Fellowship)

Thanks to Volkan Kan for his digital remastering of the photographs.

Contents

The Town Groups

1st Ashcombe	(Weston-Super-Mare)
1st Milton	(Weston-Super-Mare)
1st Weston	(YMCA)
2nd Weston	(St Saviour's)
	(Etonhurst)
	(Clarence Park Baptist)
3rd Weston	(District Troop)
	(St Paul's)
4th Weston	(Etonhurst)
	(St Saviour's)
5th Weston	(Worlebury)
	(Christchurch)
6th Weston	(Kingsholme School)
	(Milton)
	(Brynmelyn School)
7th Weston	(Christchurch)
	(Uphill)
	(Ashcombe)
8th Weston	(Worle)
	(Weston)
	(Hill Road Methodist)

9th Weston	(Victoria Methodist)
	(Emmanuel/Mendip)
10th Weston	(St Martin's Worle)
	(The College)
11th Weston	
12th Weston	(Boulevard Congregational Church)
13th Weston	
14th Weston	(Corpus Christi, Roman Catholic)
15th Weston	(Petergate School)
16th Weston	
17th Weston	(County/Grammar School/ Broadoak School)
18th Weston	(Good Shepherd)
19th Weston	(St Jude's/Milton & Worle)
20th Weston	(Moorland Road Congregational Church)
	(Milton Methodist)
21st Weston	(Sunnyside Methodist)
22nd Weston	(St Peter's School)
23rd Weston	
24th Weston	(Hill Road Methodist)
25th Weston	(St John's)
26th Weston	(Holy Trinity)
	(Salvation Army)
27th Weston	(Salvation Army)
	(Bourneville St Andrew's/Birnbeck)
28th Weston	(Lancaster House/ Holy Trinity)
29th Weston	(St Peter's Milton)
30th Weston	(Wadham Street Baptists)
31st Weston	(Church of the Latter Day Saints)
32nd Weston	(Oldmixon)
33rd Weston/	(1st Worle)
1st Worle	(1st North Worle)
	(1st Worle Village)
34th Weston	(Baytree School)
2nd Worle	(Meadvale)

The Village Groups

Bibliography

Springhall J 'Youth, Empire and Society', London, Croon Helm, 1977

Lord Baden-Powell R 'Scouting for Boys. A handbook for instruction and good citizenship' Oxford, Oxford University Press, Reprint of 1908 version in 2005,

Thurman J 'The Patrol Leaders Handbook', Rochester, Staples, 1950

Gilcraft 'Wolf Cubs', London, C Arthur Pearson Ltd, 1928 (1958)

The Boy Scout Association 'The Senior Scout Handbook', London, The Boy Scout Association, 1948 (1951)

The Boy Scout Association 'The Road Ahead', London, The Boy Scout Association, 1945

Weston-super-Mare Local Association 'Report of the Scout Commission of Enquiry',
Weston-S-Mare A E Allen, Oct 1946

Kingsmill A 'A School in the Forties. Weston-super-Mare Grammar schools 1940-49', Nottingham, Karanfil Press, 2005

Archives

Anderson J Axemen Axe District Scout Band 1983-2001

Coombs A Axe Scout District Archive 1950-present (1910-50 for North West District)

3rd Weston (St Paul's) Scout Group Archive 1928-93

18th Weston (Good Shepherd) Scout Group Archive 1931-37 (part of the 3rd Weston Archive)

Cooke R & Perriman D 19th Weston (St/Jude's/Milton & Worle) Scout Group Archive
1932-43 & 1948-1999

Harris P 24th Weston (Hill Road) Scout Group Archive 1942-2000

Biddulph D R 29th Weston (St Peter's) Scout Group Archive 1963-99

Wedmore Scout Group 1st Wedmore Scout Group Archive 1919-current

Hart C 1st Uphill Scout Group Archive 1951-2002

A note on terminology

Like most organisations, the Scout movement has a number of shorthand terms which for the sake of brevity during the text are utilised. Below is a list of the terms and their meanings for those readers who may need a reference to the terms.

ABSL	Assistant Beaver Scout Leader
ARSL	Assistant Rover Scout Leader
ACM	Assistant Cub Scout Master, the term was used until 1967, to describe an adult who assisted with the running of the Wolf Cub Pack.
ACSL	Assistant Cub Scout Leader. Master was replaced with 'leader'.
ASM	Assistant Scout Master
ASL	Assistant Scout Leader.
BST	Boy Scout Troop
Boy Scout	A member of the movement aged between eleven and eighteen used during the years 1908-67
BSL	Beaver Scout Leader
CM	CubMaster or CubMistress
DC	District Commissioner appointed to oversee a District
ADC	Assistant District Commissioner
GSA	The latest term used to describe anyone who assisted in any of the sections but does not need to undergo formal training, replaces the term Helper
GSM	Group Scout Master, appointed from 1928 onwards to oversee the operation of the Scout Group.
GSL	Group Scout Leader, replaced the GSM term from 1967.
RSL	Rover Scout Leader
Rovers	The older section for young men aged eighteen to twenty five
RSC	Rover Scout Crew
Sea Scouts	Scouting that had provision for water orientated activities
Senior Scouts	The section was formed in 1945 for boys aged between fifteen to eighteen, which operated either

	as a separate section or, where numbers were too few, as a distinct Patrol within a Troop. Patrols were named after Great adventurers or heroes, examples include Guy Gibson and Captain Scott.
SSL	Senior Scout Leader
SG	Scout Group
WCP	Wolf Cub Pack
Wolf Cubs	Members of the movement aged between eight to eleven from 1916-67, post 1967 referred to as cub scouts.

Key dates

The registration of Wolf Cub Packs, Scout Troops and Rover Scout Crews was until 1919 done locally. After this date National Headquarters began to register these sections. At this point in time each section was registered independently, so although a Wolf Cub Pack and Boy Scout Troop may be called, for example, 7th Weston, they were two separate entities, the Boy Scout Troop was registered with the number 15043, and the Wolf Cub Pack 9591. With the creation of Scout Groups in 1928, these individual sections were brought together under a Scout Group, led by a Group Scout Master, in itself a new title. All Groups that were operating at that time were reassigned a new number, for example, the above mentioned 7th Weston was given the Group number 4234. From this point forward the numbering of all successive Scout Groups dates from this numbering system. The fact that we have Groups now numbered such as 46632 for the 1st Bristol Muslim Scout Group reveals that since 1928 46632 Scout Groups have been registered, of which around 10,000 are providing Scouting today. Although the number and title, such as 10th Weston or 69th Bristol, may be reassigned, the Group registration number is not. Each new Group gets a unique number.

As we know, the Boy Scouts were started in 1908. BP's initial test camp was exactly that, to test out his ideas. The earliest Troops that can be traced back to 1908, and there are some groups out there that can trace an unbroken history back to those early days, such as the 55th (St Mary's) Bristol Scout Group. Following the rapid take up of Scouting before the Great War, younger brothers of Scouts began to ask for a section for themselves, some pioneering Troops started a junior section. However it was not until 1916 that Wolf Cubs were officially started. The next development in the movement was the formation of Rover Scouts in 1919, which sought to extend the Scouting experience for boys aged over eighteen. The development of Senior Scouting was not undertaken until the closing years of the Second World War when experiments were undertaken to provide a senior Troop for boys aged between fifteen to eighteen. This section went 'live' nationally in 1945. Probably the greatest change to the movement was implementation of the Advance Report in 1967 which, following several years of investigation and questionnaires, saw the disbanding of Rover and Senior Scouts to be replaced with the Venture Scout Unit. The age ranges were also adjusted with the Troop catering for boys aged between eleven to fifteen and a half/sixteen, whilst the newly formed Venture Scout section catered for boys up to their twentieth birthday. The loss of the Rovers was keenly felt amongst some. Although the Rover section had never been numerically strong, it numbered less than the total of warranted leaders, the comradeship that it engendered is still fondly remembered by old Rovers to this day.

Among other changes the Advance Report sought to strengthen Groups which had either insufficient leaders or young members through consolidations (amalgamations). The terminology was also changed with the words Wolf, Boy and Master being dropped. Leaders would be the term used for all adult warranted leaders henceforth.

Further developments saw the nationwide introduction of Beaver Scouting for six to eight year olds in 1984, although this model had been running since the late 1960s in Northern Ireland. Initially the new section was an associate member of the movement, although it was soon to be brought into the Scouting family officially. The original scarves were turquoise and worn nationally, irrespective of the Group colours. This was changed and Group scarves were adopted by the Beavers. During 1991 probably the most fundamental change occurred when girls were allowed to join the Scouts. In Weston, 2nd Worle were the first Group to adapt to this change. This was a voluntary policy until January 2008 when all Groups had to take in girls into any section. The vast majority of Groups had already done so by this time and found that mixed membership had its advantages.

Changes were again on the cards in 2002-04 with the disbanding of Venture Scout Units to be replaced by District based Explorer Scout Units (or cells) to cater for young people aged between fourteen to eighteen and a County based Network for eighteen to twenty-five year old members. The latter had a few teething troubles and most Districts now have a cell of Network Scouts.

Over the years the movement has reviewed and updated its progressive training programme, with the original Scout First Class and Second Class giving way to the Scout Standard and Advanced Scout standard, before again being revamped into the Scout Award, Explorer and Pathfinder Scout awards and, finally, in 2002 into the present system of challenges and activity badges. Above this all has been the highest Award available, the Chief Scouts Award for Scouts and the Queens Scout Award to members of the Seniors, Ventures and now Explorer section. The Duke of Edinburgh's scheme runs alongside the Scouting awards and many Groups take advantage of this scheme.

Foreword

Welcome to this history of Scouting around the Mendips, or rather the segment of the Mendip Hills that was roughly covered geographically by the North West and later Axe Districts. There is still enough material to ensure at least another book about the Scout Groups that met on or under the shadow of these beautiful hills and which belong to other Districts, for example, Bath, Clevedon and the other half of the North West District which is now named Gordano District, or even further to parts of the current Sedgemoor District.

For those readers who are curious to know what inspired the author to undertake this project, it grew out a keen interest in history, coupled with an active role in the Scout movement. The project developed in three stages; the first and second stages did not reveal just how large an undertaking this was to become. The initial idea germinated from a desire to record the history of the recently amalgamated 29th Weston (St Peter's) Scout Group, where I had been a Cub, Scout and later a Venture Scout, between 1985-94. I had started my Scouting experience as an eight year old Cub in Yardley, Birmingham, at the 261st Birmingham Scout Group, Scouting being in the family, as my father had been a Cub Scout and my Uncle was still actively involved in the City's Scouting community, as GSL at 34th Birmingham Scout Group. My recollections of my Scouting days are of happy memories of campfire cooking, activities and sleeping out under canvas, the inevitable wet camps, the occasional tent blowing down whilst I slept through the incident, much to my leaders' amusement. The discovery of a Scout's two favourite things, fire and water, continue to be a feature of my Scouting, as I still enjoy in participating and leading campfires as well as raft building. For some reason most people can recall their first camp. For me that was a weekend Cub camp at Goblin Combe in 1986, in more or less sunny weather. The highlight of the weekend, apart from the food - I still have a passion for camp stew - was the archery session using home made bows.

I have been a Leader in the movement since November 1999, having been a Scouter in Weston, Barnsley and currently Bristol and Taunton, working with every section from Ventures down to Beavers and I enjoy the challenge and rewards that all these sections offer.

In the autumn of 1999 the 29th Weston had recently amalgamated with the nearby 19th Weston Group and I decided that before the memory of the Group faded away that an effort should be made to record the history of our Group. The process began with the tracing of former leaders, including Mrs Babs Atherton, Mr Delwyn Cox, the founder of the Group, and Mrs Ayliffe, Mrs Dunstone and Mrs Sparkes, whose late husbands had been the original leaders of the Group. Following up this work it quickly became apparent that several leaders had been connected with other Groups, particularly the 24th Weston (Hill Road) Group. Rather than leave that material out I decided to expand the research to other local Groups, starting with the neighbouring 19th Weston, where I was a sometime member of the Celts Venture Scout Unit, and then moving on to include the 3rd Weston (St Paul's), where I started out in my leadership role as a Unit Helper, stepping up to the warranted position of Assistant Venture Scout Leader, and later Assistant Scout Leader.

Around 2001 the notion that writing a history of all the Groups within the District would be a worthwhile project struck me. Little was I to realise that it would take over six years of research, with encouragement from former leaders, resulting in over seventy Groups being recorded ranging from the very start of Scouting in the Mendips through to the present day, 2008, and a bedroom full of memorabilia and records. I have thoroughly enjoyed my research. The opportunity to meet new people and discuss a favourite mutual pastime has been a delight, as have the anecdotes, recollections, and photographs that have been shared. Much of the material has come to me from individual members, both past and present, of Scouting who have shared their recollections with a very grateful author. Documentary evidence has been utilised in conjunction with oral history to try and create an interesting account of the history of Scouting. However, as the early years are beyond living memory now thus, up until the conclusion of the Great War, I have had to rely upon fragmentary documentary evidence.

The earliest oral testimony comes from a former Redhill Scout, who was a Scout in the mid 1920s and recalled attending the Arrowhead Park Jamboree in 1929.

The documentary evidence has been greatly augmented through the loan of several Scout Group archives, namely the Weston Groups; 3rd (St Paul's), 17th (Grammar School), 19th (St Jude's/Milton & Worle), 24th (Hill Road) and 29th (St Peter's), alongside the village Groups at Uphill and Wedmore. The latter is well worth a read as the photograph album and diary of their trip to France in 1924, now in the Somerset Records Office, reveals a fascinating look at Scouting during the interwar years. The 24th Weston (Hill Road) archive, carefully kept by Mr Pete Harris, is particularly useful as it provides insights into how a Troop operated during the Second World War, while the St. Paul's archive reflects the long and illustrious history of Weston's oldest Group, recording the acquisition of the first dedicated Scout Headquarters within the town, though originally brought by the 18th Weston (Good Shepherd) Scout Group which met during the 1930s, as well as providing a vast amount of information on Scouting activities within the Group and District for over forty years.

A great deal of material has been consulted and incorporated into trying to provide an accurate and historically factual account of Scouting in and around the Mendips. The author has left several

Groups out of the book, as they pass briefly in and out of the District and can be better served by incorporation into a study of Sedgemoor District Scouting. Further, the northern half of the old North District, now Gordano Scout District, covering Backwell, Clevedon, Nailsea and surrounding villages has not been included, as to do this region justice would require a separate book. For the sake of brevity, I have streamlined some of the archival and oral material, trying to give an equal amount of space to all the Groups. There is sufficient material and scope to write separate histories of several Scout Groups in their own right, for example a book could be produced for each of the following Groups; 3rd Weston (St Paul's), 19th and 24th (Hill Road) and 1st Uphill Groups from their own records.

This book focuses on the histories of individual Groups, rather than the District as a whole. This is partly due to the availability of documentary evidence that I had access to. District events have predominantly been patched together through Group sources such as leaders meeting minutes, fliers and recollections of interviewees, hence their somewhat patchy nature.

Needless to say, any mistakes or omissions are my own. Hopefully the reader will enjoy the reading as much as I have enjoyed the research and writing of the book.

Yours in Scouting

Duncan R Biddulph
Former Weston Scouter
69th Bristol (St Joseph's) and West Hatch (Taunton) Scout Groups.

Chapter One District History

The formation of the first Troops of Boy Scouts in the resort and its surrounds dates from 1909, a year after the publication of Baden-Powell's handbook 'Scouting for Boys' which was serialised in six fortnightly instalments by the publishing magnate Arthur Pearson, who provided support for Baden-Powell in the early years. The 1907 experimental Brownsea Island camp which took place between 29th July and 9th August in Poole Harbour was organised by Baden-Powell to test out his theory of training boys to be constructive citizens of Edwardian society and historically rests in the milieu of concerns over the decline of the British as an Imperial Nation, the 'physical deterioration' question that had been exercising society in the twilight of the Victorian period. Deep concerns were expressed regarding the health and fitness of the lower social orders for military service, partially instigated at the shock of realising that a large proportion of volunteers to fight in the Second Anglo-Boer (1899-1902) were unfit for military service. The seeds of Boy Scouting germinated in the combined culture of concern about the climate of 'imperial decline', whilst at the same time the Boy Scouts inherited the pastoral 'myth' of open air woodcraft alongside a paternalistic longing for class harmony, which sought to break down the social barriers of the late Victorian British class culture, stressing patriotism to one's country over divisive perceptions of class distinctions. Perhaps the greatest value of this would be seen in the espirit de corps of the Rover Scout section.

The publication of Scouting for Boys, priced at four pence per issue, shortly after the conclusion of the Brownsea camp was far reaching, probably achieving as much as any other contemporary work in refashioning attitudes of adult youth workers. The Boy Scout Scheme was initially set up to fit into the existing organised youth movements, such as the Boys Brigades, the Anglican Church Lads Brigades and Young Mens Christian Association (YMCA) programmes. However with groups of boys spontaneously reading Scouting for Boys and forming Patrols, then seeking suitable local adults to act as SMs, reveals the extent of the impact that Scouting for Boys was having. So far there has been no direct evidence for this scenario occurring at local level. However it is a probability that it may have arisen and the evidence has not survived, based upon evidence from other parts of the country, notably the north London boroughs of Islington and Enfield.[1]

The YMCA was to provide a base for the scheme and it is no accident that many early Troops were sponsored by the YMCA within their communities. Local examples of such an occurrence include the Weston, Clevedon, Bristol and Taunton YMCAs which were amongst the earliest Scout Troops to register. Other early supporters in Weston-Super-Mare, like elsewhere in the country, include a number of clergymen with Troops being provided with a place to meet and assistance in providing leaders such as the examples of St Saviour's, Christchurch, Victoria Methodist and St Martin's. The large number of private schools in the resort also bore fruit for Scouting with early Troops operating at Etonhurst, Kingsholme, Ashcombe House and Clarence House, though the latter was to convert into a cadet force two years later. Up until the beginning of the 1970s private school sponsored Groups were still operational, and the 17th Weston (Grammar School/Broadoak) continued to meet until the early 1990s. The present siting of the Ashcombe Scout and Guide Group headquarters at the local primary school continues the long tradition of good working relationship between schools and Scouting.

The earliest documentary evidence for Scouting in the resort comes from the final months of 1909 with three leaders recorded as being warranted, one of whom, C T Wright, was named as SM of the 1st Weston (YMCA) Troop. It is not recorded what Troop

[1] J Springhall 'Youth, Empire and Scoirty', London, Croon Helm, 1977, pp. 56-62

the other two men were leading. With the springing up of Scout Troops across the country it was necessary to set up local advisory committees, the appointment of travelling inspectors and development of a bureaucracy to cope with the rapid expansion of Scouting during the early years. The amalgamation of these local committees into County Scout Councils and the subsequent Districts soon followed. Weston's District. known as North due to its geographic position in the north of Somerset County, was formed on January 13th 1910[2] under the registration of Weston-super-Mare and District Local Association, in Somerset. Geographically, the area covered by the Local Association was much larger than that covered by the present day District of Axe, ranging from Weston down towards Burnham and eastwards to Harptree. Col. H T Daniels was appointed the DC and Major Griffiths the Chairman of the Association. Several Local Associations existed within the District, besides the Weston Local Association there were Local Assocations for the Clevedon Scouts and a further one covering the Axbridge area. The borders of the District remained the same for many years aside from minor changes in boundary around the Blagdon area with the formation of Mendip District in the early 1930s[3]. Signatories of the formation of the Weston Local Association include Mr Jackson-Barstow, with Major Griffith Davis, Col. Temple-Cole, Reverends Lloyd, Westhead, H H Doombar, M I Holme, Redding, William, Rev Canon Yates and Rev Preb Thompson along with Dr Hooper and Messrs A Parson, T H Webb, A R N Joseland, C Clarke, C T Wright, G E Wollen, N Partridge and Miss Jackson-Barstow. Some of these men were SMs to the early Troops.[4]

From its initial formal start in November, with the issuing of a warrant to Mr C T Wright as SM at the 1st Weston (YMCA) Boy

[2] Copy of Form B Local Association Returns, 1920, (Courtesy of The Scout Association , Gilwell Park, Archive)
[3] Copy of Registration papers of 1st Cheddar(Gilwell Archives)
[4] Copy of Weston Boy Scouts Byelaws of the Local Association (Gilwell Archives)

Scout Troop, Scouting soon developed in the area and by the outbreak of the First World War Weston had thirteen Scout Troops. The majority of the early Troops were either sponsored by local educational establishments, with private schools including Ashcombe House, Clarence, Etonhurst and Kingsholme supporting Troops, or by the Churches, with Troops at Christchurch, St. Saviour's, St. Paul's and St. Martin's (Worle). Early village Troops known to have been in existence include Cheddar, which formed in August 1910, led by Mr A Paul, and Winscombe which opened in 1913 under the leadership of Mr H Weeks. Other village Troops formed during this period, although a paucity of records does not reveal when they were formed. Yet by 1918 village Scout Troops were operational in Banwell, Burrington, Congresbury, Churchill, Hewish (under the leadership of Mr W Bell), Langford and Rickford as well as at least ten Troops operating in Weston. A great many of these Troops, particularly in the villages, were to disband during the period 1919-20, perhaps a reflection that their leaders did not return from the conflict or that the post Great War period saw other challenges to recruiting and retaining leaders. Those Troops that remained witnessed the Patrol Leaders taking much greater responsibility for the Troop.

A sea change in public attitudes can be traced following the Great War with a challenge to the patriotic militarism of the pre-war period. The Boy Scouts under Baden-Powell were quick to pick up on this current, with an emphasis on international Scouting and the birth of International Jamborees, the first being the Arrowehead Jamboree at Birkenhead in 1929, which was attended by local Scouts. The Crystal Palace rally of 1919 showed the Scouts coming of age and presented an opportunity to showcase the movement to a wider public.

During the 1930s Scouting nationally went through a period of contraction, which reflected itself at the local level. The period between 1931-39 saw more Scout Groups disband than formed.

Ironically a local effort to start Scouting in several locations including Brighton Road in Weston, West Harptree, Hutton and Locking in 1939 would be a short-lived as these Groups closed down as the war effort and a shortage of leaders took its toll. By 1940 twenty-two Groups had been formed in Weston, although they were not all in operation at the same time and several numbers were reassigned to new Groups as old ones disbanded.

World War Two placed a great strain on Scouting as leaders were called up for service both in the forces and in civilian roles in supporting the war effort. This, coupled with a large influx of evacuee school children during the first years of the war, placed some considerable strain on those Groups that were able to remain operational. Several evacuee boys joined the recently formed 24th Weston (Hill Road) Group whilst others joined other local Groups. Through the war years there is a dearth of information upon Scouting activities, with the exception of the aforementioned Hill Road Group. The 1st Weston (YMCA) and 3rd Weston (St Paul's) Group records have either not survived or, as is perhaps more likely, were not kept during the war period. Other Groups that continued to meet throughout the war years include the 17th Weston, 2nd Winscombe (Sidcot School) and possibly the 22nd Weston (St Peter's School). Wartime Scouting faced a number of restrictions with petrol and food rationing being felt. Ingenious methods of creating Scout uniforms were also undertaken. As khaki cloth was hard to come by, so old uniforms were pressed into service and in the case of the newly formed 24th Weston (Hill Road) Group, their ASM, Bert Glass, created the Group scarves by dying triangular bandages red and mauve and sewing the two halves together. The concerns of parents and travel rationing meant that most camps were kept close to home with black out conditions being applied after dark. Scouting also played a part in the war effort with Scouts assisting in farming camps, as recalled by former members of the 17th Weston (Grammar School) Troop. Some Groups went out of existence altogether. Mr Alan Banwell recalled how he left the

Wedmore Troop to join the local Army Cadet Corps during the war years, feeling it was his duty to help.

Efforts at reconstruction were underway in 1944 with several Groups reforming, such as the 21st Weston (Sunnyside) Group. 'The Road Ahead' in Somerset Scout report sought to reconstruct Scouting for the post war period with requests for disbanded Groups to be reopened when leaders had been demobbed. Typically most Groups reformed some time between 1946-49. Perhaps the most important of the decisions of the Road Ahead report was the proposal to divide the old North District into two Districts, with a new District being formed in the south centred upon Weston-super-Mare and the surrounding villages. The District came into existence six years later in 1950, being named Axe after the river that flowed through a large part of the District, under the leadership of Colonel H Harvey, as the District Commissioner.[5]

As Weston grew in the post-war years with new housing estates being built around the southern end of the town so the membership of Scouting grew with existing Groups expanding, as well as new Groups starting up. A particularly fruitful period of expansion was during the mid 1950s to 1969 when the District doubled the number of its Groups. Several of these Groups were reformations whilst others, such as the 27th Weston (St Andrew's) Bourneville, 28th Weston, 29th Weston (St Peters) Milton and 30th Weston (Wadham St Baptist), were fresh Groups. In the villages Banwell had a third and fourth attempt at sustaining their Scout Group, whilst a new Group formed at East Harptree and Wedmore Cubs reformed under the leadership of Mrs Vera Banwell. A decade later a fresh round of new formations, albeit on a reduced scale, would witness provision for Scouting in Sandford, the Meadvale estate in Worle and Bleadon. In addition several existing Groups would expand their sections with the 3rd,

[5] Copy of District Registration Form (Gilwell Archive)

19th, 24th and 32nd Weston having two Packs. Alongside the expansion of Cub packs the top end of the movement, the Venture Scout section, also expanded with several new Venture Units being formed between 1983-88. The creation of a new section, Beaver Scouts, in 1984 for boys aged between six to eight was a slow germination period which took off in the District several years later. Interestingly many of the early Colonies were in village based Groups with Banwell pioneering the first Colony which formed in 1986. Congresbury Scout Group started two Colonies catering for thirty six boys two years later, with Burrington and Wrington and Locking Groups opening their sections the following year. Over the next four years seven Colonies were opened and Axe appointed their first ADC Beavers, Mrs Eileen Nock.[6]

However, the following two decades would reveal a decline in the membership both in terms of adults and young people, coupled with Groups closing or amalgamating, declining from a high point of twenty three Scout Groups operational in 1985 down to fifteen two decades later. The largest contributing factor for the shrinkage would be a lack of volunteer adults.

[6] Axe District Directory 1993 pp. 9-36
Recollections of Mr S E Nock

Table One: Numbers of Scout Troops & Groups operational between 1910-50 in the North West District

Year	No. of Groups	Year	No. of Groups
1910	6	1935	17
1918	18	1945	18
1925	12	1950	11

Table Two: Numbers of Scout Groups operational between 1950-2005 in Axe District

Year	No. of Groups	Year	No. of Groups
1955	17	1985	23
1969	23	1993	19
1975	20	2007	15

Table Three: National Membership 1910-2002[7]

Year	Total Membership (Adults and Youth)	Membership rise/decline
1910	107986	
1918	194388	+86402
1925	305867	+111479
1935	448107	+142240
1945	412485	-35622
1955	511010	+98525
1969	534625	+23615
1975	596934	+62309
1985	623843	+26909
1995	630760	+6917
2002	466007	-164753

[7] Courtesy of Gilwell Archives dept

Early Cub Scouting

The implementation of Cub Scouting begun after the Cub Conference in 1916 and appears to have taken a few more years to bear fruit in Weston with the registration of the first Wolf Cub Packs in 1920, when Packs were registered at Christchurch and Banwell, along with the appointment of a Cub Commissioner, Miss Bisdee of Hutton. Other Packs followed in the inter-war years, some making a brief appearance such as the 18th and 20th Weston and 1st Compton Bishop Packs, whilst others endured longer with Packs continuing after the disbanding of the Troop at 4th Weston (St Saviour's). With the formation of Scout Groups, which brought together under one roof the independently operated and registered Wolf Cub Packs, Boy Scout Troops and Rover Crews, the District had several Scout Groups with a Pack and Troop, notably 3rd (St Paul's) and 7th Weston (Uphill). In the instance of the 1st Weston (YMCA), the Group consisted of a Scout Troop and Rover Crew, Cub Scouting being started in 1931 by Mrs W B Wall.

The 1930s appear to have been a heyday of Wolf Cubbing with Packs being started at several churches and schools during this period. However by the close of the thirties the number of Packs and Troops had declined and would decline further as the Second World War imposed the constraints of providing stable leadership as adults were called up for war work. Those Groups which did manage to continue Scouting included the 1st (YMCA), 3rd (St Paul's), possibly 4th (St Saviour's), 17th Weston (County School) and 2nd Winscombe (Sidcot School). A number of evacuees joined the Scouting movement locally and some stayed to the end of the war. An example of this would be the 24th Weston (Hill Road) Scout Group which formed in 1942 and included several evacuees amongst its members.

Rover Scouting

Rover Scouting, which sought to cater for young men aged eighteen and over, started nationally in 1919. Rover Scouting in the District was undoubtedly operating by the early 1920s with the 1st Weston (YMCA) having a small number of Rovers meeting in 1922. Records from the 1928 census returns indicate that twenty six Rovers were meeting at 1st Weston (YMCA) Crew.[8] In addition, the 9th Weston (Mendip) Rovers led by Mr Cuthbert Collingswood and Mr Rex Monk were formed in April 1928. Three years later a Rover Crew was formed at 3rd Weston (St. Pauls) with the warranting of Rev F A Pollard as RSL.[9] A further Rover Crew opened in June 1939, just prior to the outbreak of the Second World War at RAF Locking, under Rev J M Scutt, however this proved short-lived as the Rovers joined up to serve their country.[10]

With the cessation of hostilities in 1945 thoughts turned to reconstruction of the Rover Crews along with Scouting and society in general. The 1st Weston (YMCA) were quick off the mark in reforming their crew in 1947, meeting until 1950 before reforming again in 1960. By 1964 Mr Hibbs had taken out a warrant as RSL, continuing on to 1967 when the Rover Crew converted into a Venture Scout Unit.[11] The 3rd Weston (St. Paul's) Scout Group Rovers reformed in 1954 with Derek Bendall becoming RSL in 1958, being assisted over the lifetime of the Crew by Mr C A Hart and later with assistance from Mr A J L Day.[12] The *Report of the Scout Commission of Enquiry* in October 1946 recommended the reformation of Rover Crew at the

---

8 Group registration Papers

9 3rd Weston Group log book 1928-57 (Courtesy of 3rd Weston (St Paul's) Scout Group)

10 1st Weston (YMCA) Group registration Paper p.1
1st Locking Copy of Group registration Form C 28/06/39 (Gilwell Archives)
3rd Weston (St Paul's) Group logbook 1929-57 p. 41
9th Weston (Mendip) Registration Paper p.1

11 Copy of Group record card 1947-82 (Gilwell Archives)

12 Copy of Group record card 1947-82 (Gilwell Archives)

Locking RAF camp.[13] However this idea had to wait until nine years later, when, in 1953, Mr E P Schofield restarted the Rovers as part of a new Scout Group at the camp. Mr Scholfield was followed by Mr Jackson and Cpl P A Cricraft with LAC Walter as the acting ARSL in 1958. The Group disbanded in March 1960, to reform eighteen months later with Mr P J Davis as RSL. Although nationally Rover Scouts numbered less than warranted leaders their contribution was considerable and a strong sense of comradeship is still evident amongst old Rovers to this day. The Crews were disbanded (along with Senior Scout Sections) in 1967-68 following changes outlined in the Advance Report to create the Venture Scout Units.

Post War reconstruction plans 1944

Following a County Scout Council held in Bridgwater on 14th October 1944 to discuss the implementation of post-war Scouting, the decision was taken by the Weston-Super-Mare Local Association on 23rd October 1944 to set up a Commission of Enquiry. The Committee comprised of a Chairman and Honourable Secretary, three Scouters and three laymen and sought to find out the opinion of Patrol Leaders and Scouters via questionnaires, in addition to reports from officials within the District, including the DC Lord Teignmouth, ADCs Mr J M Townsend (Scouts) and Miss M E Hatcher (Wolf Cubs), the Treasurer Mr V E C Berkeley, Secretary Mr F J Hill and District Padre, Reverend H G Hollinghurst, as well as Mr O H Thomas, the DRSL.[14] From this process the Committee proposed a number of recommendations ranging from the division of the existing District with Weston and surrounding area becoming a separate District in its own right, which was achieved in 1950 with the creation of Axe District. Further, a new Country Association

---

13 WSM LA '*Report of the Scout Commission of* Enquiry' (Oct 1944) p. 14

14 Report of the Scout Commission of Enquiry appointed by the Weston-Super-Mare Local Association
(October 1946) pp. 3-7.

should be created covering the villages of Sidcot, Winscombe, Banwell, Wrington, Redhill, Shipham and Sandford under the supervision of either an ADC or District Scouter. During the discussions concerns were raised about the standard of Courts of Honour, resulting in the proposal for a division of the Court of Honour with the Troop Council being the forum for Troop administration and the Court of Honour being left to deal with issues of Troop "Honour". Recommendations were made with regard to Troop sizes with a healthy Troop being considered to have thirty Scouts and, for Senior Scouts, a minimum of eighteen which led to recommendations for the closure and merger of smaller less efficient Troops.[15] The policy was evidently enacted, a case in point being the merger of the 21st Weston (Sunnyside Methodist) Troop into the 24th Weston (Hill Road) Troop in 1947. The Committee also called for the reforming of Troops at Banwell, Churchill, Hutton and Langford, with groups at Cadbury House and Congresbury and the Rover Crew at Locking camp.

It is interesting to note which areas were not recommended to have a Scout Group, notably Uphill. Perhaps the thinking here was that with the 17th Weston Troop being so close at the Grammar School there was no need for provision for a village group in Uphill. Four years later Scouting returned to Uphill village. Further, no mention is made of Scouting provision for Worle or Weston to fill in the gaps where no local Scout Group existed, and no mention is made of reviving Groups that had disbanded in the town, such as the 19th Weston Scout Group, which reformed a couple of years later. This may have been omitted as plans were already in place to reform these town Groups, although the omission of a Group at Worle is interesting, Worle having to wait twenty eight years before its own dedicated Scout Group opened in 1972 with the formation of 33rd Weston (1st Worle), which today continues as 1st North Worle Scout Group.

---

[15] Report of the Scout Commission of Enquiry. WSM LA. October 1946. pp. 8-11

More mundane, yet equally important, issues to the success of post-war Scouting were discussed by the Committee including the lack of 'outdoor' Scouting taking place alongside concerns about the standard of uniform. Interestingly a strong body of opinion argued for the wearing of a beret for occasions except ceremonial when the ordinary Scout hat should be worn was one of the proposals of the Committee as was the motion that Patrol badges replace shoulder knots. Both these factors were undoubtedly caused partially by the constraints of the war years.

The District had some land at Worlebury, which may have been the site of the original 5th Weston Troop (Worlebury), and a debate ensued as to whether to sell the plot of land, which at some point presumably occurred as no further mention of the land or its use comes to light in the records. The concept of a District headquarters was mooted with a recommendation that a District headquarters be established and the number of parades was to be reduced although the first Sunday after St. George's day was to be kept for the annual parade.[16]

Within the District at the time were seven Wolf Cub Packs. The ADC, Miss Hatcher, felt that more Packs needed to be established. The Committee decided that approaches should be made to Church authorities to facilitate this. Of the seven Packs the 1st Weston (YMCA) and 3rd Weston (St Paul's) had some male leaders, the remaining five Packs had all female leadership teams. Miss Hatcher reported that Cubs were transferring to Scouts at the age of eleven and a half. To encourage better transfers to Scouts the Leaping Wolf badge was proposed as a link badge and closer co-operation between Packs and Troops was called for.[17]

---

[16] Report of the Scout Commission of Enquiry. WSM LA. (October 1946) pp. 12 & 14
[17] Report of the Scout Commission of Enquiry. WSM LA. October 1946. pp.12& 13

Changes to the movement were afoot during the final years of the war with an experiment to try out a new section, Senior Scouts, catering for boys aged between fifteen to eighteen who would either form a separate section where there was sufficient leadership and numbers interested, or form a patrol within the Troop for senior boys. The 1st (YMCA), 3rd (St Paul's), 17th (Grammar School), and 24th (Hill Road) Scout Groups began to experiment with the scheme. The Hill Road experiment was shelved temporarily in early 1945, before being resumed a few months later and ran successfully for three years until Mr Glass departed from the Group. Seniors at the other Groups proved more long term with Messrs Chris Copp, David Abraham and Ian Sutton taking the new sections. Senior Scouting sought to provide more adventure and encourage a greater self reliance in its programme.

The golden age of Scouting 1950-67

Scout membership grew during the 1950s and 1960s as the effects of the post-war baby boom fostered a rise in young people who wished to join the movement. This trend reflects itself in the District with new Groups forming and existing sections expanding. New Groups were started on the Bourneville estate, the Salvation Army Citadel in Carlton Road, Lancaster House School, St Peter's Church in Milton and Wadham Street Baptist Church. Other Groups reformed including Groups at St Jude's Milton, St Peter's School, Banwell, Uphill and 1st Winscombe.

Table Four: Groups operational at the forming of Axe District in 1950

Reg No.	Name of Group	Reg No.	Name of Group
4229	1st Weston-super-Mare (YMCA)	27602	25th Weston-super-Mare (St John's)
4230	3rd Weston-super-Mare (St Paul's)	12770	2nd Winscombe (Sidcot School)
4231	4th Weston-super-Mare (St Saviour's)	25391	1st Banwell
11558	17th Weston-super-Mare (Grammar School)	27723	1st Cheddar
26263	19th Weston-super-Mare (St Jude's)	27724	1st Hutton
21240	24th Weston-super-Mare (Hill Road)		

The DC Col. H Harvey served thirteen years before handing over to Mr R J L White, formerly of 3rd Weston (St Paul's) Scout Group, who remained in post until a motor accident in 1968 forced Mr White's retirement. He was succeeded by the GSL of 1st Weston, (YMCA) Mr F Haynes, in whose time the District shrunk geographically as the county changes in 1974 saw the District southern boundary being redrawn at Bleadon, with the formation of the County of Avon. Groups south of this line formed part of the Sedgemoor Scout District and included 1st Axbridge, 1st Brent Knoll, 1st Cheddar, 1st Shipham and 1st Wedmore.

In 1985 the Beaver section was introduced into the District with six colonies in existence by 1991, being located in the main in the villages, with Colonies at Banwell, Burrington and two at Congresbury, and other Colonies at Hutton and Locking. The appointment of the first ADC Beavers, Mrs Eileen Nock, a former CSL, took place in 1988. She supported the Locking Group's search for a new leader, with Carol Draper coming forward to take over from Julia Shaw. The first District Beaver event for the most recent section of the Scouting family was held at Sandbay in 1988 with a pirate themed fun day where the Beavers made pirate hats, had face painting and races followed up with a barbeque. The day was attended by seventy Beavers from Banwell, Burrington and Wrington and Congresbury.

Over the next eleven years of Mrs Nock's term as ADC, thirteen new Colonies were started although by 1999 the number of Colonies had dropped to sixteen following the disbanding of the second Colonies at the Congresbury and 19th Weston Groups. Mrs Nock passed the reins over to Mrs Jane Deacon, who had been the BSL at the 24th Weston (Hill Road) Group before moving on to her District post.[18] Like her predecessor, when Mrs Deacon retired she went into the Axe District Scout Fellowship, which aims to support Scouting within the District. The position of ADC Beavers has not been filled since Mrs Deacon stood down, although the role is shared equally between Mrs Carol Pepper and Mrs Wendy Pearson, both leaders with 1st North Worle Scout Group and DBSLs.

Patrol system

The Patrol system was in accordance with Baden Powell's ideas set out in Scouting for Boys, whereby Scouts were organised into Patrols which had a distinct name, usually after animals and birds. Patrol names included Badgers, Falcons, Foxes, Kestrels, Peewits, Otters, Ravens, Seagulls and Wolves to name a few.

[18] Mrs E Nock Correspondence 1999

District Beavers Sandcastle Competition

District Beavers

Royal Visit, August 1977

Chapter Two: Scout Group histories

1st Ashcombe (Weston-Super-Mare)

01/04/00
Reg No. 46441

Scarf: Red and black halved.

This Group was created with the merger of the 1st Weston Cub Pack and 24th Weston (Hill Road) Scout Group at the start of the 21st century. At the time of creation the Group was meeting at the United Reformed Church under the leadership of GSL Tony Brown and consisted of a Beaver Colony led by Karen Trevitt, although this was short lived and disbanded soon afterwards. The Cub Pack was led by CSL Richard Spindler, with Martin White and Keith Dudley holding ACSL warrants. Martin succeeded Richard who left the Pack in 2002. At the time of the Group's formation the Troop was led by Tim Harris, who stood down in 2002. A search for new leaders resulted in the author offering his services and recruiting a team at Easter 2003 comprising of fellow ASL David Poole, with Diane Biddulph taking a Troop Helper certificate and David Biddulph as an occasional Troop Helper. The Troop had stood at around a dozen Scouts prior to this time and, although initially shrinking, it expanded to around eighteen Scouts two years later. The Troop undertook a number of camps and activities during the three and a half years, from Easter 2003, mounting two summer camps, the first a joint Scout, Guide and Brownie camp at Huish Woods, with members of Banwell Troop in attendance. The following year the Scouts camped at Beaudesert, again inviting the Banwell Scouts. David Poole and the author became involved with helping the Banwell Troop in the autumn of 2003 as their leader was struggling. Following the departure of Banwell SL the two leaders ran both Troops and offered activities and camps to members of the

Troops until David Poole moved over to take on the leadership of 1st Banwell in late 2005. Further camps undertaken by 1st Ashcombe Troop included a camp at Woodhouse Park, several camps at Huish Woods and an indoor camp at the 34th Birmingham Scout Group headquarters (where my uncle had been a long serving GSL) when they attended the National Indoor Shooting Centre at Wolverhampton and went ice skating. The Troop twice attended the Malvern Challenge camp, as well as holding several sleepovers, following the Group's move to their new headquarters at Ashcombe School in late 2004. The Ashcombe Troop started with two patrols, Falcons and Panthers, which was joined for a time by a third Patrol, Cobras. Activities undertaken by the Troop included kayaking, caving, climbing and archery.

The Troop took in its first three female members in 2004 when Sophie, Stephanie and Shanna joined the Troop, shortly afterwards two other girls joined. Following the departure of David Poole, his younger brother, Brian, joined the leadership team taking out an ASL warrant. Keith Dudley, who had been an ACSL in the Pack moved up to join the Scout section in 2005. Following the author's departure from the Troop at the end of 2005, the Troop was led jointly by Brian Poole and Keith Dudley, although Mr Dudley was to move to 1st Locking Troop within a year, taking about half of the Troop with him. Brian Poole and Diane Biddulph continued to take Scouts, with assistance from the GSL, Tony Brown. The Troop participated in the Triple Troop Camp held in 2007 at Cranham Scout Centre along with the Banwell and Winscombe Troops under the leadership of Banwell SL, Dave Poole.

Following the departure of CSL, Richard Spindler in 2002, the Pack was led by the experienced Mr Martin White, with assistance from several ASCLs including his wife Mrs Joanna White, Messrs Keith Dudley, Neil Bidwell, and later Ms Sheridan Pemberthy, who had been a leader in Gibraltar, as well as a number of parents, of whom Mrs Elaine Borthwick joined as a warranted leader. The Pack held an annual Summer Camp, including the Forest of Dean, Bishops Lydeard and Mafeking Hall in South Gloucestershire and participated in the Giant Sleepover at their headquarters. The Pack strength ranged between twenty to thirty Cubs.

The Beaver Colony had been led by Mrs Trevitt, who moved on in 2002. The Colony disbanded temporarily as no new leaders could be found. The section was restarted following a recruitment drive by the Group, with four leaders coming forward.

1st Milton (Weston-Super-Mare)

18/07/99
Reg No. 46345

Scarf: Blue with yellow trim

This Group was formed by the amalgamation of the 19th and 29th Weston Scout Groups. The Group scarf reflects the histories of these two former Groups merging the colours of the 19th with the badge of 29th (St Peters). The GSL at the time of the amalgamation was Nigel Ball who shortly afterwards was appointed ADC Scouts. This left the Group without a GSL until Paul Greatorex was appointed. He had previously held an ASL warrant with the Troop. His wife, Joanna, led one of the Beaver Colonies. The other Colony was led by Alana Nuttycombe who was succeeded by Gemma Stacey. Ms Stacey had assistance from her friend Amy Brokenshire who held an ABSL warrant. Both were former members of the Venture Scout Unit. One of the Group's longest serving leaders is Mr Chris Wiseman who has been a Colony Helper for close to fifteen years. Both Beaver Colonies, like the Cub Packs, are very popular with the young people of the area and operate at full strength of twenty-four Beavers.

The 19th and 29th both had Cub Packs which continued after the merger. The Lynx Pack has had a stable leadership team which in 2000 consisted of Kevin Chisholm as CSL, Sarah Glen as ACSL and Barrie Robbins as a Pack Helper who later stepped up to an ACSL warrant. Sarah Glen took over the reins following Kevin Chisholm's appointment as SL and Zoe Heath took out an ACSL warrant. The Leopard Pack was led by Debbie Symons, however she stepped down and Helen Hender and Amanda Smart both hold ACSL warrants and run the Pack jointly before leadership passed to Marianne Stacey, Gemma's younger sister.

Pete Grant, SL, and Neil Osborne, ASL, ran the Troop until 2002 when they moved on to form the District Explorer Scout Unit based at the Group under the name of Saracens, taking the name from the old 29th Venture Scout Unit of which Neil was a member. The Troop numbers have tended to be in the high 20s with peaks in the higher 30s and such a large Troop has attracted a team of ASLs to assist Mr Chisholm including Mark Hodder, Rachel Stafford, Ant Buck and Natalie Shirfield.

Upon amalgamation the two Venture Scout Units merged and took the name of Inquisitors. The Unit was led by Carl Warren with Joe Holdaway as AVSL for a while. Later Christina Pople joined the Unit as a Unit Helper. The Unit had use of the Venture room at the HQ in Drysdale Road. The first Unit Chairman was Ian Stone with David Biddulph serving as Unit Treasurer. In 2001 the Inquisitors took in several former members of the recently disbanded Phoenix VSU. The Unit disbanded in September 2002 when the latest changes to the Movement were implemented.

1st Milton have a large number of Scouters involved in running the various sections who are "home grown" having come up through the Sections, mainly the Venture Unit.

1st Weston-Super-Mare (YMCA)

25/11/09-01/04/00
Reg No. 10356

1928 4229

Scarf: Dark blue with light blue trim

The 1st Weston-super-Mare Boy Scout Troop, sponsored by the YMCA, is the earliest recorded Troop formed in Weston-Super-Mare. Although the exact date of registration is unknown it is highly likely that the Troop was in existence some time around the late summer of 1909, as there was a delay between the formation and registration of a Troop. The first identifiable leader of the Troop was Mr C T Wright who was warranted on November 25th 1909. Other early warranted leaders include Mr A B Pepper and Mr G Jeffree, although which Troop they were attached to was not recorded.[19] The following year Mr Wright had passed the leadership over to Mr H T Palmer whilst he moved on to start the 3rd Weston District Troop, which also met at the YMCA headquarters adjacent to Grove Park at the northern end of High Street. The following year, 1911, Troop meetings were being taken by Mr Stratton Smith who is recorded as SM in 1911, although he handed over the Troop to Mr F G Simmons in April. Both the 1st and 3rd Weston Troops are referred to as District Troops between 1910-13. Mr Wright returned as leader of the Troop some time during the First World War, remaining with the Troop until 1922. Mr William Holder succeeded as SM remaining in post for three years, before moving on to assist with other Scout Troops within the resort. Over the years he was active in 9th Weston, 10th Weston and supported efforts to form 24th Weston although he did not take a warrant within that Troop.

---

[19] Early Somerset Warrants 1909-39 (Gilwell Archives)

The Troop suffered its share of good and bad fortunes, with a low ebb in the autumn of 1922, possibly due to a change in leader, as the Troop is recorded as having only nine boys under the leadership of SM W Holder and ASM Noel Partridge. Change was again on the cards when Mr R S Wort, known by his nickname of 'Dickie', took over the leadership of the Troop, remaining with the Troop for fifteen years. In addition to his Scouting commitment Mr Wort also held the position of General Secretary of the YMCA. Over the next six years the Troop numbers expanded rapidly from nine to fifty Scouts with a Rover Crew being formed with a membership of twenty six young men who assisted with the operation of the Troop.

The Troop and Crew were registered as a Scout Group, with Mr Wort being appointed GSM, in November 1928. Mr Wort had the assistance of Mr Lewis James as an ASM.[20] Four Patrols can be traced during this time; Otters, Lions, Owls and Nightjars, [21] although with a Troop of fifty it was very likely that other Patrols existed. As the average size of a patrol was eight members, it can be surmised that perhaps another four Patrols were in operation around this time. One of the names from the Troop trophy is of particular note, Mr Don Hunt, who was Patrol Second (P/S) of Owls Patrol in 1934.[22] His grandsons were both members of the Group as Scouts and Ventures and later taking out roles within the Group with Mr Dave Hunt becoming an AVSL whilst his brother Mr Mike Hunt served as Group Chairman.[23]

A brass band was started in 1923, and practiced in the basement of the YMCA so as not to disturb the other activities taking place in the headquarters. The initial instruments comprising of eight cornets were presented by a local benefactor, J J Barstow-

[20] Copy of The Boy Scouts Association Form F, 15/11/28 (Gilwell Archive)
[21] Copy of Form F 15/11/28 (Courtesy of Gilwell Archives)
[22] YMCA Patrol Trophy 1928-33 & 1988-98
[23] District Directories 1990-1999 Courtesy of Mrs A Coombes (District Archive)

Jackson, the Chairman of the Local Scout Association as well as a prominent local landowner. The band performed for fundraising efforts on behalf of the Scouts which included a performance at the Assembly Rooms with a young John Bailey,[24] who later become the editor of the Weston Mercury, as a band member. Mr Wort, himself a skilled cornet player, was a key part of the Group's band.

The success of the Group continued with the formation of a Wolf Cub Pack in 1931 under the leadership of Mrs W B Wall.[25] However a change of Cub leader occurred in 1933 as the County minutes record N Bloxall of 1st Weston (YMCA) Cub Pack attending County meetings. [26] It is a possibility that, with the departure of Mrs Wall, N Bloxall continued on as leader of the Cubs, although the Pack does not have another registered leader until 1948. However, from the local association report in 1944 it is evident that the Pack was still operational, having an all male leadership team.

Mr K Ellsbury took out a warrant as SM in 1938, though two years later he had been called up for war service and the leadership of the Scouts reverted to Mr Wort for a short duration until he departed in 1940. The position of GSM was soon filled by the Reverend Shipley, nicknamed "Ship", seeing the Group through the hardship of the wartime years. This Group was one of a small band of Groups that managed to remain operational throughout the period of hostilities with the Patrol Leaders taking on a much greater responsibility for Troop life. [27] Members of the Troop during the war years who later took out warrants include Mr Tim Redman and Mr Derek Tottle.[28] Rev. Shipley held the

---

[24] J Bailey 'Weston-super-Mare look back with laughter' pp. 79-80

[25] Early Somerset Warrants 1909-39 (Gilwell Archives)

[26] Somerset Boy Scouts County meetings attendance book, from 05/08/33 (Tangier Scout Centre Archive, Taunton).

[27] Misc Notes from Mr R Ivens p.1

[28] Interview Notes Mr E F Redman & D Tottle

post of General Secretary of the YMCA as well as being the GSM.

With demobilisation after the Second World War, the Troop regained the services of leaders coming back from the war, such as Eric Hibbs who upon return from the army in 1947 took over the leadership of the Troop until October 1949 when he was appointed RSL of the reformed Rover Crew, although the Crew had a short existence and disbanded within three years. Mr R E John, of Johns the bakers based in Whitecross Road and later Winterstoke Road, took over the reins of the Troop, succeeding Mr Hibbs, until moving to Bridgwater with his job in 1958. He later returned to the Group as GSL.[29] Mr Hibbs again took over the Troop until reforming the Rover Crew two years later handing over to Mr Don Andrews, who had previously been an ASM with the Troop since 1954 and before that had been an active member of the YMCA. Mr Andrews became one of the longest serving leaders within the District serving over thirty years as a warranted leader. Mr Andrews is remembered by several former leaders in the District for the Scout Leader training courses he ran in the 1980s, where he divided fellow leaders into Patrols on Saturday mornings[30]. Over the years the Troop had a number of Assistant Leaders including; Trevor McCann, Don Andrews, S Hall, P Baker, H Hammond, S Cobbe, A R Carver, A Bevan, F J R Furneaux, J Hynds, Chris Copp, E F 'Tim' Redman, Derek Tottle[31], D Perriman, A Diamond and R Craddock, the latter two shared the leadership of the Troop when Mr Andrews retired in 1988.[32]

---

[29] The Scouter 1938 (Gilwell Archive)
[30] Recollections of Mr D R Andrews
[31] Copy of Group warrants (Gilwell Archive)
[32] Recollections of Mr D Andrews
Copy of Group Warrant records (Gilwell Archive)
Recollections of Mr E F Redman
Recollections of Mr C J Copp

Mr V E C Berkeley took the helm in 1949, having previously been the GSM at the 17th Weston (Grammar School), remaining with the Group for seven years. For a short period Mr Johns led the Group between 1956-58 before handing over to Mr Frank H Haynes, who had previously been a Leader with the 126th Bristol (Sea Mills Scout Group), and worked for BAE systems as a commercial manager with 'a gift for organising', and was appointed GSM in 1958, a post he held for thirteen years before being appointed DC between 1969-76 when he was called to higher service. His nickname of 'Beaver' came from his time as Scout in the Tile Cross area of Birmingham where he was the PL of the Beaver Patrol.[33] Normal camping was resumed after the war with the Troop camping at a number of sites in the early 1950s including Lilstock in Somerset (1952). Three years later a training weekend was held at Shipham which included a 1st class hike from the farm behind Cheddar Church back to camp. A major fundraising initiative took place around this time with the arrival of a new GSM, Mr F Haynes, which resulted in the purchasing of six new Patrol tents to replace the three aging First World War bell tents brought from the Army by the Group. The new tents, made to order by Yeo Brothers Paul in Bristol, were first used by the Troop at their Summer Camp at Sampford Brett in 1959.[34] The 1960s saw the start of a link between the YMCA Scouts and a Swedish Scout Group, with the Weston Scouts attending a Swedish Jamboree camp in 1964[35] which, amongst a number of lifetime friendships, included the meeting and subsequent marriage between Bob Craddock and Cunilla.[36] The Swedish Scouts under their SM Mr R L Romnell, returned the visit three years later, camping with the YMCA Troop at

[33] Recollections of Mr D Andrews
Recollections of Mrs M Haynes 12/09/07

[34] Recollections of Mr D Tottle

[35] Recollections of Mr D Tottle

[36] Recollections of Mrs M Haynes

Allerington on the Quantocks on Lady Gass's land with a total of one hundred and seventy five in camp.[37]

The Cubs acquired the services of Miss B E Baker in 1951 and later Miss D Neath served for three years. In October 1960, Mr V Crane was appointed CM with a team of ACMs including Miss Baker and Mrs Pughe. Mr Crane departed in October 1964 handing over the reins to Mrs E D Marley, with assistance from Miss Gabriel and the recently appointed Miss F D Bennett, Mr S F Cooke and Mr S Hoke.[38] The Pack again had a change of leader when Mrs 'Babs' E Holley (nee Baker) succeeded Mrs Marley as Akela at the Pack in 1967, with Miss Gabriel and Mrs Pughe continuing to assist. Mrs Holley continued as Akela until 1981, culminating thirty years of service with the Pack, when she passed the responsibility of leadership to Mrs Diamond.[39] The Group and Pack were fortunate to have a dedicated team of leaders who remained with the sections for a considerable time. Mrs Diamond served nineteen years as Akela, during which time she was assisted by a number of ACSLs and Pack Helpers including; Mrs Cunilla Craddock, Mrs Janice Allen (nee Redman), Mrs Christine Robinson and Mr Martin White, who had been a Scout and Venture with the Group.

Since being reformed in 1960 the Rovers at 1st Weston continued to meet right up to the implementation of the Advance Report of 1967. The Group formed a Venture Scout Unit under the leadership of Mr E F 'Tim' Redman, the founding leader of the Ventures, at that time called 1st Weston YMCA Venture Scout Unit. He was assisted by Mr Chris J Copp, who had previously been an ASM in the Troop.[40] The Ventures appear to have ceased

---

[37] Recollections of Mr D Tottle
[38] Copy of Somerset County Directory 1964 p.14 (Tangier Scout Centre Archive, Taunton) Copy of Group Warrant records (Gilwell Archive)
[39] Copy of Somerset County Directory 1967 p.5 (Tangier Taunton, Somerset Scout Archives)
[40] Interview with Mr Redman May 2004

to meet in 1972 and remained inactive until being reformed in 1983 under the name Jabbewocks V.S.U. led by Mr Roger Furneaux who handed over to Mr David Hunt in 1995.[41]Mr Hunt remained with the Unit until 2001 whereupon the leadership passed to another former Scout from 1st Weston, Mr Martin Crandon, a member of Seagull Patrol and later PL of Seagulls. The Unit finally disbanded in 2002 around the time of the latest changes in the movement.

During the ninety one years that 1st Weston operated it benefited greatly from the long term leadership which provided stability at the Group, with the average length of service from leaders being between ten to thirty years active Scouting. Regrettably the Troop disbanded in 1998 as no new leaders could be found to continue the section and two years later the Pack amalgamated with the 24th Weston (Hill Road) Scout Group as their long serving leaders were retiring with insufficient leaders remaining to continue the Pack. During the lifetime of the Group it had a reputation as one of the foremost Groups in the District, which was undoubtedly augmented by the commitment and skills of the long serving leaders

Scout Patrol names from 1928-33 and 1981-90	
1928-33	1981-90
Lions	Eagles
Nightjars	Kestrels
Otters	Owls
Owls	Seagulls

[41] District Directory 1993 p. 25

2nd Weston Troop (St. Saviour's)

15/03/10-1919 (BST)

The vicar of St Saviour's, the Reverend H S Chamberlain, was one of the original supporters of Scouting in Weston, founding a Troop in March 1910. Reverend Chamberlain's warrant dates from March 15th 1910, as does Mr R Burns, who held an ASM warrant. The Troop's leadership changed in 1919 with the departure of Reverend Chamberlain and the arrival of the Reverend Canon Yates[42]. The same year also witnessed the Troop exchanging its registered number with the 4th Troop (Etonhurst) Troop[43], no explanation as to why this change had occurred can be located by the author.

2nd Weston (Etonhurst School)

1919-24 (BST)
24/01/45-47 (WCP)
Reg No. 22514

From 1919 to 1924 the title 2nd Weston Troop was reassigned to Etonhurst School, located at 35 Beach Road under the leadership of Mr G E Wollen who was a co-owner and teacher at the School, as well as being the SM.[44] The last record of Mr Wollen as SM is from the 1922-23 Weston-Super-Mare directory.[45] Whether the Troop carried on for a while after Mr Wollen's departure under another SM is not known. The Troop had disbanded by 1925 as the title 2nd Weston was reassigned. The School would have one more attempt at Scouting in the closing year of the second World War when a short-lived Pack was opened by Mr D H Mille-

---

[42] pp71 1911 Weston-Super-Mare Directory (Weston Library Local History Archives)
[43] Copy of District Papers 1920 (Gilwell Archives)
[44] Weston Trade Directory 1919 (Weston Library)
[45] Weston-Super-Mare Directory 1922-23 p. 56 (Courtesy of Weston Library)

Barstow as CM and Mr D Hickbey as the ACM, with nine Cubs, although it disbanded within two years[46].

2nd Weston (Clarence Park Baptist Church)

10/01/25-31/03/28 Form E
Reg No. 15328

The number of 2nd Weston was reassigned within a year of the closure of the Etonhurst Troop with the registering on October 1st 1925 by SM, Mr R E Monk of the Clarence Park Baptist Scout Troop with a membership of ten Boy Scouts.[47] The Troop's activities are mentioned in Mr Ray Green's book on the history of Clarence Park Baptist Church, with the formation of the Troop recorded in the minutes of the Deacons meeting. However, later some friction arose between the Scouts and the Church with a report in the Deacon's book of "there being a little friction between the Scouts (*and the Church*) and the SM was asked to ensure that the Scouts went straight home after their activities finished. But that the Church was very grateful for their help for a few weeks when the man who pumped the organ walked out at short notice"[48].

The Troop visited Cheddar Gorge in August 1925 whilst camping nearby at Winscombe. The following year the Troop camped at Stanton near Bridgwater for a weekend at the invitation of 3rd Weston (St. Paul's) Troop. The Troop participated in the District camp held in 1927, along with other Weston Troops.[49] There is a change of SM in 1928 and shortly afterwards the Troop folded. Mr Monk moved to Emmanuel Church and helped found the 9th Weston Scout Group. At that time he was working as an upholsterer at Podger and Son in Weston.

---

[46] Copy of Form C 24/01/45 (Gilwell Archive)
[47] Copy of Troop registration (D R Biddulph Scout Archive)
[48] R Green 'Christ's People at Clarence Park, 1900-2000' pp18-19
[49] Photograph album of Mr R Monk (courtesy of Mr B Faraghar)

3rd Weston (District Troop)

1910-13

This District Scout Troop registered in 1910, met at the YMCA, initially being led by Mr C T Wright with Mr A M Roberts as an ASM. The following year Mr Stratton-Smith is recorded for a brief period as taking both the 1st and 3rd Weston (District) Troops before handing over the 3rd Weston Troop to Mr F G Simmons in April. By the end of 1913 the 3rd Weston District Troop had folded as the number was reassigned to a Troop forming on the southern end of the town at St Paul's church.

3rd Weston (St Paul's)

17/01/14 (BST St Paul's)
31/09/21 (WCP)
Pack Reg No. 4365

(1928 Reg No.) 4230
Scarf: Maroon with gold border

The 3rd Weston (St Paul's) Boy Scout Troop registration date is unknown, but it is very likely to have been linked with the issuing of a SMs warrant on January 17th 1914 for Lt Colonel Temple-Cole at 3rd Weston (St Paul's) Boy Scout Troop. The Troop was meeting at the Whitecross Hall, which was St. Paul's Church hall. Shortly afterwards Lt Colonel Temple-Cole was called up for the Great War. Despite the loss of their leader the Troop continued to meet throughout the war years. With the cessation of hostilities in 1918 the Troop's fortunes improved. Lt Col Temple-Cole returned and two years later Mr H R Kirk joined as an ASM in

May 1920.[50] A year later Mr C T Wright joined the Troop as SM with the promotion of Lt Col Temple-Cole to the position of ADC[51]. On the 21st September the Wolf Cub Pack was registered by acting CM Mr H R Kirk with thirty nine boys on the membership roll[52]. The Pack was one of the earliest recorded Packs to form in the District. Earlier Packs which formed were the 7th Weston (Christchurch) and 1st Banwell, both having formed the previous year.[53] Mr Wright left the Troop in October 1922, returning to the 1st Weston (YMCA) Scout Troop and handing over to Mr W Smith, who was appointed SM a month later.[54] However change again was on the cards in 1926 when Mr Kirk took over the reins of the Troop, whilst Miss Gwen E Ball took out a CM warrant. [55] The following year Mr J Spence joined the Troop holding an SM warrant.

The 3rd Weston-super-Mare (St. Paul's) Scout Group was registered in 1928, comprising of a Wolf Cub Pack numbering eighteen boys with the Troop strength standing at a dozen. [56] This was a decrease in the membership from the start of the decade. Mr Kirk, the GSM, remained with the Group for a short while before resigning in June 1929, moving on to start a Scout Group at Langford.[57] Miss Ball continued to lead the Wolf Cubs with invaluable help from ACM, Mr Leonard Griffiths. The Troop was led by SM Mr Albert W Collins, residing in Uphill, with assistance from ASM Mr Eric Stevens of Langford Road. The Troop appeared to be inactive for a period at the end of 1928 and restarted during the spring of 1929.[58] The recently reformed

---

[50] Mr R S Ivens) *Misc. Notes on Scouting in North Somerset*, 22/10/04
[51] Notes taken from the *1921-22 Weston Trade Directory* (Weston Library)
[52] Copy of Form F 30/09/21 (Gilwell Archives)
[53] D R Biddulph *Misc. Notes from Gilwell* (Gilwell Archive)
[54] Mr R S Ivens *Misc. Notes on Scouting in North Somerset*, 22/10/04
[55] D R Biddulph *Misc. Notes from Gilwell* (Gilwell Archive)
[56] Copy of *Form F* Annual Group Re-registration dated 15/11/28 (Gilwell Archive)
[57] D R Biddulph Notes taken from *The Scouter* warrants section (Gilwell Archive) Copy of Form C 24/09/24 (Gilwell Archives)
[58] 3rd Weston (St Paul's) Scout Group logbook 1929-57, p. 4

Troop held their first camp over the weekend of Whitsuntide, attending the Somerset Jamboree at Wells with ASM Stevens, Patrol Leaders Stevens, Curry, G Tanner and R Adams present. The camp made a strong impression on those attending who particularly enjoyed the camp fire and boxing competition finals held in the Bishop's barn, yet some dissatisfaction was expressed over the stony ground underfoot which deprived the Scouts of a good nights sleep.[59] Several members of the Troop including Scouts Bruford, Collins (the son of the SM), Griffith, Kingham and Stacey undertook a hike from the headquarters in Whitecross Road to the old quarry above Manor Road where an afternoon of tracking was undertaken. Mr Stevens led the Troop on the monthly church parades to St. Paul's, in those days a good turnout for church parades was the norm, whilst in August Scouts; Clarke, Fear and Pearson attended the Scouts coming of age Jamboree at Arrowe Park in Birkenhead.[60] During the summer recess the Troop lost the services of SM Collins and also ASM Stevens in September 1929, leaving the freshly appointed GSM Reverend E L Noel-Cox to run the Troop.[61] He remained with the Group until moving away in February 1930,[62] whereupon Mr Stevens, who had a son in the Troop, returned to the Group, remaining with the Troop until 1932. Other new faces included Miss B Gilbert who joined the Pack as CM in June 1929 remaining until the following August. With the departure of Miss Gilbert the Pack ran without a CM although Miss Linda A Bray had been recruited and appointed in September as an ACM in the Pack.[63] The following month Mr R J L White, known in the Group as 'Stoker', was appointed as an ASM, initially joining the Troop as a games instructor.[64] Mr White was to show great dedication to the Group, during his time becoming SM in 1936

[59] 3rd Weston (St Paul's) Group logbook 1928-57 pp. 2-4 (Courtesy of 3rd Weston St Paul's) Scout Group

[60] 3rd Weston (St Paul's) Group logbook 1928-57 p. 5

[61] *The Scouter* Vol. 23 p. 438 (Gilwell Archive)

[62] D R Biddulph *Misc. Notes from Gilwell* (Gilwell Archive)

[63] *The Scouter* Vol. 24 p. 474 (Gilwell Archive)

[64] D R Biddulph *Misc. Notes from Gilwell* (Gilwell Archive)

and, later, GSM as well as undertaking responsibilities within the District including; Honorary Secretary, ADC Scouts and finally as DC in the 1960s.[65]

The Troop expanded rapidly during 1930, rising to thirty-five members by February divided into five patrols; Cuckoos, Curlews, Owls, Peewits and Woodpigeons. The same month a very successful joint dance was held between members of the Troop and the local Guides which raised £8 for Troop funds. Efforts to form a Troop band also paid off with two donations, one from Mr G Whittaker whose gift allowed for the purchase of a bass drum and sticks and the other from the ladies of the Church of the Good Shepherd who raised £5 which paid for eight cornets The band was trained by Mr Baker, their first parade being held on the second parade Sunday of April where the band "acquitted itself well, despite the inclement weather".[66] The band's first official appearance was on Easter Sunday when they led the Group to St Paul's church at 3pm. Following the service the Group retired to Clarence Park where the Group were 'potted at' (photographed) reflecting the first recorded effort at a Group photograph that became a tradition within the Group over the years. By this time the Troop had reached full membership with forty-eight Scouts and closed its waiting list. Later that month the band led the Group to a parade at the County School grounds in April where they were inspected by Scouter L Emery of the Uphill Troop. [67] During the 1930s the Troop ran a newsletter called the 'Signal Fire' which served as a means of communicating and publicising the Groups achievements.[68]

With the expansion of the Troop new appointments were necessary within the ranks resulting in PL George Harrison of

---

[65] 3rd Weston (St Paul's) Logbook 1928-57 p. 15
District Directories 1963-69 Mrs A Coombes (District Archive)

[66] 3rd Weston (St Paul's) Group logbook 1928-57 p. 15

[67] 3rd Weston (St Paul's) Group logbook 1928-57 pp. 12-16

[68] 3rd Weston (St Paul's) Group logbook 1928-57 p. 27

Curlews being appointed Troop Leader with P/S Fear of Peewit being appointed as PL of the Eagle Patrol. He was succeeded by Scout R Hewlett as P/S of the Patrol and P/S Pearson to PL of Owl Patrol. The Troop embarked upon a more outdoors programme as the summer months came with a series of wide games in Weston woods such as capture the treasure on May 20th in addition to cricket games and badge work. The annual Whitsuntide County Jamboree was held at Weston cricket ground in 1930 with a large contingent of the Group being present. Preparations for the Troop Summer Camp that was to be held at Pensford in early August included a medical examination of the boys in the Troop on Tuesday 29th July, when only two boys were declared unfit to attend the camp. The camp was held at Mr Sperrings' farm with the camp being pitched in true Scout spirit in the pouring rain. Most of the camp was given over to hiking, as well as a trip to Pensford colliery and a flight in an aircraft from Bristol airport at Whitchurch. The Troop paraded twice over the week of August 2nd to 9th to the local churches at Publow and Pensford, the latter being located on an island in the middle of the river.[69]

An influx of new leaders which took place during the thirties helped to expand the activities offered by the Group, with Mr O H Thomas (previously SM of 1st Axbridge Scout Group) becoming GSM following the departure of Rev Noel-Cox, and Mrs A M White as CM, both warranted in July 1931. The Reverend Frank A Pollard, a rare breed of leader who held multiple warrants, took out a RSL warrant in October, whilst simultaneously being the GSM of both the 17th Weston (County School) and 18th Weston (Church of the Good Shepherd) Scout Groups. Rev Pollard remained with all three Groups until March 1933 when he moved away from the resort, although he continued his Scouting elsewhere in Somerset.[70] In 1932 Mr Stevens moved from the

---

[69] 3rd Weston (St Paul's) Group logbook 1928-57 pp. 24-27

[70] D R Biddulph *Misc. Notes from Gilwell* (Gilwell Archive)

Troop to become SM of the recently formed 18th Weston[71] (Church of the Good Shepherd), which retained strong links with the 3rd Weston as many of the Group's Leaders had been Assistant Leaders with the 3rd Weston. Miss L A Bray was soon to follow Mr Stevens to the 18th Weston as CM. [72] With the departure of Rev Pollard the St. Paul's Rover crew was supported by the Reverend H F C Higgs who took out a RSL warrant in December 1935 and, like his predecessor, held the warrant of GSM at the 18th Weston. To assist with badge work the Troop had divided into two segments for parts of the training, based upon the requirements for the First and Second Class badges and the King Scout Award. Advanced badges such as the Ambulance badge for the Senior Scouts were gained and the Troop prepared for a display in bridge building for a forthcoming display. National events were marked by the Troop, including the R-101 airship disaster of October 5th 1930 with the loss of forty eight lives, when the Group officers and principle colours wore mourning colours for the October 12th Church parade in memory of the victims of the disaster.[73] The Group attended the annual Remembrance Day memorial as the following month's Church parade coincided with Remembrance Sunday where the Group was joined by the freshly formed 17th Weston (County) Scout Group.[74] Further the Group were also honoured by the election of ASMs Messrs Stevens and White to the Local Assocation as Assistant Treasurer and Assistant Secretary, which the Troop recalled as being a high honour.[75]

A change of Troop night occurred in February 1931 with Troop nights moving from Tuesday to Thursdays to accommodate those Scouts who were attending night school. The band received a gift of two bugles from Mrs Perry and Mrs Ward. Perhaps the

---

[71] D R Biddulph *Misc. Notes from Gilwell* (Gilwell Archive)
[72] D R Biddulph *Misc. Notes from Gilwell* (Gilwell Archive)
[73] 3rd Weston (St Paul's) Group logbook 1928-57, p. 30
[74] 3rd Weston (St Paul's) Group logbook 1928-57 pp. 30-31
[75] 3rd Weston (St Paul's) Group logbook 1928-57 p. 44

highlight of the year was the inspected of the Troop on March 5th by officers from the Somerset Light Infantry who reported very favourably on the smartness and conduct of the Scouts. In the following month, as part of their civic duties and to reflect on the close ties between the St John's Ambulance brigade and the Troop, the Patrol Leaders turned out for the dedication of two new St John's ambulances on the beach lawns. The following year saw the Troop celebrating a number of successes, with the Scouts winning the Jeffrey rifle shield, and the Handicraft shield. However the highlight of the 1932 Whitsun County Jamboree held at Corsten, had to be the visit of Lord Baden-Powell, with the camp being voted the best camp ever by the Scouts.[76]

The struggle to find a meeting hall on several occasions over the next few months as the Whitecross hall was booked for other functions may have laid the seeds for the Group to look for its own headquarters. However on the positive side the Group were able to succour a camping field from Mr Lance at Hutton from June to August, although wet weather rather spoilt the opportunity to undertake outdoors scouting at the field. To go with the use of the field came the bonus of new camping equipment in the form of a gift of a new trek cart to replace the Troop's aging cart, donated by Mrs Buckley, a friend of the Troop. The Troop's fortune continued to improve further when Scout S Baker achieved four firsts for his handiwork for camper, carpenter, cook and fretwork at the County Jamboree Craft Display. Three Kings Scouts Awards were gained by PLs Burrows, R Fear and P/S H Lane, being presented at a meeting at Hucker's field by DSM Joseland.[77] Annual Camp was held at the end of August in an effort to obtain better weather which seemed to pay off, as the camp at Hangleton near Brighton enjoyed good weather for most of the week.[78]

[76] 3rd Weston (St Paul's) Group logbook 1928-57 pp 54-55
[77] 3rd Weston (St Paul's) Group logbook 1928-57 pp.35- 41
[78] 3rd Weston (St Paul's) Group logbook 1928-57 p. 42

In 1933 the Troop took in C M Hyssett, a former Sea Scout from the now defunct 6th Weston. The same year saw the resignation of Rev Pollard from his Group warrants as he had been promoted to an ADC. He duly visitied his old Troop to invest two Rover Squires, sporting his white feather (the mark of an ADC) in his hat.[79] The following autumn the Troop entered Scouts A & J Bowering, A Greenland and C Hyssett as the Troop's representatives at the County swimming competition. In contrast to the achievements of the Troop and Crew, the Cubs closed for a number of weeks following a poor turn out, with only one Cub, C Bennett turning up for a Pack meeting. Dissatisfaction was expressed about the abilities of the Cubs, with a comment in the Logbook that stated "new recruits make better Scouts than Cubs from this Pack."[80] After a period of twelve years the Pack was suspended.

The Rovers met on a Monday, post war the Crew moved to a Tuesday night, whilst the Troop met on a Tuesday from 7:30pm. Band practice was held on a Wednesday evenings. The Rover Crew at this time had continued to expand and provide service to the local community with the Rovers being asked by Mrs Graves-Knyfton of Uphill Court to manage her woods. This was to prove beneficial to the Group, with a steady supply of Scout staves and pioneering poles, in addition to a new flagpole and new benches being made from the timber felled in the Graves-Knyfton estate woods.[81] The Crew was proving to be popular, with sixteen members the following year, (1934), of which three were taking out ASM warrants. That year was to be one of their best years with the Crew taking home the County handicraft trophy in June and winning all classes in the County swimming competition in September. Subscriptions in October 1934 were set at 4 shilling a year, or a penny a week for the forty eight weeks that the Group held meetings. The Troop at this time comprised of five Patrols,

[79] 3rd Weston (St Paul's) Logbook 1928-57, pp. 68-69
[80] 3rd Weston (St Paul's) Logbook 1928-57, p. 71
[81] 3rd Weston (St Paul's) Logbook 1928-57, pp. 71-77

with a membership of thirty-eight Scouts, named after birds, with R Fear serving as Troop Leader. However the Group had to give up their camping field, 'Oatlands' at Windwhistle Lane, which was purchased by the council for building purposes. The Group were to share the Drove Road recreation ground.[82]

December 1934 Patrols

Patrol Name	PL	P/S
Curlews	J McGill	D Clarke
Eagles	W Mogg	Vacant
Owls	C Hyssett	R Dorrall
Peewits	A Smith	E Baumann
Woodpeckers	J Wheway	A Bowering

In 1935 Troop leader R Fear stood down. He was succeeded by Frank Wheeldon, who had recently returned from a 25,500 mile trip to attend the Melbourne Centenary Jamboree in Australia, where he went bushranging for four days, sailed a yacht in Sydney harbour, climbed mount Buffalo on a pony and took tea with Scouts from seventeen other nations.[83] The same year saw a very rare honour to be bestowed upon a Scout, with the presentation of the Cornwell badge which commemorates Scout Jack Cornwell's heroism in the Battle of Jutland, and is regarded as the 'Scout's V.C.', to B L Bonning, who had faced twenty operations and lost a leg due to blood poisoning. Colonel G Flemming, Chairman of the Weston-s-Mare and District Boy Scouts Assocation, presented the award alongside a guard of honour from the 3rd Weston Troop. Others in attendance included Mr JJ Jackson-Barstow, Mr J Milligan, Bristol County Commissioner and other notables.[84] TL Brian Bonning was called

[82] 3rd Weston (St Paul's) Logbook 1928-57, p. 87
3rd Weston (St Paul's) Logbook 1928-57, Rev. F A Pollard Group Report 11/12/34p. 98
[83] 3rd Weston (St Paul's) Logbook 1928-57, p. 100
[84] 3rd Weston (St Paul's) Logbook 1928-57, p. 102

home in 1941. The Group made use of the summer months on the Uphill cricket field, setting up a standing campsite where ASM White, as usual, spent as much time sleeping under canvas as possible, declaring that he would prefer to sleep out all year.[85] That year Rev Pollard departed to pastures new, moving to Portishead Nautical school and the Rev. Higgs was appointed curate of the Church of the Good Shepherd. He proposed a new departure for fundraising, a fete jointly run by the 3rd Weston and 18th Weston Groups, which although not as successful as the Scouts would have hoped they remained optimistic that the next year's fete would bear better fruit.[86]

Mr White was promoted to SM in May 1936, and in addition to the existing Fear brothers J and R Fear, who held ASMs warrants, Stoker White recruited further leaders for the Troop with Mr S C Baker taking out an ASM warrant. This gave the Troop three ASMs, some of whom had come through the Troop and Rovers.[87] It was decided that the Troop would camp at the Plymouth Jamboree which was to last for ten days and would include a visit by the Chief Scout, as well as coinciding with navy week.[88] Mr R J Fear stood down the following year, whilst Mr Bewdley-Bull took out a SM warrant, (though whether this was an indication that the number of Scouts led to the formation of a second Troop or that the Group felt that two SMs would be advantageous is unclear). In the spring of 1938 Mr Braithwaite and, later on that year, Mr J C Bowering were appointed ASMs in the Group.[89]

The Good Shepherd Troop which in 1936 comprised of two patrols was to meet with the St Paul's Troop, as the Rev Higgs was unavailable to take the Troop meetings, and was conducting a

---

[85] 3rd Weston (St Paul's) Logbook 1928-57, p. 103
[86] 3rd Weston (St Paul's) Logbook 1928-57, p. 103
[87] 3rd Weston (St Paul's) Logbook 1928-57, p. 109
Early Somerset Warrants 1909-39 (Gilwell Archive)
[88] 3rd Weston (St Paul's) Logbook 1928-57, p.109
[89] Early Somerset Warrants 1909-39 (Gilwell Archive)

search for a new SM. This evidently proved unsuccessful, as the Troop folded into the St Paul's Troop soon afterwards.[90] Miss Bray returned to the Group as CM in 1938 after the disbanding of the 18th Weston Scout Group, being assisted by Mrs M Rogers holding an ACM warrant.[91] The Troop was operating a Senior Patrol for older Scouts prior to their move to the Rover Crew on the occasion of their seventeenth birthday. However it was recorded that the Senior Patrol should be discontinued in Septemeber 1936, owing to First Aid lectures. These lectures were held in conjunction with the 5th Weston (Christchurch), 17th Weston (County School) and 18th Weston (Good Shepherd) Troops.[92]

The Group were preparing for a Scout Concert in the winter of 1936 with the GSM Mr Thomas and his wife undertaking an operetta, which included the Rovers singing 'In Town Tonight' and their humourous "Four Dancing Daughters' sketch, which featuring four of the largest Rovers and went down exceedingly well. The concert raised £6 6s for Group funds.[93] In 1937 the Group decided to hire the same camping field as the previous year at last year's rate of £5, charging 3 pence per week or a penny a night camping fees to those wishing to use the site and ensuring that a rota of leaders was available to ensure that each night was covered.[94] SM White proposed that TL J Page should apply for an ASM warrant as ASMs Baker and Fear were soon to depart and that B Bonning should take the Pack after Mr Fear left, duly taking out an ACM warrant.[95] At the same time the mastership of the band was declared open, as Mr Baker had to stand down due

[90] 3rd Weston (St Paul's) Logbook 1928-57, p.109
[91] D R Biddulph 'Misc. Notes from Gilwell' (Gilwell Archive), 2004
[92] 3rd Weston (St Paul's) Logbook 1928-57, p. 112
[93] 3rd Weston (St Paul's) Logbook 1928-57, p.111
[94] 3rd Weston (St Paul's) Logbook 1928-57, p. 113
[95] 3rd Weston (St Paul's) Logbook 1928-57, p. 115

to pressure of work commitments. Mr K Fear was to take on this role in January 1938.[96]

No record was kept in the Troop log during the war years and little can be ascertained about the Troop activities during this period beyond the fact that the Troop continued to meet. The Troop had several evacuee boys who joined the Scouts, such as "Freda" Worman who was a pupil at the evacuated Miteham School, who paid a visit to the Troop in June 1946 whilst on holiday in the resort.[97]

The Troop was in camp at Spaxton when the war ended with the defeat of Japan and the Scouts attended the VJ celebration service at Spaxton Church. Whilst in camp the Troop assisted the farmer, Mr Hawkins, with his barley harvest and on Thursday entertained seventy visitors on the annual visitor day at camp. Back to normal Scouting and the Troop attended the Local Assocation Youth Service on the beach lawns, parading from Walliscote School, with both the YMCA and St Paul's bands in attendance.[98] The Troop was now meeting on Monday and Friday evenings, a pattern that was to continue for many years.

In 1946 the Troop said goodbye to David Abraham, he starting his National Service in the army, who had been with the Troop since 1940, retaining the leadership of the Curlew patrol for two years and five months. Upon completion of his National Service, he rejoined the Group being appointed SSL in 1955. Afterwards he served as GSL.[99] The Group, like other Scout Groups the length and breadth of the country, was to face challenges with leaders being called up to undertake National Service. However a good proportion of these young men returned to take warrants or help in other ways with the St Paul's Group which had always

[96] 3rd Weston (St Paul's) Logbook 1928-57, p. 116

[97] 3rd Weston (St Paul's) Logbook 1928-57, p 137

[98] 3rd Weston (St Paul's) Logbook 1928-57, pp 123-124

[99] 3rd Weston (St Paul's) Logbook 1928-57, p. 130

enjoyed a strong community spirit amongst its members, both past and present.

The Group acquired the services of Mr Noel Partridge, nicknamed 'Pip', who had been a Scouter in the town from the early days. He was officially warranted as a Lone Wolf, a Scouter who was not attached to any particular Group, although he had strong ties with the 3rd Weston and regularly assisted them on Troop nights and with camping, until moving away to London.[100]

Following the war, the Troop revived their football and cricket teams, with the football team taking the moniker 'Saints'. These two sports teams over the years had varied fortunes, playing a variety of local teams, both Scouting and non-Scouting organisations, for example the Bourneville, Bleadon and Boys Brigade cricket teams, whom the Troop's squad beat in the 1948 season.[101] The Troop played an away game against the 3rd Burnham Scouts who beat the St Paul's boys 4-1.

The St. Paul's Troop Summer Camp in 1948 was held at Moretonhampstead with four Patrols in attendance, Curlews, Woodpeckers, and Woodpigeons in addition to the Peewit Patrol from 14th Bridgwater Scout Group. The Woodpecker's patrol won the camp patrol competition whilst overall the Troop achieved a Camping Standard Certificate from the ACC for Devon Scouts who mentioned in his report that he found a "very good camp indeed", with the Senior Scouts winning high praise from the inspection for their camping skills. The Scout Troop continued to expand the following year with the formation of a seventh Patrol named Swan. Further successes included the awarding of Scout Cord on July 9th to Gordon Grove, the first Scout in Weston to receive the award.

---

[100] 3rd Weston (St Paul's) Logbook 1928-57, p. 169

[101] 3rd Weston (St Paul's) Logbook 1928-57, p 183 & 206

The Troop had always had good relations with its sister organisation, the Girl Guides, with periodic joint dances and meetings with local Guide Troops such as the Moorland Road Guides and, later, the 16th Weston (Grammar School) Guide Troop, led by Captain Miss Hughes.[102]

The Troop was proving to be very popular and by the close of 1948 was attracting fifty boys to the Friday night meetings. Success in numbers was not limited to the Scouts. The Pack continued to expand rising to thirty-six boys and then topping fifty on a regular turn out during the early 1950s. The Pack was ably led by ACM, and later CM, Bryan Jones with a team of adult helpers which over the years included Guides Ann Bray and Babara Murell in 1946. Later helpers and leaders included the aforementioned Ann Bray, who took out an ACM warrant, Mrs O'Flynn, Mrs Jenkins, Mrs Herridge and Scouts. A long waiting list of forty names was causing some headaches for the leaders and a second Pack was started. Both Pack meetings were reduced to an hour each, running from six to seven and from seven to eight from Tuesday May 31st 1949. This experiment proved to be unsuccessful as the Cubs in the later Pack was inevitably late in finishing. [103].

[102] 3rd Weston (St Paul's) Logbook 1928-57, p. 240
[103] Group Annual General Meeting Reports 1948-49 (Weston Library)

Patrol names 1945 through 1975

Year	Patrol	PL	PS/APL
1945	Bulldogs	J Hollies	
	Eagles	B Chamber	
	Owls	R Neil	
	Woodpeckers	C Chritchard	
	Woodpigeons	B Jones	
1948-49	Bulldog	Colin Lewis	Clifford Hart
	Curlew	Alan Maynard	Peter Kent
	Owl	Terry O'Flynn	Russell Kinsay
	Swan	John Hughes	David Horler
	Tiger	Michael Webber	Kenneth Payne
	Woodpigeon	Michael Partridge	A Baker
	Woodpecker	William Williams	Henry Smythson
	SS Wingate	David Tremlett	John Horler
	SS Scott	Philip Clark	Peter Gee
1954	Bulldogs	R Hadley	D Sanders
	Curlews	F Davis	D Finch
	Owls	R Davis	P Bevan
	Woodpeckers	P Smith	D Wilding
	Woodpigeons	P Andres	D Robert
	Swans	D Gibby	D Eastoe (Acting)
	Tigers	D Langford	
1975	Bulldogs	Robert Hooper	Paul Havindon
	Eagles	Tim Rose	
	Panthers	Adam Cashmore	Graeme Barnes
	Swans	Graeme Tozer	Mark Green
	Woodpigeons	William Stribling	Philip Warren
	Woodpeckers	Nigel Meredith	Chris Beuley

In 1959 two successful parties were held with the 17th Weston (Grammar School) Scout Troop on December 17th and February 18th. In addition the Senior Scout Troop held a meeting with 229th Bristol (St. Aldhelms) Scout Troop in January. The return visit in June by the Bristolians took the form of a cricket match which 3rd Weston won by one run! Amongst the normal activities of the Senior Scout Troop of hiking, camping and advanced badge work they undertook a blindfolded night-hike being dropped off in

Winscombe and having to make their way back to Weston, which they did by 3am. A training camp for the Court of Honour (the original title for the Patrol Leaders Council) was held at Shiplate at Mr W H Poole's farm over the Easter week and Patrol camps continued over the summer months. The usual sites for these camps included Uphill Castle Cricket Club, Hutton, and Shiplate amongst others. The Troop participated in the first Somerset County Jamboree held since 1939, at Ilminster where the Troop was presented with a Good Camping pennant. The Annual two-week Summer Camp was held at Castle Farm Farleigh Hungerford with the six Patrols attending camping in a large meadow loaned to the Troop by Messrs Greenhill brothers. Only 'trained' boys (those who had passed their tenderfoot badge and above) were invited to the Summer Camp. The camp was visited and inspected by the local DC Lt F H Miles R.N.V.R. who commented on the very high standard of camping by the Troop. The weather was very hot and thus bathing and swimming in the river adjoining the site was a very popular pastime.

The Troop's cricket and football teams had many good games under the captaincy of N Partridge and Andrew Trott. The annual Local Association Athletics Sports saw the 3rd Weston take second place behind 17th Weston. Work on the headquarters continued with the completion of the extension to the Gilcraft Den to the tune of £450 fundraised through a series of initiatives from the Parents Committee including jam jar recycling, book and jumble sales and whist drives. John Mitchell took out an ACM warrant with the Pack in 1950[104] with additional occasional assistance provided by Scouts Geoffrey Cooke and Norman Andres. The Troop continued to meet twice weekly on Monday and Fridays with Kenneth Deacon the only Scout to attend all the meetings during the last year. During the year Alan Maynard became Chairman of the Troop Court of Honour. New recruits

[104] 3rd Weston (St Paul's) Group Logbook 1929-1957 p. 222

into the Troop included Derrick A Langford, who later held warrants within the Group including ASM, SM and VSL.

A ceremony was held on September 9th to officially open the extension to the Gilcraft Den by Mr V W Allan, a local Scout Group Trustee. On Armistice Day, November 11th, the eleven members of the Group who gave their lives were remembered in a service at the Den with the Rover flag being carried by a pre-war Rover, Vic Stevens, a contemporary of some of the fallen. Mr A Clark became the new Chairman of the Parents Committee, with the Committee continuing to do sterling work on behalf of the Group with whist drives and jumble sales to assist in fundraising. Mr A Griggs from the Somerset Youth Service showed the Troop the latest Scouting film titled "the Knights of Freedom" on December 2nd, which was greatly appreciated by the Troop.

Over the camping season six patrols held good weekend Patrol camps at locations ranging from the DC's back garden to the more usual haunts of Uphill Cricket Club, as well as the annual pilgrimage to the County Jamboree that year held at Nettlecombe Court near Williton where the twelve Scouts attending achieved a Good Camping pennant. Other activities included a cycling tour camp through Devon and Cornwall by Scouts A Maynard, G Grove, D Baker, E Tillbrook and D Horler. Through the kindness of "Sgt" J Green of 14th St. Mary's Bridgwater Scout Troop, Scouts G Grove and M Partridge, (both 1st Class Scouts), joined his Troop camping at Druens near Rotterdam, Holland from the 10th to 26th August. Six Scouts headed off to Pimm, Sidmouth for Annual Camp, where on visitors day the Troop received one hundred and forty guests and entertained them with games, which the guests were invited to join in, camp tea and camp fire songs and stunts. Making use of the natural surroundings the Scouts bathed several times in the river Otter, using the river for wide-games and challenges such as getting the patrol across the river on stretchers, passing fire across the river and a blindfold crossing of the Otter. Members of the camp support team included R

Kinchin and Peter Neathway manning the medical department whilst stores was run by J B Haynes, A Trott, R Kinsay, J Hull, E Osborn and M Partridge with N G Partridge assisting with the implementation of the programme.[105]

Subscriptions for membership of the Pack in 1951 stood at 1d weekly or 4s annually for Cubs whilst Scouts were charged 2d weekly or 7s 6d annually. A three-day camp was held at Uphill for the older Cubs, which went without a hitch, with the Pack enjoying the annual Christmas party, Cub Morris winning the fancy dress competition. Cubs Douglas Roberts, Robert Parson, Maurice Alder, David McGuire and Michael Page gained their Second Stars; which was an achievement as none had been awarded in the District the previous year. The Pack won first place at the Local Association Athletic Sports held in June on the Grammar School field. In November, CM Bryan Jones was called up to do his National Service. In his absence Mrs Ann Kinchin and Messrs Hancock and Windebank, the Pack treasurer, kept the flag flying, the latter two having joined the team during the year. Scouters Miles Kinchin and Ann Bray tied the knot at St Saviour's on November 26th at noon with Scouting friends and family in attendance.[106]

Mr A Griggs returned to show another Scout film "the Gang Show" on January 26th with members of the 1st and 17th Weston Troops invited resulting in a large turnout. The DC visited the Troop on November 3rd, presenting two ASM warrants to two old PLs, Eric Osborn and Peter Neathway, who had just returned from National Service. Bob a job week raised £22 11s 19d for Troop funds with D Langford earning 22s 6d and Woodpigeons Patrol earning the most for a patrol with £6 4s 6d. The Scouts did not confine their handyman skills to Bob a Job and took on the repainting of the outside of the Den. Scouts Norman Andres and

---

[105] Group Annual General Meeting Reports 1948-49 (Weston Library)
[106] 3rd Weston (St Paul's) Group Logbook 1929-57, p. 244

Gordon Grove and M Board of the 17th Weston Troop were selected at County level as part of the Somerset representatives to the British contingent at the Jamboree in Austria, reflecting on the quality of Scouting being undertaken at 3rd Weston (St Paul's). Camping, the highlight of the life of the Troop, continued to be popular over the following years with regular attendances at Jamborees. The Burnham-on-Sea Jamboree held on the Whitsun weekend of 1951 was particularly memorable as a former GSM of the Group the Rev. Pollard gave the address. The following Somerset Jamboree held at Bath was inspected by the Chief Scout Lord Rowallan. Patrol camping continued unabated over the summer months with annual camps taking place near Westbury in Wiltshire in 1951, Timberscombe in 1952 which a French Scout, Gerald Audre Saint-Supery of 13th Bordeaux Troop attended as a guest. Other activities at Timberscombe included Scouts Michael Bickell, Robert Barley, Terry O'Flynn and Barry Oakley undertaking a special expedition. The Troop performed a camp good turn to the local farmer by building two dams across the stream and assisted in the fruit harvest. Outdoor activities included meetings held at the "tips" and at Uphill Castle Cricket Club field. A more unusual event for the Troop was the attendance of Mr G S Burton, ADC Scouts in Tanganyika, who gave a talk on Scouting in Africa and brought along some exhibits. He continued to attend Troop meetings for the duration of his stay in the resort. King and Queen Chief Scout Awards were gained by Michael Bickell and Barry Oakley. The 3rd Weston Scout Band with Mr Abraham at the head leading the twenty drummers while Norman Andres led the Buglers, had the high honour of leading the annual St. George's Day parade through the town and received much praise.

During 1952 nineteen boys were invested in the Pack, which attended two rallies on the Grammar School field, the first on September 22nd where the Pack came second, and 12th July when the Pack came 4th. However, to make up for that, the Cubs easily won the Wolfshead Trophy on June 6th at the Local Association

Athletic Sports Day. The Annual Camp held in July was a success despite heavy rain and thunder on the second night which the Cubs slept through!

The Parents Committee received a new Chairman, Mr V G Alder, and Mrs Bickell became the Secretary. The Committee continued to assist in fundraising and supporting the Group. Derek Langford was appointed as Troop Leader in September and played the big drum for the first time when the Group paraded to the Harvest Festival service held at the Church of the Good Shepherd. Jonathon Frankpitt was appointed to the PL-ship of Bulldogs and attended with eight of his fellow PLs and PS the Court of Honour weekend held over the 14-15th October at the Den. During the same month ongoing training hikes were held for those Scouts working towards their First Class Badge. The DC, Col. Harvey, visited the Group to present warrants to David Abraham SSL and John Hill, a former Scout who had left the town in 1940. Upon his return he promptly offered his services to his former Troop and took an ASM warrant. Mrs Jenkins had become a regular Helper with the Pack, working alongside CM Wing Cmdr Hancock. The fundraising efforts were directed towards repairing the roof of the Den, with the last of the bill paid off in October after a successful rummage sale brought in £25 to Group funds. The following month the Group gathered for their memorial service, led by the vicar of St Paul's at the Den. Old Scouts Jack Smith and Jack Bowering were present, the former read Psalm 23 and the latter the list of the St Paul's fallen from both World Wars. Bobbie Hadley and Derek Sanders sounded the last post and reveille.[107]

Michael Partridge, whilst on leave from his National Service with the army in Malaya, called in to see his old friends. The Seniors were practicing their Morse code. Mr Griggs showed a series of Scout films at the Den, including: "Call yourselves Scouts", "Way to Adventure", "Inside Information" and "1st Class

[107] Group Report 1955-56, p. 1

Journey". The Troop went carolling around the District on December 19th in the process raising 16s for the Children's Society.[108] In the first month of 1956 a number of visits took place between the St Paul's and RAF Locking Rovers, including an interesting talk given by Bristol County Commissioner John Birkett. The St Paul's Rovers repainted the canteen at the Den as part of interior redecoration that was taking place at the Den. The Cub party was well attended with forty Cubs present. The two competitions held during the party were won by Christopher Pound, for best fancy dress with Nigel Probert taking the top place in the campfire sketch. Mrs Jenkins was presented with her ACM warrant at the start of the monthly Church parade. Clifford Hart took charge of the colour party in March whilst the Rovers provided assistance for over two months to Mr Rousfell who had suffered a stroke. The Troop continued their season of hiking, with ASM John Hill's route around Sand Bay and Woodspring Priory being regarded as the best of the hikes. With the coming of spring the Group was again generously given use of Uphill Castle Cricket Club field. Sectional meetings were held out of doors with the Troop practicing pioneering skills constructing an aerial railway, with bridge laying over the ditches undertaken by the Seniors. The Band, numbering eighteen strong, led the St George's Day District Parade to Wadham St. Baptist Church repeating this task in July for the Girl Guides parade to Kewstoke Church.

The Group said au revoir in May to brothers John and Maurice Gay who were emigrating with their family to Australia. Later John was to send the Troop a selection of Australian stamps. A training camp was held at Charterhouse on Mendip with Scouts from the 1st and 17th participating, though it appears that the Group did not send a patrol to the Somerset Jamboree that year. On June 21st Derek Bendall was appointed a Rover Mate. Three days later the Group posed outside the Den for their annual

[108] Group Report 1955-56, p. 2

photograph taken by one of their own, Clifford Hart, following Church parade.[109] The Annual Camp was held at Manor Farm, West Kingston in the Cotswolds with Pip Partridge, a former Scouter of the Group now residing in London, joining the Troop in camp for the week. A patrol of 24th Weston Scouts under the care of Peter Neathway camped with the Troop over both weekends, with the campers attending the local Church service whereupon they made up four-fifths of the congregation. The weather was at times rough and the Troop proved their worth in selecting the sheltered spot which did not suffer any flooding during the sudden downpours.[110]

The Pack continued to be popular with prospective new boys being asked to attend the first meeting of September. With the formation of the 27th Weston (St Andrew's) Pack the Group decided that preference should be given to boys from the St Paul's parish who wished to join. During the year Cubs Richard Jacobs and Brian Goodyear gained all thirteen proficiency badges offered by the Boy Scout Association, which required a lot of hard work by both Cubs. The Pack was unable to retain the Sports trophy for a sixth year and twelve boys were due to move up into the Troop. The Troop invested fifteen boys into the Troop with 2nd Class Awards being presented to D Ashton, R Cooke, R Hayman, D Thompson, A Golding, T Leslie, B Young and W Osborne, whilst Scouts D J Austin, P Andres, L de Looze (who with his brother had arrived from the Isle of Man), D Easton and D Sanders achieved their First Class Scout Awards, with twenty two proficiency badges being presented. As usual the year witnessed instruction given in metrology by Wing Cmdr Hancock and medical training by the St John's Ambulance instructors. The Seniors had a very successful year with suppers being enjoyed at Hutton Quarry and the Beach with the Seniors undertaking the Mechanics badge which included several visits to the electrics

[109] Group Report 1955-56, pp. 2-3

[110] Group Report 1955-56, p. 3

works on Locking Road. J Austin, who was that rare instance of an outsider being invested into the Senior Troop, and D Langford were on the cusp of completing their Queens Scout Awards. A number of hikes were undertaken such as from Shiplate back to Weston along the river Axe, a two day excursion around Dunster before the Annual Camp at Timberscombe, during which the Venturer badge was attempted with a twenty-four hour period of exploration.[111]

Mrs Fear and Mrs Davies, who ran the Troop canteen, presented the Group with a new Union Flag, which was dedicated and blessed during September's Church parade.[112]

The Rover Crew regularly met on alternative Tuesdays in their room. New members Michael Loud, Robert Bailey and Richard Davies were inducted into the Crew as Rover Squires after the service of dedication held on April 4th, followed by their vigils at St Paul's church. In keeping with the rules, their investiture took place in private the Tuesday after their vigils. Philip Halford was also received into the Crew at the same time. Rover Michael Partridge, prior to his departure for his period of National Service, gave an account of the national camp he attended at Celle in Germany with fellow Rovers Bob Bailey, Peter Smith, Peter Taylor and Derek Langford being guests of the Wunsdorf Scouts, who had camped with the St Paul's Troop at their 1953 Annual camp. Michael was presented with a prayer book by the Crew. To the Crew's delight, Russell Kinsay was able to return after a period of serious illness. A number of meetings with the RAF Locking Rovers and their Leader Peter Merryman took place. The St Paul's crew attended the County Rover Moot held at RAF Locking over the weekend of 18-19th June. The Rovers Christmas good turn involved present giving at Weston Hospital.

---

[111] Group Report 1955 p. 2

[112] Group Report 1955-56, pp. 3-5

Clifford Hart and Derek Bendall were nearing the end of their time of National Service, with the Crew looking forward to welcoming them back home.[113]

In September 1955 the Troop had a membership of sixty-eight Scouts, although Troop attendances averaged forty to fifty Scouts on Troop nights, Monday and Fridays. Eleven Scouts were awarded their Fire Fighter badge after a course of instruction held at Weston fire station. In addition to the monthly Church parades and those Scouts who were confirmed and attending communion service on the second Sunday on the month at 8am at St. Paul's, a small group of Scouts held a regular Scouts Own at the Den on Sunday afternoons between 3-3:30pm. Pip Partridge showed a lantern slide show of the Group history and especially the previous Annual Camp at Colyton (1954) to friends and supporters on February 22nd. The Troop travelled up to Bristol to watch the 229th Bristol (St Aldhelm's) Gang Show "We'll live forever" on December 10th. In addition to the Annual Camp several weekend camps were held including patrol camps and a number of Saturday day hikes, though the latter were not as well supported as they had been in previous years. Two new ASMs were appointed; Douglas Davies and John Hill, who later moved to Ilminster continuing his Scouting with the Ilminster Troop.[114] The band continued to practice on Monday evenings between 8:0-8:30 pm with John Hill leading the Bugles and David Abraham in charge of the drums. Barry Oakley handed over to Derek Langford on the bass drum this year.

The Troop's pedal cart, Weston Wizard, designed and maintained by a former Scout, Bobbie Williams, entered and came second in the Troop heats in the regional finals held on Weston seafront in 1956. The Group were the only Group to own their own HQ. Work continued on improvements and maintenance with Michael

---

[113] Group Report 1955 p. 1

[114] Group Report 1955 pp. 3-4

Loud and the Rovers repainting the Scout sign on the outside of the Den. The exterior was repainted during twelve afternoon or evening sessions by many willing volunteers. The Troop Trek Cart was in need of restoration. The tug of war rope was missing, after twenty years or so of surviving Boy Scout activities.[115]

The Troop continued to be active with John Hall succeeding Derek Langford as SL. By the mid 1970s the Troop had Curlew, Bulldogs, Eagles, Panthers, Swans, Tigers, Woodpigeons and Woodpeckers. Although a year later with a lower number of Scouts in the Troop, Curlews and Tigers were disbanded. The same time saw T Letherby, I Lorriman and G Hill promoted to SPLs.[116] The Troop was providing a varied programme, ranging from a backwoodsman ship evening at Uphill quarry, through to caving, canoeing, wide-games, including joint meetings with the 7th Weston (Uphill) and 27th Weston Troops and providing a five-a-side football team to play friendly matches against the Rotary Club Boys Home as well as working towards the progressive training scheme of Scout Standard and Advanced Scout Standard. The PLC would later decide that only upon completion of the Scout Standard could an APL be invested, whilst a PL had to be a holder of the Advanced Scout Standard in order to be invested.[117]

The membership fee for the Troop was set at 5 pence per week, although within a few years it rose to 20p, with a quarter of the subscription fee going to Patrol funds, whilst the rest went into the Troop funds. Fundraising activities included paper drives, with one successful attempt netting £80 for the Troop. The annual sponsored night hike was undertaken, on at least one occasion the profits were given to the RNLI,[118] whilst on another occasion the funds went towards the Troop's Scotland trip fund.[119]

---

115 Group Report 1955 pp. 2-5
116 3rd Weston PLC Minutes Book 1974-86, pp. 2 &, 8
117 Ibid p.30
118 3rd Weston PLC Minutes Book 1974-86, p. 5
119 3rd Weston PLC Minutes Book 1974-86, p. 14

The Troop joined in the first Axe-Jam held over the weekend of May 15-17th 1975, and the Troop entered a team for the B.P competition.[120] The following year they participated in the District camp codenamed operational Battle Axe held over the weekend of March 26-28th at Burrington, where the Troop were represented by R Hooper, A Cashmore, P Havindon and P Warren.[121] The Scouts were keen players in the District events, entering the annual Sports day, swimming gala and Be Prepared competitions regularly winning the swimming gala in 1976 and the five-a-side competition the following year. The Scouts were especially delighted to win the Stoker White trophy for swimming, the first time the Troop had won the trophy which had been funded through a legacy left by Stoker White's estate. [122] The annual night hike organised by PLs Hooper and Tozer, took place over the night of November 12th with the Scouts hiking from Christon Church to Shipham Scout HQ in 1976.[123]An interesting aside is the discussion of forming a Troop on the Oldmixon estate, as many boys were travelling from the estate to attend St Paul's meetings. The idea was to be discussed further. Presumably nothing came of the idea as no further mention is made within the PLC minutes.

Rob Hase, who was later to become SL of the Troop, achieved his Chief Scouts Award alongside fellow PL, Colin Money, who were both presented with their Awards by the County Commissioner on District Camp.[124] Both Scouts were selected to attend the forthcoming World Scout Jamboree.

The Troop noted that Woodhouse Park was charging 10p a head for a day visit to the campsite. Some time later it was noted in the

[120] 3rd Weston PLC Minutes Book 1974-86, p. 14
[121] Ibid p. 22
[122] 3RD Weston PLC Minutes Book 19754-86 p. 21
[123] Ibid p. 31, 58 & 62
[124] Ibid p. 65

minutes of the PLC that the Patrol Leaders Room was for use by the PLs only, after it had been used and left in a mess, much to the disgust of the PLC.[125] Subs by 1980 had risen to a pound a month, these days it stands at around two pounds plus per week. The Troop brought itself a minibus in 1982 for the cost of £57. It was to prove uneconomic to keep and was disposed of later.

After many years the patrol names, some of which had been in existence since the 1920s, were changed in 1982 with Ravens, Hawks, Eagles and a Beaver patrol replacing the older patrols of Bulldogs, Woodpigeons, Panthers and Swans. The names were changed again in 1985 with a reversion to the more traditional Patrol names of the Troop. Since that time the Troop have generally kept Bulldog, Woodpecker and Tigers patrol names in circulation.

Changes of Patrol names 1982-85	
Swifts	Tigers
Eagles	Eagles
Falcons	Bulldogs
Ravens	Panthers
Hawks	Woodpeckers

John Hall departed from the Group in 1981. The PLC presented him with a clock for his services to the Troop. Dave Palmer succeeded him as SL.[126] Following Dave Palmer's departure in 1984, the leadership of the Troop passed briefly to Rob Hase, who had been an ASL since 1981. He left the Troop in December 1985. The GSL Mr John Moon ran the section for a while until a leader could be found.[127] Although the Troop did not have a SL for some time, the Troop continued to meet, with Ian Stocker running the Troop. He was followed by Neil Williams who was

125 Ibid 10/11/80 p . 91
126 Ibid 17/03/81 pp.92-93
127 Ibid c. Feb 1984, p .125

active in the early 1990s before Dave Perriman joined the Troop in 1994 remaining until June 2000, when he 'hung up his woggle'. Dave Perriman continued to help with the Troop as a Skills Instructor. He took out an ASL warrant in 2005 when the age bar on holding a warrant was lifted and he still serves with the Group, having been actively Scouting for over fifty years.[128] Nigel Neads, a 'home grown' Scout currently leads the Troop, with assistance from Tom Longhorn, who like Nigel was a Scout with the Troop.

Mr L.H.D. Abraham was appointed GSL in 1971 succeeding the long serving Stoker White. Mr Abraham had previously led the Senior Scout Troop and remained as GSL until his untimely death in November 1983. Mr John Moon took up the reins the following month, remaining in post until ill health forced his resignation in October 1994. Mr Moon continues to take an active part in the local District, serving as a member of the Scout Fellowship. The Group ran without a GSL until John Hall transferred from 1st Hutton Scout Group, where he had been GSL, taking the same role at the 3rd Weston. Mr Hall remained with the Group until 2004. Since then the role of GSL has remained vacant.[129]

Mrs P M Jenkins, who started helping with the Pack in October 1955[130] and had a son in the Pack, was appointed CM in 1960, a post she held for two years before handing over to Miss Tunstall, a fellow ACM, who took the Pack for about year. Mrs Day soon followed before the leadership settled down with Mr R G West leading the Pack for most of the 1970s. A year later a second Pack was formed and it is probable that from this period the Packs were named Stoker White and Wingate Packs, Mrs C G Lane took a warrant shortly afterwards leading the second Pack. Both Packs had had a change of leaders by the end of the decade,

[128] Mr Perriman's Recollections 2004
[129] District Archive Mrs A Coombes
[130] R H L White 3rd Weston (St Paul's) Group Report 1955-56 p. 1 & 2

with the 1979 District Directory listing the two Packs, referred to simply as 'A' and 'B' Packs. Miss Letherby was Akela of the 'A' Pack whilst the 'B' Pack was without an Akela.[131] The Group had two ACSLs at this time, Mrs D Parker and Miss J Thomas. The second Pack remained operational until the mid 1980s, when a shortage of leaders led to its demise.

The Pack was being led by Mrs Julie Taylor in 1993. However two years later the experienced Devina Dexter, who had served as an ACSL in the Pack, having previously being involved with 2nd Uphill, 1st Banwell and 32nd Weston Packs, took the helm. When Mrs Dexter moved away from the resort the leadership passed to Mrs Sharon Hall, wife of John Hall. She had been a leader with the Hutton Cubs prior to her move to the 3rd Weston 'Stoker White' Cub Pack. Mrs Hall has continued to lead the Pack, which is one of the more popular Packs, regularly having thirty six Cubs, ever since except for a brief break[132].

The Group formed a Beaver Colony in 1993, which was jointly led by Mrs Debbie Perry and Mrs Wendy Marsh. Mrs Perry remained with the Colony until the late 1990s. Miss Julie Roberts took out an ABSL warrant in 1994 and four years later her mother, Mrs Kathy Roberts, joined the Colony becoming BSL. The Colony has been strongly supported by the Roberts family with Darren Roberts lending a hand whilst his father, Mr Alan Roberts served as Group Chairman at the close of the last century.

The Senior Scout Troop

The Group officially started a Senior Scout Troop in late 1946 which started on Wednesday 2nd October,[133] being led by Mr Haynes who was invested as SM (S) by ADC Senior Scouts, Mr Joseland, on Friday 17th January 1947. Early members of the

---

[131] 3rd Weston (St Paul's) leader warrants 1947-82 & Axe District Directory 1979, p. 8
[132] Axe District Directories 1998 , 2001, 2004 & 2007
[133] 3rd Weston (St Paul's) Logbook 1928-57, p. 142

section included Miles Kinchin, Peter Neathway, Eric Osborne, the TL Geoff Cooke, Brian Jones, J Horler and Alec Kingsmill of the 17th Weston (County School).[134] The Section met initially on Wednesday evening though this soon changed to Tuesday evenings after Cubs and by 1950 shifted again to a Thursday evening.[135] Following Mr Haynes in the leadership of the Senior Troop was Mr L H D Abraham, known as 'Dickie' who took the helm in 1955 having run the section since 1950. By this stage the Senior Troop had its own room within the headquarters. This Section catered for Scouts aged between fifteen to eighteen and was implemented at the end of the Second World War. Two Patrols were formed in the Troop named Wingate and Scott after Major General Orde Wingate, the leader of the Chindits campaign in Burma, and Sir Robert Scott the Antarctic explorer. Senior Patrol names were named after British heroes. The Troop undertook a considerable amount of hiking; other activities included a bridge building competition held at Uphill, with such badges as the Venturer and Despatch Rider badge being undertaken during 1959. The Seniors joined the Scout Troop for their annual summer camps as well as holding their own camps. Many boys from the Troop moved on to the Seniors, whilst some others such as John Moon and, later, John Hall, joined after moving into the area. A very ususual exception was the acceptance of John Austin, who later served for many years as a Scouter at 17th Weston, who was received into the Senior Troop directly from outside, which his SSM, Mr Abraham, commented was a very rare occurance.[136] Mr Abraham was assisted by two Leaders during the time he ran the Seniors, C A Hart and, later on, Richard Ivens, who both came through the ranks in the Group.[137]

---

[134] 3rd Weston (St Paul's) Logbook 1928-57, p. 148

[135] 3rd Weston (St Paul's) Logbook 1928-57, pp. 151 & 231

[136] R J L White '3rd Weston (St Paul's) Notes on 1954-55', p. 2

[137] Senior Troop logbooks 1958-67 (St Paul's Group Archive)
Group warrant papers 1949-82 (Gilwell Archive)

On Friday 5th September, with the whole Group present, Terry O'Flynn was presented with his King's Scout Award by the DC, Colonel Harvey, and four Cubs came up to the Troop having completed their Leaping Wolf badge. The Leaping Wolf badge was the idea of the Scout Commission of Enquiry of 1944 and was the forerunner of the later link badge which sought to encourage a better transfer between the Pack and Troop.[138]

Senior Scouts in 1960[139]

Wingate	**Scott**
G Harrison (PL)	J Frankpitt
R Ivens (P/S)	J 'Dapper' Day
A Richardson	D Osborne
J Moon	P Steff
D Smith	R Bewdley-Bull
D Swingler	

The Rover Crew

Efforts to restart the Group's Rover Crew were first mooted on Tuesday 31st May when the Senior Scouts met to discuss the forming of a Crew, as several members were reaching that age. The first meeting appears to have taken place on Tuesday 15th November, with Mr Kinchin and the SM present, as well as Rovers Brian Jones and John Mitchell.[140] The Crew was to have a

[138] WSM L.A. 'Report of the Scout Commission of Enquiry', Oct 1946, (A E Allen, Weston 1946), p. 9
[139] L H D Abraham, 3rd Weston (St Paul's), Senior Scout Logbook 1958-67, 04/09/60
[140] 3rd Weston (St Paul's) Logbook 1928-57, p. 215

brief existence, lasting less than two years.[141] It lay dormant for three years according to the Group census. The Rovers reformed three years later,[142] and along with the Senior Scout Troop, continued unbroken until 1967 when the Advance Report was implemented.[143] This saw the closure of the Senior Scout and Rover Crew sections, being replaced by the new section known as Venture Scouts which operated in units catering for young people aged sixteen to twenty-one.

Saint's Venture Unit

Discussion within the Group revolved around whether St Paul's could sustain a Group based Unit in its own right or whether they would have a shared Unit which had access to the old Seniors room. The Venture Unit was started in 1971, taking the name of 'Saints' which had been a moniker for the Troop football team in earlier years. Leaders during this time included Mr John Moon, Adam Cashmore and Robert Lowdnes. During this period the Unit undertook a number of foreign trips in their coach, highlights of which included swimming in the Med in 1983. The Saints continued to meet until 1990, when the Unit disbanded.[144]

The Unit remained dormant until being restarted with the encouragement of the GSL John Hall in late 1999. The first meeting was held in the autumn with Lesley Hunt as VSL. Assistant leaders and helpers included Steve Taylor, Penny Jeffries, Rob Hase and myself. Members of the Unit between 1999-2002 included; Chris and Claire, David Deacon, Heather, Paul Simons, Kirsty and James Hall, Nigel Neads and Stephen. Most of the members came from the Group, however several

[141] 3rd Weston Group Census 1947-82, p. 1 (Gilwell Archive)
[142] Copy of Group census data 1947-75 (Gilwell Archive)
[143] Copy of 3rd Weston (St. Paul's) Census data 1947-82 (Gilwell Archives)
[144] Axe District Directory 1979, p. 8, Mrs A Coombes District Archives & Group Leaders Warrants, 1947-82

members who had been Scouts under Lesley Hunt joined from the Hill Road and Bleadon Scout Troops. The Saints attended several weekend camps including the Avon Moot in 2000 and the Northamptonshire 'Nailer' Jamboree in 2001. The Unit closed along with the other Venture Scout units in the District in 2002 with the implementation of the new Programme and age ranges. District based Explorer Scout Cells catering for the age range fourteen to eighteen were formed, although not at the 3rd Weston Group.

The Group continues, currently comprising of a strong Beaver Colony and Cub Pack. The Troop although slightly more depleted in numbers than in times past, continues to provide active Scouting. Like most long term successful Groups the continuing story of 3rd Weston's Scouting success is down to the loyalty of its leaders, with much of the current Troop leadership coming from former Scouts. Some things do not change in Scouting, the St Paul's Scout Group's ability to recruit from within being one of these factors. The Troop is on the cusp of celebrating eighty years of non-stop Scouting, with the Group soon to be celebrating their 100th anniversary on January 17th 2014.

The Gilcraft Den

The Group headquarters was originally purchased by the Rev Pollard for use by the 18th Weston (Good Shepherd) as well as 3rd Weston (St Paul's) who had use of the headquarters from 25th December 1932.[145] Following the disbanding of the 18th Weston in 1936 efforts were made by members of the 3rd Weston (St Paul's) Group, co-ordinated by Stoker White, to retain the Gilcraft Den as their Group Headquarters.[146] With the Group secure and established at the Totterdown Road site, fundraising efforts were undertaken to expand their headquarters over the

[145] 3rd Weston (St Paul's) Logbook 1928-57, p. 64
[146] 3rd Weston (St Paul's) Logbook 1928-57,

years with extensions ranging from the building of the current kitchen and side rooms used for Senior and Rover Scout sections and provision of a toilet block and lobby at the front of the hall. Later a garage and storage was constructed for the Group's equipment. Discussions regarding the replacement of the hall are mentioned in the Group's minutes although this resulted in improvements rather than a wholesale rebuilding. One quote from the 1950s put the cost of a complete rebuild at £2000 to £3000, a considerable amount to raise in those days.

4th Weston Scout Troop (St. Saviour's)

15/03/1910-24 (BST)
13/06/23-21/06/66 (WCP) Reg. No. 6155
(1928) Reg. No. 4231

Scarf: Yellow

Following the reorganisation of the District in February 1919 the Troop swapped its number with the Etonhurst Troop, being known as 4th Weston-Super-Mare (St Saviour's) Boy Scout Troop, which continued for a further five years before disbanding, presumably due to a lack of leaders following the departure of their SM, Canon Yates.[147]

Shortly before the Troop closed a Wolf Cub Pack was started, registering with IHQ on June 6th under the watchful eye of CM, Miss Mary G Hiley, with twelve Wolf Cubs at the time of registration. Throughout the Pack's existence it numbered between eighteen to twenty-four Cubs in three to four sixes.[148] Five years after the Pack formed it had expanded slightly and acquired the services of Miss M Steed as an ACM[149] By 1932 Miss M E Hatcher was running the Pack as CM, a post she held in

[147] Copy of District census of 1920 (Gilwell Archive)
[148] Copy of Form F 13/06/23 (Gilwell Archive)
[149] Copy of Form F 15/11/28 (Gilwell Archive)

addition to being appointed DCM. She had assistance from Miss G F Francis and Miss M Osmond, the latter held an appointment only briefly from April to November 1932. Miss Francis was to return to the Pack as Akela after the Second World War. Miss Franklin, whose Cub name was Baloo,[150] joined Miss Francis in the running of the Pack holding an ACM warrant. Members of the Pack over the years have included Cyril Hart, Philip Robinson, Philip Holley and A Mosley, the latter won the Somerset County Scouts swimming competition in 1945.[151] Mr Philip Holley joined the Pack as a member of White Six in 1953 being invested on October 19th having passed his tenderpad test. During his time in the Pack he recalled that the Pack had about eighteen Cubs in three sixes and that the Cubs wore blue jerseys, his jersey being hand knitted by his mother. Another member of the Pack at this time was Graham Middle who along with Philip attended the Cheddar parade in 1956 as a flag bearer. The Pack joined in the Gang Show at St Jude's Hall as well as Cub sports days held at Ashcombe Park during these years.[152]

Miss Francis later was appointed ADC Wolf Cubs for the town and worked alongside Mrs Banwell who held the joint role of ADC Wolf Cubs for the rural area of the District and CM of the 1st Wedmore Pack.[153]. Miss Francis and Miss Franklin ran the St Saviour's Pack for many years and are recalled with affection by their former charges. Miss Francis stood down as Akela in 1963 handing over to Mr Allan Marshall who had previously been a Helper with the 1st Uphill Scout Group, his connection to the Pack was through his son who was a member of the Pack. Miss Franklin continued to assist for another year before retiring, leaving Mr Marshall as the sole leader of the Pack. Struggling to find additional leaders the decision was made to amalgamate the

[150] Recollections of Mr P Holley 15/09/07
[151] Copy of the 1945 Somerset County Directory p. 11 (Courtesy of the Tangier Centre Archive)
[152] of Mr P Holley 15/09/07
[153] Interview with Mrs V Banwell

Pack with the nearby Hill Road Pack in June 1966 when six boys from the St Saviour's Pack joined the 24th Weston (Hill Road) Scout Group, alongside their Akela.[154]

Isle of Wight National Senior Scout Rally c. 1950s

2nd Weston (Clarence Park Baptist Troop). 1925 Troop with trek cart

[154] Interview Notes with Mr & Mrs Marshall on 12/05/04

3rd Weston (St.Pauls) Scout Group c.1950

3rd Weston (St.Pauls) Kit Inspection c. 1950

4th Weston Pack (St Saviour's) at Cheddar 1956

5th Weston-Super-Mare (Worlebury)

24/10/10-1922

The earliest reference of the Worlebury Troop dates from October 1910 when Mr S Smith was appointed SM, making it one of the earliest Troops to form. The Troop had a change of leader the following year with Mr C T Wright recorded as SM. Presumably he retained the leadership of the Troop until the outbreak of the First World War.[155] Following the cessation of hostilities, the Troop struggled to find a leader, the position of SM was still vacant in 1920[156]. Little more information has been located regarding this Troop and it is probably that it disbanded some time in the early years of the 1920s. However a plot of land, which may have been owned by the Troop, was still held by the

155 Copy of 1914 Weston Trade Directory p 52 (Weston Library)

156 Copy of District return Form B & I 15/04/20 (Gilwell Archive)

District until being sold following the Second World War.[157] The number was reassigned in 1927 to the Christchurch Scout Troop.

5th Weston (Christchurch)

23/03/27		Reg No. 16070
	(1928)	Reg No. 4232
25/04/33-WWII		Reg No. 15167

The Reverend W M Skrine started a Troop for boys from his parish which met in the Alfred Street Mission Hall. The Troop grew slowly and steadily over the following year with an increase from twelve to fifteen Scouts. The Troop's fortunes continued to improve with the arrival of Mr H W Hinsley as a probationary ASM in October 1928, at the same time Reverend Skrine was appointed GSM.[158] The Troop was still active in 1930 when it took in the 10th Weston (the College) Troop[159], although it appears that the Troop disbanded two years later, perhaps due to the loss of their leaders.

Within the space of a year another attempt was made to support Scouting within the parish when the curate, Reverend P H Slocombe, started a Troop comprising of six Scouts. The Troop again met in the Alfred Street Mission Hall (later the Church hall). The sponsor was the Rev. E Roberts, vicar of Christchurch. Mr C V Stevens joined as an ASM at the start of 1935 and the following year Mr E V Hancock took out a warrant as SM in the spring, remaining with the Troop until 1937, although early in the year the Reverend Slocombe stood down as GSM. It is probable that the Troop disbanded shortly thereafter due to a lack of

157 Weston BSA Local Association 'Report on the Scout Commission of Enquiry', Weston-S-Mare Allen, Oct 1946, p.12
158 Copy of registration Form C, 23/03/27, (Gilwell Archive)
159 Copy of Form F 1930 (Gilwell Archive)

warranted leaders.[160] By the end of year Mrs Froggett had opened a Wolf Cub Pack, although she resigned the position the following year, moving to become CM at the 7th Weston-Super-Mare (Ashcombe Pack), the Pack continued to meet with CM Miss I Holloway. The Pack closed some time during the Second World War.[161] This appears to have been the end of Christchurch's direct support of Scouting as no further efforts to start a group are mentioned in the material viewed by the author.

6th Weston-Super-Mare (Kingsholme School)

29/07/12-23

Kingsholme School, which opened in 1904 and was located at the top of Arundel Road, formed a Boy Scout Troop to cater for the members of the school in the summer of 1912 under the leadership of SM Mr Muir[162], Two years later Mr F A Bateman was recorded as the SM. He was a teacher and joint owner, alongside Mr C A Bracknell, of the school.[163] The Troop remained active until 1923, after which no further mention is made of the Scouts at Kingsholme School. The following year the number was reassigned. The School colours were predominantly green with yellow, so it is feasible that the Troop colours reflected this.

Later on, during the Second World War, there appears to have been a Cub Pack operating at the school, as recalled by the late school historian, Mr Christopher Norman, who attended Kingsholme school from 1942 to 1947 and who belonged to the Cub Pack before moving on to 1st Weston (YMCA) Troop.

[160] Notes taken from The Scouter (warrants) 1935 (Gilwell Archive)
[161] Copy of the 1939 Somerset County Directory p. 29 (Courtesy of the Tangier Centre Archive)
[162] Copy of Warrant Cards for Somerset 1908-14 (Gilwell Archive)
[163] Notes from Weston Trade Directory 1914 p. (Weston Library)

Unfortunately little more has, so far, come to light on this Group.[164]

6th Weston (Milton)

Fd: 19/11/1924-1927 Reg No. 13232

The second Troop to bear the title 6th Weston was registered with Imperial Headquarters in the winter of 1924. Troop meetings were being held at the home of the SM, Stanley Kitchen, at 2 South Terrace, Milton (now Salisbury Road). The formation of the Troop in lower Milton perhaps came about as there were sufficient boys interested in Scouting from Milton and Worlebury to continue Scouting in the locality (the 5th Weston Worlebury) Troop had gone out of existence a few years previously). The Troop had nine Boy Scouts and an ASM, Mr Charles Millier, although the Troop operated for a short two and a half years before disbanding, perhaps due to a lack of a suitable meeting place.

6th Weston (Brynmelyn School)

11/07/1927-1933 Reg No. 16471
(1928) Reg No. 4233

This Troop of Sea Scouts, formed in July 1927, was the last Sea Scout Troop to be formed in the resort. (The first Sea Scout Troop, 9th Weston, met at Victoria Methodist Church). The Troop's headquarters was Brynmelyn School, located at number one Landemann Circus, where Mr Cyril A Lund was a Schoolmaster as well as SM to a Troop of sixteen boys. He was

[164] Corr. Mr C Norman 13/05/04 (Biddulph Archive)
Weston-S-Mare Directory 1915 (Weston library)

assisted by ASSM Mr Walter Edwards (on probation)[165]. The Troop was assigned the new number of 4233 in 1928 and Messrs Lund and Edwards were still Group Scouters, although the numbers of Sea Scouts has dropped to ten.[166] No date of closure is recorded for the Troop. However Mr C A Lund was not mentioned by the time of the 1931 Weston census and the Troop went out of existence in 1933.[167]

7th Weston-Super-Mare (Christchurch)

1914-24

Like most early Troops, little information has been found regarding the 7th Weston Boy Scout Troop which formed some time in 1914 meeting at Christchurch Mission Hall, located at the top of Ashcombe Park Road, under the leadership of Mr J J Lovell.[168] The 1914 Weston Trade Directory records that the Troop met on a Thursday night from 6:30pm, however beyond this snippet of information little more can be gleaned regarding this Troop.[169] Mr Lovell is not mentioned in the 1924 Weston-Super-Mare directory, thus the author suspects that the Troop had folded by this time. The number was reassigned two years later.

---

165 Copy of Troop form C record 11/07/1927
166 Copy of Annual Group Re-registration, Form F, record 15/11/1928
167 3rd Weston (St Paul's) Logbook 1928-57, p. 68
168 pp53 1914 Weston-Super-Mare Directory (Weston Museum Archives)
169 Weston Trade Directory 1914 p40 (Courtesy of Weston Library)

7th Weston (Uphill)

01/06/1926-33	(Troop) Reg No. 15043
28/06/1927-33	(Pack) Reg No. 9591
	(1928) Reg No. 4234

Uphill's first effort at Scouting can be traced to the summer of 1926, when in June 7th Weston Boy Scout Troop was recorded meeting at the Old School Room, Uphill. The Troop was off to a good start with three leaders, Rev S Rowland-Hosbons who was the Troop President and Chaplain, in addition to being the Vicar of St Nicholas Church, George J Gillham was appointed SM, being assisted by Charles T H Howe with a Troop of thirteen Boy Scouts.[170] The following year a Wolf Cub Pack of seven boys was formed also called 7th Weston under CM Lewis Emery which met at the Old School Room. With the formation of Scout Groups in 1928 the Boy Scout Troop and Wolf Cub Pack were registered as a Scout Group bearing the title 7th Weston (Uphill). However, a change in the leadership had occurred with Mr Howe being appointed SM, a position he held for a year before standing down in August 1929 swapping to an ASM warrant, whereupon Mr Emery took over the leadership of the Troop, [171] In 1928 the Group strength stood at thirty-five, with twenty-two Boy Scouts, ten Wolf Cubs and three Scouters, Mr Emery, Mr Howe and an ACM.[172] The Group ceased to operate around 1933, likely due to the departure of the leaders. The following year the title 7th Weston was reassigned to Christchurch (Ashcombe).

The 1st Uphill Scout Group which formed in 1951 changed their title from 1st Uphill to 7th Weston (1st Uphill) between 1963-85, showing a recollection of the earlier village Group, though another reason stated was that the Group wished to be nearer to

[170] Copy of Troop Registration Form C 01/06/1926
[171] Somerset Warrants 1909-39 (Gilwell Archive)
[172] Copy of Form F 9Scout Group Registration) 15/11/28 (Gilwell Archives)

the front of the parade to hear the band in the days when Groups paraded in alphabetical order, hence Uphill was near the end of the parade.

7th Weston (Ashcombe Park)

19/03/1934-12/01/1938 Reg No. 16129

The Group was attached to Christchurch, meeting at the Ashcombe Road Mission Hall, hence the name of Ashcombe, for four years from 1934. Although it was registered as extinct in January 1938 it appears to have ceased to meet in the latter half of 1937.[173] The title 7th Weston may have been given to the Group as a remembrance of a previous 7th Weston (the original) between 1914-24. The 5th Weston Group was also sponsored by Christchurch during the 1930s and the Church had two Scout Groups operating at the same time in two different locations, the only Church to support two Groups simultaneously since the very early days of Scouting in Weston, when the YMCA had sponsored two Troops, the 1st and 3rd Weston Troops.

The Ashcombe Group was led by Mr and Mrs Froggett, the Group's sole Leaders, who lived next door to the Mission Hall. Mr W Froggett held the warrant of GSM with his wife as CM to a Pack of twenty-two boys. Mrs Froggett had previously briefly been CM at 5th Weston (Christchurch) before joining her husband in forming the Group. The Troop membership stood at three at the time of registration, although that is likely to have risen as new recruits and Cubs moving up boosted the numbers. A Girl Guide Troop and Brownie Pack also operated at the same venue and the 3rd Weston Brownies ran for a number of years after the closure of all the other sections from the venue before moving to

[173] Copy of Form F, 25/11/37 (Gilwell Archive)

other premises. This Brownie Pack is still operational, now meeting at Weston's United Reformed Church in the town centre.[174]

8th Weston-Super-Mare (Worle Troop)

15/10/14-23

Very little is known about the 8th Weston Troop (Worle) which opened in October 1914 other than the few references from the Weston Trade Directory of 1918 and an early SM warrant for Mr J Marsh[175] and the 1920 Local Association Return.[176] Mr Marsh was the Troop's leader for its nine year existence, as no evidence can be found for the continuation of this Troop after this date when Mr Marsh stood down.

8th Weston (Trinity Mansions)

16/06/1926-30/11/27 Reg No.15110

The number 8th Weston was reassigned three years later to a Troop under the leadership of General Sir Charles Warren who held the warrant of SM and Mr F Townsend as an ASM. Mr Townsend's warrant was cancelled in November and Sir C Warren was briefly appointed an ADC in 1927 shortly before he was called to higher service.[177] Very little information is known about this Troop, other than a note on the registration form with a

---

[174] Weston Trade Directory 1936 p (Weston Library)
Copy of a letter referring to 7th Weston-Super-Mare (Ashcombe Pack) dated 25/11/1937

[175] Weston Trade Directory 1918 p (Courtesy of Weston Library)

[176] Copy of Local Association Return sheet (Gilwell Archives).

[177] Misc Notes Scout History from Mr Richard Ivens p. 2

reference to Troop registration Number 7085 when the Troop disbanded.

8th Weston (Hill Road Methodist)

09/08/1934-31/02/1939 Reg No.16528

The 8th Weston-Super-Mare (Hill Road) was registered in the summer of 1934, having been meeting for a few months prior to registration by Mr J Dudman, who held the position of SM to a Troop of six Boy Scouts amongst whom were PL Dudman, son of the SM, and A Glass[178]. The following year Mr Dudman became the GSM, with Miss Olive Helliar taking a warrant as CM of the Pack of eight Wolf Cubs. The Group continued to offer Scouting to members of the Church and local community until 1939, although numbers appeared to have dwindled towards the end of the Group's life and perhaps explains its closure.[179] Three years later the 24th Weston (Hill Road) Scout Troop was formed at the same location, led by Mr A (Bert) Glass and Mr Doug Raymond.

9th Weston-Super-Mare

Fd: 1914-25

This Troop was organised by Victoria Methodist Church starting in early 1914 and soon gained the services of Stanley Ball as an ASM.[180] Mr B Webb was also connected with the Troop. The Troop was Weston's first Sea Scout Troop and remained operational throughout the First World War. Whilst their SM, Mr Ball, was on active duty the Troop was led by Mr Webb. Members of the Troop in 1917 included Gordon Couch, who became a Weston Hotelier, L Potter, H Couch, L Couch, G

---

[178] Recollections of Mr A Glass
[179] Notes from the Scouter 1935 (Gilwell Archive)
[180] Early Somerset Warrants 1909-39 (Gilwell Archive)

Couch, C Hillman, H Parsons, C Frost, L Limmer, N Hillman, E Buckley, W Robertson, W Frost, Hugh Parsons and P Harding. Little is known regarding the Troop's activities during the War Years, although like other Troops of this vintage they assisted in home defence, including coast watching. One recorded trip was a day trip out to Brean Fort in 1917. A change of Leader occurred in 1920 with Mr W Holder as SM until 1922. Beyond this time little more is known about the Troop which had disbanded by 1928.

9th Weston (Mendip Rovers & Emmanuel Scout Group)

Fd: 20/04/1928-39 Reg No. 18253
(1928) Reg No. 4235

Mendip Rovers

This Rover Crew is the first independent Rover Crew that the author has records for and formed in spring 1928. Mr Cuthbert Collingwood held the position of RSL being assisted by Mr Rex E Monk with an initial membership of eight Rovers in the Group, which were holding their meetings at the Albert Hall. This building was demolished in the 1960s to make way for the Town Hall extension[181]. At the time of re-registration in winter of 1928 the Rover membership had dropped by one to seven and Mr Collingwood was the sole leader. Mr Monk may have started the Scout Troop around this time. The Rover Group was closed in 1938, though according to the correspondence "owing to Church reorganisation this section has not been meeting for some time"[182]. Attempts were being made by the ADC Scouts and the Honourable Secretary to stop the Rover Crew from completely folding, although they would appear to have been unsuccessful.

[181] Copy of Registration Form C 20/04/1928
[182] Copy of Form F dated 15/11/1928

The Scout Troop

A Scout Troop also met at the Albert Hall under the Leadership of Mr Monk who worked as an Upholsterer for Podger and Davis. Henry Allen, whose father was the superintendent at the gas works, took out an ASM warrant with the section. The Troop had three Patrols, Eagles, Otters and Owls, who met on Wednesday nights. Warren Casey, whose father was an RSPCA Inspector, was the Troop Leader and a member of the Rover Crew. PL Donald Bailey joined the RAFVR in WWII and became a Squadron Commander. The curate of Emmanuel, the Rev. Burns, was the Troop Padre and Noel (Pip) Partridge was a 'Lone Wolf' (a Scouter not attached to any one Troop), though he was connected with the Troop and later with 3rd Weston (St Paul's) Troop.[183] Another member of the Troop, Mr Bindon, reminisced about "attending a West Country Jamboree at Corsten near Bath (in 1935) where the Troop won a Good Camping Pennant" and he recalled Christmas hikes over Wolvers Hill and Banwell where for 2/6 they could buy a Christmas lunch with cider[184]. The Troop were keen campers, with camps taking place around the West Country and beyond. Joint camps were held with the Watchet Sea Scout Troop under the leadership of Mr Norman, the local baker, and later an Easter camp at Max Mills Farm, Winscombe in 1928 with the 10th Weston Troop. The farm was a favoured spot for Mr Monk and the Troops he was connected with. Camps were held at Bleadon in June 1932 and later at Ludlow in Shropshire where the Troop held their summer camp followed by an October camp back at Max Mills Farm in the same year The Troop were off to Kernow (Cornwall) the following year for their Summer Camp held at Mevagissy, whilst 1934 saw the Troop camping at Canada Combe with their Padre Rev. Burns. Further activities over the year ranged from hiking on the Quantocks to Patrol camps for

[183] Misc Notes North Somerset compiled by Mr R Ivens 25/10/04 pp 1-2
[184] Misc Notes North Somerset compiled by Mr R Ivens 25/10/04 p 2

Eagle and Otters Patrols. The Group stayed closer to home the following year holding their Summer Camp on the Quantocks and visited Watchet and Minehead. The following year the Troop set off for the St George's Day Annual Service in April at Windsor Castle, camping outside Windsor for a night enroute to the service the next day, where the Troop were reviewed by His Majesty King George V. They were the only representatives from Weston in attendance. Their Annual Camp that year was held in Devon with the Troop camping at Colmbrook and visited Clovelly, the Lorna Doone valley, Fishguard and Badgeworthy waters. The Troop mounted a camp to Scotland in 1937 as well as visiting Gretna Green. The Troop and Rovers were regular attendees of the annual Somerset Jamborees held over the Whitsun weekend, including the 1930 Weston, 1932 at Glastonbury, "which was attended by Scouts from Norway, Sweden and a few other countries"[185] 1933 at Taunton, with three Patrols in camp, and Corsten near Bath in 1935. Scout Griffiths won the Henry Butt trophy for swimming in 1931 much to the Troop's delight. The Troop folded in 1944, Eric Atkinson may well have been the Troop's last leader.[186]

10th Weston (St Martin's)

Fd: 1914-1924

In 1914 a Troop was formed at St Martin's Worle by the Reverend I Holme, who was vicar at Worle Parish Church. The Troop continued to meet until 1924 when the Troop disbanded, presumably due to a lack of leaders. Beyond this very little information is known about the Troop.

10th Weston The College

[185] Mr Monk's photo album 1925-38 (Courtesy of Mr R Faraghar)

[186] 3rd Weston (St Paul's) Logbook 1928-57, p. 124

Fd: 23/11/26-1930 Reg No.15637
(1928) Reg No 4236

The Troop number was reassigned within two years to the College Troop which opened in November 23rd. At the point of registration the Troop started out with the two Scouters, Mr Noel Partridge as SM and Mr J G Stevens as ASM, with twelve Boy Scouts. Two years later the Troop re-registered and a new number was assigned, the 1928 Group number 4236 with Mr William Holder SM with nineteen Scouts in the Troop. In 1930 the Troop folded into the 5th Weston (Reg. No. 4232).

11th Weston-S-Mare

No record known

12th Weston-Super-Mare (Boulevard Congregationalist Church)

Fd: 06/12/27-15/05/33 Reg No.9977
(1928) Reg No 4237

A Wolf Cub Pack formed under the leadership of 'Akela' Miss Ethel Powell and Assistant CM Miss Edith Shaddock and had seven Wolf Cubs sponsored by the Boulevard Church[187] opposite the Weston Mercury offices. In 1928 the Pack re-registered having expanded to sixteen Wolf Cubs under the leadership of Miss E Powell, who was the only leader.[188] Miss Powell can be traced to 1933 in the District records until her warrant is cancelled

[187] Copy of Pack Registration Form 'F' 06/12/27 (Gilwell Archive)
[188] Copy of Pack Re-registration Form 'F'15/11/28 (Gilwell Archive)

in April [189] and presumably the Pack also folded at this time. In 1933 1st Banwell folds with the registration form recording the Troop folding in Group No. 4237 12th Weston-Super-Mare. Presumably at this point in time the Group had a Scout Troop operational, although it probably disbanded some time later.

13th Weston-S-Mare

No record known

14th Weston (Corpus Christi)

Fd:	1919-20	
	02/12/29-WWII	Reg No 10516
	20/03/46-31/04/49	
	18/08/1969-1980	39451

Scarf: Yellow with white trim

Very little is known about this Troop's first founding other than a reference from the Roman Catholic Church of Corpus Christi records from 1919 when "a Scout Troop was formed"[190]. The Troop's headquarters was assumed to be at the Church Hall in Carlton Street. The Troop does not show up in the District Register of April 1920 and so had evidently disbanded.

A second effort to provide Scouting at Corpus Christi was underway in the final year of the 1920s with the Group registering in December 1929, led by Mr Fernand Tasnier as GSM and Mr Ellis Pope holding an ASM warrant with fourteen boys in the Troop at the time of formation. In the following year Mr Tasnier

[189] The Scouter Vol. 1933
[190] The Story of Corpus Christi School 1899-1961 (Weston Museum Archive)

stood down in October with Mr H R McClelland and Miss I Hawkins joining as SM and CM respectively in September[191]. Mr McClelland remained with the Troop until 1932 when Mr Tasnier returned to the Troop until May 1934. The new leaders in the Troop were Mr J J Mason as SM and Mr J Gallop as an ASM both remained with the Troop until December 1937 and with no further warrants issued for the Troop leadership, it is likely that the Troop had folded. Miss Hawkins stood down earlier in the year in February after seven years service, handing over to Miss M C Phelps. Although no record of Miss Phelps warrant's date of issue has been located, she attended a County Scouters meeting in 1936. [192] By 1937 the Group was down to Group Scoutmaster the Reverend W H Hustable and a Wolf Cub Pack under the leadership of Miss M C Phelps and the Group folded some time during the war, probably due to a lack of leaders.[193] The Troop's meeting place was the Parish Hall in Carlton Street. This building along with the Chapel was demolished in the 1960s to make way for the Dolphin Shopping Centre development.

A third, short-lived, attempt at running a Cub Pack was undertaken in the mid to late 1940s with the formation of a Wolf Pack being led by Miss E R M Barry meeting at Corpus Christi School in March 1946. The Pack continued to meet for three years before history repeated itself and the Group again went out of existence.[194]

On August 10th 1969 the 14th Weston reformed and was registered with Headquarters ten days later. The Group comprised of four Scouters, three Instructors, fourteen Cubs and fifteen Scouts. The Leaders were Mr Edward Jack, the GSL, and Mrs Mary Lim as

---

[191] The Scouter Vol. 24 1930 p. 474 (Gilwell Archive)

[192] Notes from The Scouter 1932-34 (Gilwell Archive)
Notes from Somerset Boy Scouts County Scouter's Meeting 08/02/36 (Tangier Scout Centre
Archive, Taunton)

[193] Copy of the 1939 Somerset County Directory p. 29 (The Tangier Archive)

[194] Notes from Lapsed Group Logbook (Tangier Scout Centre Archive, Taunton)

CSL. Mr Alexander Jack and Mr Antony Bambo took the Troop being warranted as SL and ASL respectively. The Troop disbanded in 1978 due to a lack of leaders whilst the Pack continued to meet for another year with Nick Ryan running the Cubs.

15th Weston-Super-Mare (Petergate School)

Fd; 05/12/29-WWII Reg No. 10543

Petergate School supported the aims and ideals of Scouting which was regarded as an extension of the curriculum in some ways and formed a Wolf Cub pack in late 1929. Mrs M K Conner took Pack meetings with assistance from Miss Enid Juteman. A dozen boys were members of the Pack at the time of registration.[195] In 1933 the Pack gained the services of Miss G E Crooke as ACM[196]. A year later she took over the leadership of the Pack for a year before resigning in 1935.[197] Mrs Conner returned to lead the Cubs, remaining with the Pack until it disbanded. The last record from the archives is from 1939. The Pack folded in World War II as it is not mentioned from 1945 in the District Directories.[198]

---

[195] Copy of Group Registration Form 'C'05/12/29 (Gilwell Archive)
[196] The Scouter Vol. Feb 16th – Mar 15th (Gilwell Archive)
[197] The Scouter Vol. Aug 16th – Sept 15th (Gilwell Archive)
[198] Copy of Somerset County Directories 1939 p. 29 & 1945 p. 21 (Tangier Centre Archive)

16th Weston-Super-Mare

No record has been located for a Group bearing this number. Considering that the 15th and 17th are formed in 1929 and 1930 respectively it can be surmised that if a Group bearing the title 16th Weston was started it never got off the ground. No documentary evidence has yet come to light to support the existence of the Group.

17th Weston-Super-Mare

Fd: 04/06/30 (County School) Reg No. 11558
13/05/48 (Grammar School)
22/01/74 (Broadoak) – 1993 Form E

Scarf: Maroon and Gold halved

The 17th Weston County School was formed on June 4th 1930 with a membership of fourteen boys led by SM David C Hughes.[199]. In the autumn the Group saw a change of leaders with the appointment of Rev Frank Pollard as GSM and Mr F K Hanham who remained with the Troop for a year as SM. The Reverend Pollard also held the position of RSL at the 3rd Weston-Super-Mare (St Paul's)[200]. With the departure of Mr Hanham the Troop was led by the long serving Mr F J Hill, who was known in the Troop as 'Fud' being recalled as quite a character. By 1939 Mr Hill had been appointed DSM and GSM whereupon he handed over the running of the Troop to a fellow teacher at the County School, Mr H C Wood, nicknamed "Splinter". Fellow

---

[199] Copy of Form C, 04/06/30 (Gilwell Archive

[200] Misc Notes North Somerset compiled by Mr R Ivens 25/10/04

leaders within the Group included the Woodwork Master Mr Robinson.[201]

During the war years the Group continued to meet and assisted in collecting the harvest and attended farming camps by digging up potatoes on the Fitzhead camp held near Milverton in 1944 as recalled by former Scout Mr Ken Tucker who was a member of the Peewit Patrol. His PL had the surname of Peacock and later took Holy Orders.[202] In May 1948 the 17th County School changed to Weston Grammar School and the 17th Weston was re-registered with headquarters. The Group formed a Senior Scout section to cater for boys aged 16 to 18, in line with the national post war review of Scouting which led to the formation of a Senior Scout Troop which was ably led by SSL Mr I Sutton who recruited Mr Philip Robinson to join him as an ASSL, succeeding Mr Sutton upon his retirement. Other members of the Seniors include Mr Richard Ivens, (currently Avon Scout County Archivist) who was a member of the Troop and Senior Scout Troop before moving to take an ASSL warrant at 3rd Weston (St Paul's).[203]

1958 witnessed a change in the leaders. Mr I Davies took the helm as GSM with Mr K W Cottam in charge of the Troop assisted by Mr D H White an ASM warrant.[204] By 1960 the Group seemed to be going through a lean patch with only Mr Davies and Mr Sutton as the warranted leaders[205], presumably Mr Davies was running the Troop in the absence of warranted leaders for that section. The following year Mr B D Stearn had been recruited to join the Troop as an ASM with Mr Sutton still leading the Senior

[201] Misc Notes North Somerset compiled by Mr R Ivens 25/10/
Copy of Somerset County Directories 1939 p.29 (Tangier Centre Archive)
Recollections of Rev'd Piper 04/09/07

[202] Recollections of Mr K Tucker 03/09/07

[203] Recollections of Mr R Ivens

[204] Copy of Somerset County Directories 1958 p.9 (Tangier Centre Archive)

[205] Copy of Somerset County Directories 1960 p.11 (Tangier Centre Archive)

Scout Troop.[206] The Group's long serving GSL, Mr John Anderson, who taught at the Grammar School, joined the Group's leadership team in 1960 as SM for one year, before moving up to GSM following the departure of Mr Davies, a position he held for thirty-one years, making Mr Anderson one of the longest serving members of a Group[207]. Prior to his involvement with the 17th Weston, Mr Anderson had been a Wolf Cub and Boy Scout in London where "my friends in the 5th East Ham (London E6) wanted me in. I joined on July 3rd 1930, then went into Scouts in 1934".[208] By 1963 the Group's new team of leaders had settled in with Mr J S Anderson at the helm being awarded the "Long Service Award, Medal of Merit and Silver Acorn" for his services to Scouting[209]. Mr R Ashley took over as SM with assistance from Mr John Austin, a former 3rd Weston (St Paul's) Senior Scout and a member of the Grammar School staff, who joined the Troop in 1963 as an ASL (he did not take out a SL warrant) and ran the Troop in conjunction with his friend Mr Anderson and from then on the Troop really took off. The Troop joined in all the District events, as Mr Anderson recalls, "we were in everything and did everything".[210] The Troop were fortunate to have the services of a band of Assistant Leaders and Helpers, including Mr Austin's younger brother, Mr Paul Austin, which allowed the Troop to undertake a wide range of activities and camps, who was a leader with the 1st Uphill Group. The Troop travelled to these events in the Scouters' fleet of cars and as Mr Anderson recalls "had a splendid camping record, and our experience and stable leadership helped very much in this direction"[211]. The Troop camped in the summer holidays, at Easter and at Christmas, the latter often being held on top of Brent Knoll in snow. In addition the Troop also "enjoyed many

[206] Recollections of Mr J Anderson 03/05/04
[207] Recollections of Mr J Anderson 03/05/04
[208] Recollections of Mr J Anderson 03/05/04
[209] Recollections of Mr J Anderson 03/05/04
[210] Recollections of Mr J Anderson 03/05/04
[211] Recollections of Mr J Anderson 03/05/04

wide-games and activities held in the countryside before the southern end of Weston was built up"[212].

The Senior Scout Troop was at times dormant and awaited the impetus of a keen Scout who wished to gain his Queen Scout Award to come and persuade Mr Robinson to restart the Troop. Two boys who did this were Harry Creamer and Raymond Goold, the latter was awarded his Queen Scout Award in 1962 by the DC Col. H Harvey in Ellenborough Park, as well as attending the year's St George's Day service at Windsor Castle. Other earlier award holders included Troop Leader Kenneth Piper who received his King's Scout Award in 1946, the same year that David Bailey of the 24th Weston (Hill Road) Group achieved his Award, both Seniors attended the St George's Day at Windsor.[213] The Seniors enjoyed camping attending the annual Scout Troop camps as well as undertaking their own expeditions such as camping at Overstowey in 1963 where three Seniors and Scouts cycled to the site whilst Mr Robinson drove the kit wagon. The camp is memorable as it was the final camp that the Group's 'parachute tent', a tent made from a World War II parachute which had a thin membrane and thus was quite cold to sleep in, was used. They also participated in the two County Jamborees held locally at Uphill in 1966 and Cheddar two years later. In addition to camping, the older Scouts participated in the pedal cart races that were organised within the District, entering a car called Schweppes, the inspiration for the name being culled from the recently released advert for Schweppes on television, perhaps demonstrating the power of advertising.[214]

The Unit started out as a successor to the successful 17th Weston's (Grammar School) Senior Scout Troop and from its formation in 1968 it was a successful Unit with a large number of members. The Unit unofficially adopted the name 'Smugglers'. Although

[212] Recollections of Mr J Anderson 03/05/04
[213] Recollections of Rev'd K Piper 04/09/07
[214] Recollections of Mr P Robinson 10/09/07

initially meeting at the Grammar School, the Unit was to rent a building in Kewstoke as their own headquarters, in what was later to become the Castle restaurant, was at that time a derelict building which was rented for an annual fee of £10 by the Ventures. Mr Robinson recalled that a lot of time was dedicated to keeping the building in good repair. Although it was cold due to the lack of heating it allowed for Ventures to meet and hold activities. However the local youths were not too helpful, regularly attempting to break into the Unit's meeting place. The Unit mounted a joint summer expedition with the 24th Weston (Hill Road) Ventures in 1972, to Germany, with Mr Robinson driving his Vauxhall Viva across France with a kayak lashed to the roof.[215]

The Unit moved on to Hill Road in 1975 and became a District based Unit. Mr Robinson faded out of the life of the Unit during the later 1970s, as Mr Teale was taking over responsibility for the Unit, later being assisted by Mr Andy Lee who took over the reins before handing over to Miss Penny Jeffries.[216] Further information about the Unit can be found in the District Venture Units section of the book.

In 1974 the 17th Weston amended their name again when the school changed from Weston Grammar School to Broadoak on 22nd January.[217] The Troop decided as part of the 75th anniversary celebrations (1907-82) to undertake a sponsored seventy-five legged race held on the Beach Lawns. The event resulted in making the local press as well as making people laugh as the domino effect kicked in as the participants fell over.[218] On April 1st 1984 the Group 'rescued' the 32nd' Weston-Super-Mare (Oldmixon) Group. The Pack, led by Mrs Skillen, continued to meet at Oldmixon Primary School and for the first time the Group

---

[215] Recollections of Mr P Robinson 10/09/07
[216] Recollections of Mr P Robinson 10/09/07
[217] Copy of Form C2 22/01/74 (Gilwell Archive)
[218] Recollections of Mr Spillane 10/09/07

had a Cub section attached to it, which continued to meet for a number of years before closing. The impending retirement of the Troop's leadership team in the early 1990s was causing concern as it was looking increasingly likely that no new leaders would come forward and this sadly came to pass when, after sixty-three years of providing Scouting at the School, the Group disbanded in 1993. One of Weston's most active and premier Groups went out of existence.[219]

9th Weston (Emmanuel) Scout Camp Dresser

[219] Copy of Form C2 01/04/84 (Gilwell Archive)

9th Weston (Mendip) River Crew at Gateway 1930

9th Weston (Mendip) Rovers Crew c. 1930

Skip Wood 17th Weston c. 1940

17th Weston Senior's Rope Bridge

17th Weston Bivvy

17th Weston Scout Group Queen's Scout Award 1964

Stogumber Joint Venture & Ranger Camp

18th Weston-Super-Mare

Fd: 16/10/31-06/01/37
(Church of the Good Shepherd) Reg No. 13225

A Wolf Cub Pack was opened at the Church of the Good Shepherd, which was an outreach Church for St Paul's Weston, on the corner of Whitting Road and Devonshire Road on October 16th 1931 having fifteen Cubs and two Scouters.[220] The Pack was led by Miss Ann Bray, who held a warrant as CM, and the Rev. Frank A Pollard, who was the vicar of the Church, who held the joint positions of GSM at both the 17th Weston (County School) and 18th Weston and RSL at 3rd Weston (St Paul's), being warranted in October 1931. Rev Pollard remained with all three Groups until the end of 1935 when he moved away from Weston. His successor as GSM, gaining his warrant in December 1935, was the Rev. F H C Higgs, whilst simultaneously holding a RSL warrant at 3rd Weston (St Paul's)[221]. In February 1936 Mr Stevens stood down as ASM and it is likely that the Troop also folded at this time, although the Pack continued to meet until January 1937 when they merged with 3rd Weston-Super-Mare (St Paul's) Group.[222] Miss Bray had started out as an ACM with 3rd Weston (St. Paul's) and after the closure of the 18th Weston she returned to her former Group as CM. Forty years after the closure of the Group the wooden Church was demolished after serving the community for fifty-four years. A block of flats now stands on the site.

19th Weston-Super-Mare

22/02/32-1943 (St Jude's) Reg No. 13695
04/05/48-11/07/2000

---

[220] Copy of Form C 16/10/31 (Gilwell Archive)
[221] From Gilwell records and Weston Library records
[222] Copy of Form C 16/10/31 (Gilwell Archive)

(St Jude's, Milton & Worle) 26263

<u>Scarf:</u> <u>Blue with yellow edge</u>

The formation of the Group was in part a reaction to the growing need for a Scout Group for the boys of Milton village, and was supported by the vicar of St Jude's the Rev E F Sherwood who took a warrant as GSM. Mr Arthur Ward and Mr Edward Thorn, who lived on the recently built Milton Brow estate, were recruited to help take Scouts and Cubs respectively. Sixteen Wolf Cubs and eighteen Boy Scouts were registered at the time of formation, with meetings being held in the Parish Room opposite the Church at the top of Grove Road. Although little is known regarding the activities of the Group it is recorded that on occasions the Scouts played cricket against the Methodist Troop, 20th Weston, on land owned by Mr Jackson-Barstow behind Christchurch Mission Hall in Ashcombe Park Road where the Snowdon Vale estate now stands. The Group regularly attended Church parades at the Church and had easy access to woods at Worlebury. However like many other Groups, the sections ceased to meet during the Second World War as leaders were called up for service.

The Group was to remain dormant for five years until being restarted in April 1948, although the Group was not registered until a month later, with a Cub Pack and Scout Troop. The latter had a short existence and disbanded temporarily around 1951. Early leaders with the reformed Group included Miss Marjorie V Boots, who started out as an ACM, though she was soon promoted to CM, departing from the town in 1954 and selling her home, Ashbrooke House, near Ellenborough Park, which became Ashbrooke School. The younger section soon acquired the services of another warranted leader when Miss G Steel of Hutton took out an ACM warrant in November 1948, serving until 1951. The role of GSM was undertaken by the Reverend E D White, who was related to R J L 'Stoker' White GSM of 3rd Weston (St Paul's), However the following year Eric Atkinson, the SM, had succeeded Reverend White as GSM. The leadership of the Troop passed to Mr W R Sharp. Despite a new leader the Troop disbanded the following year.[223] In 1951 Mr Atkinson stood down and the Group was left without a GSM for a period of fifteen years, during which time the Group was to expand and succeed both numerically and in terms of purchasing a plot of land to build a headquarters.

The archival evidence for this Group survives in considerable detail from the reforming of the Troop in 1954 onwards, the bulk of the material having been collated by their longest serving Scouter, Bob, R E Cooke known to the young people of the Group as 'Rikki'. The Group has been fortunate to have a core of dedicated leaders throughout its lifetime. Beside Bob Cooke there has been a cadre of leaders including; David Perriman, Steve Gambling and Alan Reynolds who all worked with the Scout and Senior/Venture section.

The Troop was restarted at the invitation of the DC, Col. Harvey, with the appointment of Mr E Willetts of Chesham Road North as SM, with four Scouts, his son Keith, John Gillings, John Bennett, who all came up from the Cubs, along with a new recruit David Fry. The first Troop meeting was held on Monday 24th September between 7-8:15pm. The meeting opened with the coming up ceremony with all the Pack forming a horseshoe to say goodbye to their sixers. Following the dismissal of the Pack, the Troop meeting continued, with the formation of two patrols, Fox patrol with David Gillings and John whilst the Cuckoo Patrol members consisted of Keith and David Fry. The decision was made to hold meetings between the current times on Mondays until further notice. Afterwards the Scouts listened to a talk by Skipper Willett about the tenderfoot tests. The meeting was concluded with flag down and dismissal.

[223] Copy of Form C (04/05/48) (Gilwell Archive)

The following week two more recruits attended the meeting, Allan Duckett and Malcolm Smith, both were former Cubs. The Troop elected to have a monthly patrol competition with points being awarded for smartness of uniform, games and passing badges. The first game of handball was played by the Scouts, and was to become a firm favourite with Scouts across the decades. During October the Troop grew from six to nine with Geoffrey Glimstead coming up from the Pack. David Burgess and Michael Ashman joined, the latter had been a member of the 3rd Weston (St Paul's) Cub Pack. The fledgling Troop received a gift from an unnamed well-wisher from Banwell who brought the Scouts a new flag, which was presented on the Troop meeting of the 25th October. During the first meeting of November the Troop had two special visitors, the DC who inspected the Troop before presenting the Troop with a £5 gift from the Local Association, and the vicar, Rev Knight of St Jude's. November saw the Scouts undertake their first outdoors activity, a (very wet) morning hike with tracking signs on Sunday 7th. A second hike was undertaken at the end of the month in better weather following a route from the Church hall in St Jude's Terrace, over Worlebury hill to the woods with a look around the Hill fort, returning via Bristol Road and Ashcombe Park, attended by Scouts Keith Willett, M Ashman, M Smith, A Bennett and D Fry achieving their Woodcraft badge in the process, which was the first badge undertaken by the Troop. In order to complete this badge, Scouts had to demonstrate to the instructor the following; recognition of tracking signs, playing a wide game and the ability to light a fire with one match.[224]

A key event in the life of the Troop was the investiture of Keith, John, Malcolm and Michael as Scouts on December 6th in front of their fellow Scouts and parents. The Group attended a Christmas service on December 19th with eight Cubs and Scouts along with the Leaders being present. Four days later Skipper Willett, Akela

224 Woodcraft Badge requirements (Gilwell Archive)

and a Cub undertook a good turn giving out books and presents to the children at the Salvation Army home in Clevedon Road. 1955 saw more recruits joining the Troop, most probably as a result of having attended the Group Christmas party held at the beginning of the month and strongly supported by the Parents Committee. Six new recruits attended in January, including P Hall, P Golledge, John Taylor and Timothy Wood. The Troop ordered twelve Scout berets, whilst training continued towards achieving the Tenderfoot, Second Class and First Aid badges. Further investitures took place in February for Allan Duckett, David Fry and David Gillings. By the start of spring the expanding Troop was in need of additional leaders, fortunately Kev Millward, a Rover Scout at RAF Locking, came down to lend a hand. Skipper Willett reported in the logbook that Michael Hadley was continuing to be a great asset to the Troop. The Scouts attended their first District St George's Day parade with Keith having the honour of carrying the Troop flag, eight Scouts attended. In early May two further recruits joined the Troop, Stephen Coombes and Graham Jones, who were introduced by David Fry. Stephen became a leader with the Hill Road Group in later years, whilst his friend Graham attended the World Scout Jamboree. By the end of July the Troop had grown to fourteen, necessitating the formation of a third patrol, Woodpeckers, led by M Hadley. The Troop mounted a short summer camp held locally at Windmill Hill, Hutton at Mr Tucker's Canada Farm with K Willett, A Duckett, T Wood, S Coombes, M Smith, G Jones, M Hadley and M Venn camping along with six Scouts from 1st Uphill. Shortly after the camp was pitched the DC, Colonel Harvey, paid the campers a visit, as did Peter Neathway from the 3rd Weston (St Paul's) Troop, Mr Jones and SM Collings of the Uphill Troop. The autumn saw further new members joining, with David Clothier, Ian Cross, Stephen Farr, from Kewstoke, and Ivor Jackson joining. Additional evenings were set aside outside of the regular Troop nights for additional training for boys working towards their First and Second Class badges. Further developments in Scout training were discussed in the first Court of Honour of the New Year, 1956, where it was decided that training would be conducted in groups according to ability. The focus on badge work was paying dividends with Observer badges and Second Class badges being awarded to Stephen Coombes, Graham Jones, Keith Willett and Scouts Coombes and Jones were promoted to Patrol Seconds in February.

The Patrols were encouraged to undertake their own camps during the spring and early summer with patrol camps taking place over the intervening years at Pool Farm, Banwell, Christon, a return to Watts Cottage for an Easter camp in 1957 taken by PL M Venn. A PL and PS camp was held at the usual haunt of Windmill Hill with five out of eight present, though little was apparently achieved as the programme was not followed as noted by Skip Perriman. Scouts, J Bennett, S Coombes, M Hadley, R Tirrell and K Willett camped at Cheddar over the May Day weekend for 5/6d at Broadway House with the Camping Club, of which the Scout Movement had been a founder member. At the end of the month ASM Perriman, who camped in the Scouters enclosure, and a patrol entered the Somerset Jamboree held at Yeovil over the weekend of the 18th-21st, coming away with a Second Class pennant for good camping. The Troop camped at Bishop's Lydeard at Watts Cottage with ASM Perriman in charge as Skipper Willett was away for part of the week of the 11th to 18th August at the cost of 32/3d enjoying hiking, an evening with the local Scout Troop (presumably the 3rd Taunton Bishop's Lydeard Troop) and a day trip into Taunton .

The Group paraded at St George's Day held in Cheddar, the flag bearers were S Coombes and M Venn, with D Clothier, G Jones, J Taylor and K Willett as escorts. Other parades undertaken by the Group included the annual Empire Youth Parade at Kewstoke Church with Kewstoke Guides in attendance in either May or June.

Following the summer holidays the Scouts got involved with the pedal car races selling programmes on the sea front in September. A twelve week pioneering project was undertaken which took the Troop up to Christmas. On the final Saturday in September M Venn and G Jones were working towards their First Class badge, hiking from Cheddar Head Farm to Under Knoll, Brent Knoll, to the home of the DC. The following month both boys were awarded their First Class badges, the first to be presented in the Troop. Graham Jones was promoted to PL of Cuckoo Patrol, he was presented with the Scout Cord in December and became the first Senior Scout in the Troop in a ceremony conducted by Skipper Willett and Dave Perriman. Skipper Willett departed from the Troop in March 1957 moving to Winchester with his family. The feelings of the Troop were recorded by Dave Perriman noted in the Troop log "this was a blow for the Troop and Group as 'Bill', Skipper had put much work into both". The Troop passed into the care of Dave Perriman who would remain with the Group for many years, as SM, Scouter in charge and later starting up the Axe Pathfinder Venture Unit, renamed in the early 1980s as Celts VSU.

During the summer of 1957 M Venn and G Jones participated in the preliminary Somerset Jamboree camp being held at Burnham on Sea over the weekend of 7-10th June. Meanwhile, down the road at Berrow Skip Perriman led a combined camp comprising of members of the 3rd Weston and Hill Road in addition to his own Troop at the Burnham District pre Yorks Wood camp. Malcolm Venn, Peter Bowles and Michael Griggs were invested as Senior Scouts in June. A fourth patrol, Cobras, was formed as membership continued to grow with twenty-one Scouts in the Troop. Mr Files, who had been a former SM and had a son in the Troop, joined as a Helper, whilst further assistance came from Rover Nigel Marston until he was called up for National Service. With so many new recruits it was decided to hold a Tenderfoot Camp taken by Skip at Mead Farm, Berrow over the weekend of June 20-21st prior to the Summer Camp. New recruits included; P

Bowles, G Files, R Gollicker and R James. This proved to be a somewhat wet camp, with cooking taking place on Primus stoves, undoubtedly an experience for the unseasoned campers although a good camp was had by all, including Graham Jones and Stephen Coombes who cycled out in the pouring rain to visit the camp. The August Summer Camp was held at the beautiful Holford Glen on the Quantock Hills with seven Scouts in camp, with an all day hike on the Tuesday that seemed to involve Rover Nigel Marston having the Troop in tow and whose favourite route appeared to be straight through the middle of gorse bushes, followed by getting stuck in mud at East Quantockhead as the hikers travelled round the coast to St Audrie's bay! For some the camp was cut short with only PLs J Bennett, M Venn, P/S J Taylor and Skip remaining for the last weekend and visiting Minehead.

By the close of the year, the membership of the Troop stood at twenty-five, including two transfers from the 1st Wilton (Taunton) Troop, Roger Betley and PL John Taylor. PL Stephen Coombes and PS John Taylor of Woodpeckers completed their First Class hike over the weekend of the 14th-15th September, starting out from Hutton, passing through Canada Coombe, through Christon and over Brent Knoll, camping at Shute Shelve before carrying on to Cheddar and catching the bus home. Both gained their First Class and Scout Cords on Monday 14th October. The Troop elected to hold patrol meetings until December partly to give Skip a break and to try out patrol-based Scouting. Three patrols managed to hold regular patrol meetings during the following six weeks. Upon the return to normal Troop meetings a new Troop yell was created which was:

> "Nineteenth Weston, nineteenth Weston"
> We're the Troop that is the best
> None can stop us, none can top us!
> That's the nineteenth Weston without question
> W E S T O N, Weston!"

At the start of 1958 Graham Jones was appointed Troop Leader whilst new PLs were appointed, with Malcolm Venn being promoted to PL of the Guy Gibson Senior Scout Patrol, David Clothier as PL of Foxes, and the two John Taylors taking Cuckoo and Woodpeckers respectively. The fourth patrol, Cobras, had disbanded as numbers dipped, predominantly due to several older Scouts moving up to the Senior Patrol. A dozen Rovers from the Locking Crew ran a Troop meeting on January 27th which included some novel stunts. The Troop held a joint wide game against the 27th Weston (St Andrew's) Troop on Monday 17th March, the aim of the game was to get into the St Andrew's Group HQ without getting caught which six of the Scouts achieved and the 19th were declared the winners. The three PLs attended the District PL Training camp run by the Locking Rover Crew over the weekend of May 9-11th with the Troop continuing its tradition of entering a team for the County Jamboree under wet and wild conditions, when a gale and heavy rain flooded out several Troops whilst many more stayed away from the event.

On Wednesday 5th March the Senior Troop met separately for the first time with Derek Bendall, ASM with 3rd Weston (St Paul's), attended the meetings to assist Skip Perriman. Seniors Jones, Taylor and Venn accompanied Skip in a weekend hike over the Quantocks, being recorded in the logbook as "steep and strenuous in places, especially the dash back for the train from Williton". The Sunday was Skip's 23rd birthday and this was duly celebrated with a baptism of Skip with jugs of very cold water! Wet weather in early June washed out the inter-patrol competition taking place at Manor Road quarry, with a retreat back to the Church hall. Rick Harling joined the Troop after having earned eight points at the District Troop Intersports Day and Ian Cross was awarded his Second Class badge. Further investitures followed during the summer months with Christopher Crabtree, Richard Parsons, Brendon Berkeley, Chris Golledge, Richard Venning and Andrew Garland being invested. With five Cubs coming up from the Pack, the Troop was again expanding with two new Patrols; Badgers and Ravens being formed. Patrol camping ensued with Ravens and Foxes camping at Hutton whilst Woodpeckers, Badgers and Cuckoo Patrols camped at Loxton. Evidently a wet year as all the Patrols were unlucky with the weather, which provided a tough introduction to camping for the tenderfoots. The Troop took nineteen boys on Summer Camp to Colyford with Skip and Troop Leader Graham Jones, acting as quartermaster. Ken Hibbard drove down on his motorbike to join the Troop in camp. Also in camp on the site were several other Troops including the 1st Weston (YMCA) off whom the 19th Weston had borrowed camping equipment.

Starting back in September saw further new members wishing to join with the Troop having six sets of brothers, although Jonathon and Ian Cross were attending boarding school in Surrey and attended Troop camps and weekend activities. The Troop meeting of November 17th was taken by the Rovers from Locking, whose theme was 'in darkest Africa'.

In 1968 the leadership of the Group comprised of 'Skip' Mr Hayman, 'Kim' Mr May-Miller the SL and 'Rikki', Mr R Cooke who held an ASL warrant. Efforts were undertaken at the start of the year to form a Venture Unit, which was briefly to come into existence lasting for approximately six to nine months. The group would attempt twice more to start a Unit, once in 1970 when they approached the nearby 29th Weston (St Peter's), regarding forming the Unit jointly between the two neighbouring Groups. This attempt proved unsuccessful.[225] Another attempt was considered during the mid 1970s before finally achieving long term success in 1983 with the formation of the Celts VSU.[226]

[225] 19th Weston Executive minutes 09/07/70 (19th Weston Archive)
[226] 19th Weston Executive minutes 09/01/68 (19th Weston Archive)

With the departure of the SL and CSL the husband and wife team, Mr and Mrs May-Miller, who were moving away from Weston, the Group was seeking new section leaders. Mr Cooke moved from ASL to SL to take the Troop, whilst an effort was made to find a new CSL. Mrs Jean Cooke, the wife of the SL, joined the leadership team as an ACSL, although due to other commitments she was unable to take on the role of CSL. An approach was made to Mr Perriman, a former member of the Group to assist. Although he was unavailable at that time, he later offered his services to the Troop in 1969.[227] Mr Nick Christian, who was a leader with the 29th Weston (St Peter's) Pack, moved over to take over the leadership of the Pack in January 1969.[228]. In the following March the Group Chairman, Mr Mohan, stood down and the role was taken by Mr Scarlett. The Pack was in need of extra help and an appeal yielded several new Instructors coming forward including Mr Wiseman and Mr Alan Slingsby.

The hunt for a HQ

From the late 1950s the Group began to seek their own headquarters; either an existing building or a plot of land to build their headquarters upon. As the 60s decade advanced so the need became more urgent with St Jude's Church Hall becoming increasingly unavailable for sectional meetings and for fundraising events. With the formation of the Senior Scout Troop the situation was exasperated as the Seniors could not meet at the Church Hall, they met over a mile away. During 1957 the Group made a bid for £795 that the Borough Council had earmarked to spend on something of public good in the Milton and Worle area. The Scouts applied for the money to be used to purchase the former Methodist Chapel next door to the current headquarters, although in that instance the Group were unsuccessful. The following year Mr Perriman, in his role as acting GSM, was again

[227] 19th Weston Executive minutes 23/07/68 (19th Weston Archive)
[228] 19th Weston Executive minutes 27/01/69 (19th Weston Archive)

in correspondence with the Council regarding the purchase of Milton Quarry (the old Henry Butt lime quarry, where the Ashbury Road estate now stands) as a place to site a headquarters. The group applied for funding from Somerset Youth Service and the Boy Scouts Association in addition to their own fundraising efforts, ranging from the periodic sponsored hikes to the more regular rummage sales. The Group made an application for the old Gospel Hall in the Scaurs, Worle in 1960, which was also being chased by the 1st Worle Guide Company. This effort failed as the Group were unable to accept the offer of a lease for a short term, as the Scaurs was due to have road widening work undertaken and the old Gospel Hall may have been pulled down. Efforts carried on to purchase or to rent a plot of land, with Worle Recreation ground and Milton Quarry, this time at Milton Hill, being considered. Between 1963-64 the Group was in negotiations and then submitted a planning application for the garage, 44 Upper Bristol Road, for conversion into a headquarters. Though plans were advanced this too fell at the fence as the owner withdrew the property from the market.

The Drysdale HQ

However after all the let downs the Group were offered a plot of land by Miss Price in June 1965 at the bottom the hill behind Drysdale Close with planning permission being applied for two years later with a successful application completed in April 1968. The Group mobilised its resources, both in terms of finances and manpower. Under the supervision of SL Bob Cooke, with assistance from Eric Johns and a band of parent helpers, the new headquarters rose block by block being completed in 1974. With the closure of the St Jude's Hall and Church in 1974 the Group was provided temporary accommodation by Milton Methodist Church at a weekly rent of £1.50, whilst the Group put the finishing touches to the Drysdale Close headquarters.[229] The

[229] 19th Weston Executive Minutes 16/01/74 (19th Weston Archive)

current headquarters developed in three distinct stages over the years with the main hall being constructed first. It served initially as a store hut though the Group drifted into it as their headquarters within the next few years. Further extensions appeared as funds were raised, with a kitchen and toilet block being constructed in 1975, shortly after which the Group moved in following the closure of St Jude's Church and Hall in 1974. The stone floor in the hall was overlaid with wood in 1978, whilst the final phase was completed seven years later when a large southward facing room was constructed, which was subsequently subdivided into two rooms, a Committee Room and the Venture Scouts Room with a passageway between and the kitchen was extended. The final phase of building work took place at the end of the 1980s when a garage and project room was constructed at the top of the driveway. This was largely the work of Group Committee members Andrew, a builder, and Liz Ball, whose son Steve was a member of the Venture Unit.[230]

Cubs & Scouts

The Group had not been idle whilst efforts were focussed on the headquarters quest. A second Pack was opened by the husband and wife team of Peter and Pansy Langley in Worle for boys from the area, as the current Pack was at full strength with a long waiting list. The inaugural meeting was held on March 9th 1970 as part of the 19th Weston Scout Group, with meetings being held at St Martin's Church Hall. The Pack was to become very popular and successful, with the Executive recording their thanks to the Langleys for their hard work and dedication the following year.[231] Within two years the Pack would split off and form another

[230] Correspondence 1957/68 (19th Weston Archive)
Interview with Mr R Cooke 2004

[231] 19th Weston Executive Minutes 22/01/71 (19th Weston Archive)

group, the 33rd Weston (1st Worle), today carrying on its Scouting remit under the title of 1st North Worle Scout Group.[232]

The Group were active in District events with the Packs entering the Cub Cricket and Sports Day competitions, Sixer and Seconder days held at Highbury and Winscombe along with the Activity Day at Wedmore, whilst the Troop were involved in the District pedal car races, swimming gala and Advanced Scout Standard training, the latter being a county event held at Bath. By 1971 the Group strength stood at ninety young people, (seventy Cubs and twenty Scouts)[233]. The following year a new Akela, Alan Slingsby, was appointed.[234] The 29th Weston joined the Group on July 16th in a parade to St Jude's Church. The Pack entered the Cricket competition being held at Cheddar, as well as the swimming gala where they came in second place and also planning a trip to Wookey Hole. The Troop numbers had declined sharply with the Troop down to nine Scouts, though seven boys were due up in September. The Troop did not meet in January 1973 due to a very poor turnout for the Christmas parade[235], and one boy had transferred to the 1st Worle Troop due to a clash with football practice. However, in order to try and reduce the waiting list, the Pack expanded, reaching a full thirty-six and Cubs were to transfer to Scouts from ten and a half rather than eleven from this point. By March eight Scouts had passed their Cycling Proficiency badge with Troop numbers up to thirteen Scouts.

Later in the year the Troop took in the 29th Weston (St Peter's) Troop which increased numbers to around the mid-40s. The planned Summer Camp to Chatsworth had to be cancelled as it was over-subscribed, the venue was rearranged for Brecon. At the Group AGM the DC, Mr Haynes, presented two warrants, an ASL warrant to Mr White and a CSL warrant to Mr Valentine

---

[232] 19th Weston Executive Minutes 09/03/72 (19th Weston Archive)
[233] 19th Weston Executive minutes 11/05/72 (19th Weston Archive)
[234] 19th Weston Executive minutes 11/05/72 (19th Weston Archive)
[235] 19th Weston Executive minutes 08/02/73 (19th Weston Archive)

who had started a second Pack to reduce the long waiting list. Eric Johns was applying for a Leader permit, which would bring the Troop leadership team up to four.[236]

By the following year the Troop strength stood at forty-one, which was a direct result of three Cub Packs feeding it. Mr Cooke was now short of leaders following Ray Alford's move to take over the Uphill Troop and Mr White was unavailable due to work commitments.[237] As part of the Troop's annual activities the Scouts participated in the Scout Job Week ('bob a job') raising £78.56 in 1974, of which £59.20 was spent on the Troop's capitation (membership fee).[238] The World Scout Jamboree being held in 1975 was to cost £50 to attend for the successful applicants. As a matter of comparison the 2003 Jamboree held in Thailand cost £2500 per Scout to attend. Numbers were down for the Troop camp, with only eighteen expressing an interest, though this may have been due to a large number of Scouts being involved in the Bristol/Bordeaux holiday exchange taking place. Subscriptions for the Troop rose from 75p to £1.30 during the autumn term, apparently the result of inflation and Avon Scouts County increase.[239] The Troop enjoyed a good Summer Camp, despite a wet start, with the Troop receiving a further new leader, Chris Lowther, who was in the process of applying for an ASL warrant. Scouts were developing an interest in water activities with a canoeing session at Marine Lake, which turned out to be a washout. The Krazy Kraft regatta was more successful, with their entry staying afloat for thirty-five minutes. Six Scouts had undertaken a Patrol camp under their own initiative, whilst the Troop had entered the Cricket and five a side football competitions.[240] With the Troop strength at forty-four and more Cubs coming up soon, a decision was made to divide the Troop

[236] 19th Weston Group AGM Report 1973
[237] 19th Weston Group AGM Report 13/05/74
[238] 19th Weston Group Exec Minutes 03/06/74
[239] 19th Weston Group Exec Minutes 03/06/74
[240] 19th Weston Exec Minutes Sept-Dec 1974

into two meetings, the Wednesday nights would be for boys who were working towards their Scout standard, whilst the Friday Troop night would be for the older Scouts, Chris Lowther took the Wednesday Troop which had twenty-three boys, leaving twenty-one Scouts attending the Friday Troop night under the direction of Bob Cooke. Eddie Scarlett stood down as GSL, following his appointment as DC. This resulted in a change round in the group with Bob Cooke taking over as GSL.[241] With such a large Troop the summer camp was one of the largest mounted by the Group, with thirty-one Scouts and four leaders in camp at Batcombe.

An interesting fact that stands out amongst the records of the Group was the concern felt about the impending creation of Avon County and the effects it would have in Scouting circles, they were to prove groundless, but this does reveal some of the unease felt about leaving Somerset County.[242]

The Troop had developed a regular pattern of camping with a weekend away in winter camping, usually at Barberry, a tenderfoot camp in May and the annual Summer camp. Night hiking also seemed a particularly popular activity, as was the annual Christmas party. Less frequent events ranged from such activities as a Patrol camp through to a three day expedition for the older Scouts over Exmoor for their Chief Scouts Award. John Slingsby gained his Chief Scout Award in November 1974.[243] With a large number of older boys the nucleus of a Venture Unit was beginning to emerge which would lay the foundations for the formation a year later.

The Pack had split into two with meetings on Monday and Thursday evenings, with leaders alternating. The aim was to reduce the long waiting list by the following May, this was not

[241] 19th Weston Group Exec Minutes 14/07/75
[242] 19th Weston Executive Minutes 26/10/72 (19th Weston Archive)
[243] 19th Weston 19th Weston Executive minutes 16/01/75 (19th Weston Archive)

overly successful as the Pack was at fifty-six strong in May, with thirty five boys on a waiting list. This appears to have been a District wide issue as the 29th Weston had over thirty on their waiting list. Packs were usually limited to twenty-four members.[244] At District events the Packs were continuing to do well, although the Sixers Weekend had been a bit of a disappointment, having been cancelled as the campsite was under water.[245] With the Group continuing to expand numerically additional Helpers were needed. Fortunately several offers of assistance were made with Mr Mereweather taking an Instructors certificate with the Pack, alongside Mrs Weedon who was taking out an ACSL warrant, while Brian Dunn and Paul Blocksidge took out Instructor certificates with the Troop. The Packs were offered the opportunity to learn to swim with sessions taking place at Pontins in Sandbay on Saturdays, resulting in a large amount of Swimmers badges being presented over the next couple of terms. The Pack attended the Cub Alive 1975 event held at Woodhouse Park.

Between the Cubs and Scouts the membership now stood at over ninety, making the 19th the largest Group in the District, a fact that was celebrated with over seventy Cubs and Scouts going on a coach trip to RAF Colerne for a day. The Group had also obtained the services of a Group Chaplain, the Rev. Wareing of Milton Methodist Church. The Group maintained strong links with the Methodist Church for many years, with parades being held there for Remembrance Sunday.

1983-1999 Celts VSU

The Group had been concerned about the lack of a suitable Venture Unit which had been mentioned during the early 1970s.

---

244 19th Weston Group AGM 05/05/75 (19th Weston Archive)

245 19th Weston Group Exec Minutes 04/11/74 (19th Weston Archive)

The Unit took a keen interest in caving, having their own equipment, along with several kayaks and a large raft which the Unit had sailed down the Wye on more than one occasion, as part of their annual camp. The Ventures undertook diverse activities ranging from going underground and water activities, taking part in the Three Peaks Challenge as well as hiking along the West Mendip Way and later South West Coastal path trails. The Unit drew its membership from the thriving Troop, although some members did come from outside the movement whilst a number of Scouts came from the 1st Uphill Group.

The Group celebrated their Silver Jubilee in 1982 and held a formal dinner the following January comprising of a soup starter, main course of turkey, chipped potatoes, peas, carrots and stuffing with a fruit salad and ice cream dessert being served. The DC, Mike Bell, was the guest speaker. R Cooke retired in 1987, although he remained a very active supporter of the Group as an honoury Scouter. The leadership passed to Eric John who led the Group until he moved away with his work.

As the Group entered the 1990s they were down to a single Pack with a Troop and Venture Unit (Celt's), the group had a new GSL with the appointment of John Hall in 1990. Two years later a Beaver Colony was started, which proved so popular that a second Colony was formed a year later. Mrs Emma Snook led the Planet beaver Colony, whilst Mrs Sylvia Woolley took charge of the Wild Cats Colony. Colony nights were Tuesdays and Fridays. The Colonies had with the exception of Mrs Anne Churchill, a high turn over of leaders, with Emma Snook standing down to become Group Treasurer in 1995, the same year that Mrs Diane Beckett stood down as an ABSL. It was perhaps not unsurprising that the second Colony was to disband soon afterwards due to a lack of leaders. The Cub Pack was led by Mrs Donna Savage, with assistance from Miss Catherine Lightfoot and Mrs Alison Kingscott. Although two years later a change of the Pack leadership had occurred with Miss Kate Lewis leading the team comprising of Mrs Barbara Vinicombe, Mrs Debbie Symons, and Mrs Tina Stockham. With Mr Hall's return to 3rd Weston (St Paul's) in 1993, the Group were left without a GSL for a short period until Mr Geoff Yates, who had held an ASL warrant within the Troop, took the helm until moving away the town in 1997.[246]

The Troop had struggled for some time to a have a long term SL since the departure of Mr Eric John, with a series of adults running the Troop in short succession, from Dale Smith, Patrick Fleming, who previously helped with the 24th Weston (Hill Road) Troop, Mr Steve Gamblin, a stalwart of the Group, and Mr Adrian Smith as ASLs. The Troop however had a number of Troop Helpers including Richard Parsons, Alan Reynolds, Steve Gamblin, Bill Beachgood, whilst Andrew Eddy, Chris Savage and Dave Snook provided hiking and canoeing skills. Despite the quest for stable leadership the Troop continued to be active and had a membership which seldom dipped below twenty Scouts.

Events reached a head in 1999 when the Troop had no warranted leaders and was going to disband. The arrival of Mr Nigel Ball in the District and his appointment as GSL of both the 19th and 29th Weston Scout Group's pointed to the way things were heading, as both Groups were seeking a solution to their problems, issues of leadership in the case of the 19th Weston and a suitable venue for meeting for the 29th Weston. The latter had been meeting in St Peter's Church hall since the demolition of their headquarters, the old St Peter's wooden Church, which had been pulled down to make way for the new vicarage. In July 1999 the 19th Weston amalgamated with the 29th Weston to form 1st Milton Scout Group, with the new Group meeting at the Drysdale Close Headquarters wearing the 19th Weston's scarf with the 29th Weston St Peter's badge worn on the nape of the scarf..

[246] District Directories 1993 & 1995 pp. 28-29 & 8

19th Weston Troop Camp

19th Weston Troop c. 1970s

19th Weston Summer Camp Patrol Trophy 1996

Krazy Kraft Regatta, Marine Lake c. 1975

20th Weston-Super-Mare

Fd: 02/09/32-1934 Reg No. 14377
2009 Weston-Super-Mare (Upper Milton)

The Congregational Church in Moorland Road opened a Wolf Cub Pack in September 1932 under the leadership of Mrs A Smith with six boys in the Pack. The Group was a controlled Pack, (by the Minister and Deacons) and had a short existence. Perhaps a lack of recruits led to its closure two years later, as there were several other Scout Groups operating nearby, including the 3rd (St Paul's), 7th(Uphill), 14th (Corpus Christi) and 18th (Good Shepherd) Weston Scout Groups which all had Cub Packs.[247]

19/05/36-1946 (Upper Milton) Reg No. 20777

<u>Scarf</u> <u>Grass Green</u>

The number was soon in service again being reassigned to the newly formed Milton Group in the spring of 1936 led by SM, Mr Fred Haytor, and Mr A W Collings who took an ASM warrant[248]. The Group met at the old Methodist Church on Upper Bristol Road (now housing the Co-op funeral Service). The building had been the Methodist Chapel until 1930 when the Church moved to its current location. The Troop comprised of twenty-five boys, many of whom came from the impoverished Milton Brow estate. Towards the close of the decade the Group formed a Wolf Cub

[247] Copy of Form C 02/09/32 (Gilwell Archive)
[248] Copy of Form C 19/05/36 (Gilwell Archive)

Pack, and, by the time of the Group's closure in 1946, the Pack was being assisted by former Scout D McIntyre.[249]

Mr Ken Blake, a former member of the Troop, recalled some of the highlights of the Troop's activities and its members. The Troop played the 19th Weston a number of times at cricket on Jackson-Barstow's land (where Snowdon Vale and Forest Drive estates now stand). Monthly Church parades to the Methodist Church started at "marble arch" the covered bus shelter at the bottom of Milton Brow, and the Troop paraded along the road and up the hill to the Church.[250] Scouts in the Troop included; Ken Blake, the brothers Donald and Lionel Macintyre, Donald later took an ACM warrant in the Pack, Eric Lees, Len Curry who was the Patrol Leader of the Seagull patrol, Alan Beaks, Ken Trego, Bert Collard, Bert Mason, Roy Goddard and Roy Collar. The outbreak of the Second World War effectively led to the disbanding of the Troop around 1943, as leaders and older Scouts were called up for active service. Five members of the Troop gave their lives for their country[251]. However the Cub Pack appears to have remained in operation for a while longer and is recorded as disbanding in 1946.[252] Post-war, Mr Haytor who was appointed as a DSM moved with his job from the town, working in the NHS in the Midlands, he sadly passed away at the early age of 62.

21st Weston-Super-Mare (Sunnyside)

Fd:	03/07/39-44	Reg No. 20169
	04/01/44-1947	22723

Scarf Yellow with a green diamond on the nape

[249] Notes from Lapsed Group Logbook (Tangier Scout Centre Archive, Taunton)
[250] Interview with Mr Blake
[251] Interview with Mr Blake
[252] Notes from Lapsed Group Logbook (Tangier Scout Centre Archive, Taunton)

Sunnyside Methodist Church in Brighton Road decided to form a Scout Troop in the summer of 1939 bearing the title 21st Weston-Super-Mare ('the Sunnyside Troop') with nine Scouts, led by SM Mr G J Harding. The Troop was a controlled Group, the sponsor being the Methodist Church.[253] The Troop shared the fate of many Groups during World War II including the recently formed Locking and Hutton Groups, and disbanded during the war years as leaders were called up for war work and by 1944 the Troop went out of existence for a brief period. The Group was restarted at the beginning of 1944 by the Rev. Hollinghurst. D Palmer took out an ASM warrant to a Troop of six. Boy Scout numbers expanded shortly afterwards, with Mr Robinson joining as GSM the following year. Meeting nights were at the Church Hall in Brighton Road from 7pm on Thursdays for Scouts and 6:30pm on Friday evenings for the Cubs, under the supervision of ACMs Miss Mogg and Miss D S Bond. [254] Despite a good (re)start, the Group was to struggle to attract sufficient leaders and coupled with the recommendations of the 'Road Ahead' report, which proposed the amalgamation of smaller Groups together for stability and to improve the opportunities for the members, the 21st Weston amalgamated with 24th Weston (Hill Road) in 1947.[255]

22nd Weston-Super-Mare (St Peter's School)

Fd:	03/12/40-1947	Reg No. 21971
	16/06/59-1971	34545

[253] Copy of Form C 03/07/39 (Gilwell Archive)

[254] Copies of 1944 & 1945 District Directory p. 21 (Tangier Scout Archive, Taunton

[255] Weston Trade Directory 1946/47 pp 14-15 (Courtesy of Weston Library)
Notes from Lapsed Group Logbook (Tanger Scout Centre Archive, Taunton)

St Peter's Preparatory School formed a Scout Group which, although registered in December 1940, is likely to have started in September at the start of the school year. Miss J E Leonard took the Cubs whilst Mr A Dolman ran the Troop. Both leaders were teachers at the School and resided onsite.[256] The Group managed to remain operational throughout the war as a result of having a stable leadership and attended the District Camp held at Congresbury in 1944. However three years later the Group had ceased to meet.

Twelve years after the Group had closed the Troop was restarted in the summer of 1959 with eight boys under the leadership of SM Mr Anthony E. Viney with Mr G H Torson, the headmaster of the School, acting as the Group's sponsor. Shortly after the Pack was restarted although little is known about the Pack beyond the name of their last CM, Peter Jones. With the closure of St Peter's school in 1971 the Scout Group disbanded. The school buildings were subsequently demolished and a modern housing estate now stands on the site of the grounds.

23rd Weston-Super-Mare

Very little information can be found regarding this Troop beyond a brief mention in the Hill Road logbook of 1943 which mentions the Troop arriving at the same campsite as the 24th Weston (Hill Road) Scouts at Yarborough Farm near Banwell in 1943. The Troop probably formed in late 1941 or 1942 and had disbanded by 1944. Where they met and who their leaders were is unknown at this time.

24th Weston-Super-Mare (Hill Road)

15/06/1943-01/09/00 Reg No. 21240

[256] Notes from Lapsed Group Logbook (Tanger Scout Centre Archive, Taunton)

Scarf; 1942-50 Red and Mauve halved
1950s Grey
Red and black halved

Hill Road Scout Troop was formed by a nucleus of four boys who approached Mr William Holder in November 1942 with the desire to form a Scout Troop. Two former Scouts, Mr Bert Glass and Doug Raymond, agreed to help Mr Holder in the forming of a new Troop at Hill Road Methodist Church. The Troop started meeting in November 1942 with their first event being a Christmas party held on December 22nd with guests from Milton Methodist Church's Life Boys leaders attending. The following month a Scout Committee was formed with the intention of applying for the registration of the Group. The initial members came from the Church based Boys Brigade with members swapping from Boys Brigade to form a Scout Troop, a feat repeated over a year later when the Life Boys switched to form a Wolf Cub Pack. The switch from Brigade to Scouts appears to have been triggered in part due to the view held by members that Boy Scouts was more exciting than bible study and drill. Troop meetings took place on Tuesdays for Scouting activities and, where possible, a games evening would be held on Thursdays. Having been visited and inspected the previous week by the DSM, F J Hood, the Troop Court of Honour met on February 9th 1943 from which two Patrols were formed; Seagulls led by PL David Bailey with his brother Brian as PS, while Curlew's PL was Kenneth Harris. The Troop numbers expanded, rising to thirteen members in May, with recruits; Paul Scales, John Snelling, Gordon Raymond, John Codrington, William Morgan and Eric Taylor joining the Seagull Patrol. Philip Hoskins, Peter Harris, Ronald Daniels, John Hodges and Russell Gibson became members of the Curlews.[257] However, Mr Holder was unable to become SM, so the Troop was taken jointly by ASMs Glass and Raymond. During the Troop meeting of June 22nd 1943,

[257] Hill Road Logbook 1942-46 pp. 6-8

following an inspection by the District, it was announced that the Group had been officially registered with Imperial Headquarters bearing the title 24th Weston Super-Mare (Hill Road) Scout Group to the Scouts jubilation.[258]

The Troop and their Leaders were determined to come up to the standards of the big three Troops in the town, who they considered to be; 1st Weston (YMCA), 3rd Weston (St. Paul's) and 17th Weston (County School), by 'working like the clappers'. Camping and badge work would form the core of the Troop's activities, the latter would prove to be somewhat challenging during the war years, although undaunted the Troop undertook thirteen camps around the local area, with sites ranging from Banwell, Rooksbridge and Congresbury. The first camp undertaken by the fledgling Troop was a PL and PS camp held at Mr Hawkin's Yarborough farm, near Banwell, over the weekend of June 5th - 6th 1943 with Scouters Glass and Raymond, PLs David Bailey and Kenneth Harris, PS Philip Hoskins and Scout Paul Scales in camp. The party travelled to the campsite by bicycle, their kit being towed on a home made trek cart. During the weekend the Scouts mastered the art of backwoods cooking, having abandoned such new-fangled contraptions as primus stoves after several unsuccessful attempts to brew up a cup of tea! They hiked to Crooks Peak with the required ditch jumping enroute and a session of 'flag wagging' (semaphore with flags) formed part of the weekend's activities, as did knot tying, backwoods skills and a visit from Peter Scales, Paul's older brother, a former 3rd Weston (St Paul's) Scout who was now in the Tank Corps and regaled the campers with stories about the 1937 World Jamboree as well as teaching the Scouts how to play American baseball.[259] Two weeks later the Seagull Patrol returned to the site for their first Patrol camp with the Bailey Brothers, Paul Scales and the Raymond brothers, Clarence and Gordon,

[258] Hill Road Logbook 1942-46 pp.
[259] Hill Road Logbook 1942-46 pp. 10-12

Doug Raymond's younger siblings, John Codrington, William Morgan, John Snelling and Eric Taylor in addition to the Scouters being in camp for a cost of 1/7d per camper. Highlights of the camp included a campfire, hiking around the local area, Morgan and Skipper's pioneering skills which produced a wash stand, whilst Clarence milked five cows in a morning, a job he continued for the duration of the camp, much to the farmer, Mr Hawkin's, delight.

Wartime Scouting imposed extra challenges for camping as rationing, both food and fuel, and what land could be used were factors to be considered, alongside parental concerns about having their sons close to home meant that it was not until after the war did the Troop mount a camp beyond the local boundaries, when the Troop held their annual summer camp at Youlbury in Oxfordshire from July 25th to August 1st 1946, attended by twenty six boys in four Patrols, Bulldogs, Panthers, Seagulls and Woodpeckers/Peewits[260], with badge work towards their Backwoodsman, Pioneer and Cooks badges. Axemanship and pioneering featured strongly in the programme with the resulting bridges and rafts until the inevitable happened with Scouts N Usher and R Bailey making a very satisfactory splash! During the week two camp fires were held with all those in camp attending and the Hill Road Scouts adding several stunts to their repertoire. The willingness of the Hill Road Scouts to sing and perform is also evident in their enthusiastic support for the annual Group shows held between 1945-48 where Cubs, Scouts and Leaders took a turn to sing, or perform a sketch to an audience of family, friends and well wishers.

In 1947 Mr Glass moved away from the town, Mr Robinson was to take the Troop, however by 1948 the Troop had disbanded, along with the senior Troop. Old Scouts from the early years recall losing interest after the departure of Mr Glass and Mr

[260] 1946 Youlbury Annual Camp Log p. 3

Raymond. The Troop remained dormant until 1953 when the Troop reformed under the leadership of SM Eric W Osborn who had been a member of the 3rd Weston (St Paul's) Group.[261]. Assistant Leaders included Peter Neathway, (also a former 3rd Weston Scout), Owen Rimmington and Pete Harris who held a Skills Instructor certificate. Stephen Coombes, a former 19th Weston Scout, joined the Group in 1960 as an ASM, to begin a period of service in various roles within the Group for a long time, taking charge of the Troop twice, between 1962-65 and 1971-80; other roles included assisting with Senior Scouts and then the Venture Scout Unit between 1968-71 and later serving as Group Quarter-Master. Following Mr Rimmington's departure in 1955 the Troop ran without a SM until Mr S Coombes took the helm in 1962. Between 1965-71 the Troop had several leaders including Mr A Marshall, Mr B Hadley and Mr D Skinner. The leadership of the Troop was undertaken for a period during the 1980s by Mr Eddings, who had a son in the Troop. Following his departure the Group struggled to find a long-term leader with the Troop being run by the ADC Scouts Lesley Hunt in the mid 1990s. Other leaders included Stuart Brown, whose father, Tony Brown was the GSL, and later Tim Harris took the Scouts.

The Troop was very active in District events, entering annually the pedal car races, the main guiding force and encourager of this being Pete Harris. Attendance at the District competitions for swimming, camping competitions and sports did not always result in taking home the trophy, however the Troop from the 1970s gained a reputation for their culinary skills, being well placed in the scoring and winning the county cooking on several occasions. Rafting also featured in the programme, with the Group starting a Scout and Guide raft race in the late 1980s which ran for a number of years, being well supported.

---

[261] Hill Road Pack Records pp.1 -6
Group Census 1947-82 (Gilwell Archive)

As the Troop expanded its numbers it became apparent that a Cub Pack would need to be formed and in September 1944 the Life Boys swapped to become a Wolf Cub Pack run by Miss A J Osborn (soon afterwards she married Mr Glass). The Cubs started with fourteen boys in two sixes, Grey and Red, though the Pack proved so popular that by 1947 the Pack had expanded to four sixes, with Tawny and Black sixes joining the two original sixes. The Pack held their first camp at Mr Chaplin's Moorland Farm in Worle between the 24th-26th August with ten Cubs, two Scouts and five adults in attendance.[262] The same year the Troop camped at Winterhead Farm near Winscombe as three patrols, the Seniors led by D Bailey, Wolf Patrol by PL J Hodge and Owls by J Codrington.[263] Early Members of the Pack included G Sanders, B Sillifant, J Green, M Haines, D Power, J Evans, J Davies, M Jenkins, B Drew, P, Bull, G Coles, J Locke, Groves, Kent, F Neads and K Stoyles. Assistant Leaders Mr J P T Dixon and Cyril Hart joined the Pack, with Mr Hart leading the Pack following Mr and Mrs Glass' departure until he was called up for National Service in 1951. Mr and Mrs Dixon took the helm remaining with the Group for close to fifteen years, before handing over to Miss Sunderland who ran the Pack briefly before resuming her role as an ACSL. Mr George Hind, previously a leader with the 27th Weston (Bourneville), joined the Pack as Akela in 1968 for a period of five years before following Miss Sunderland's lead and stepping down to an ACSL warrant. As the section proved so popular with a long waiting list, a second Pack was started in 1974 with Mrs Judith Sinclair taking one Pack. Both Packs continued to meet until a lack of leaders resulted in the one of the Packs closing. In 1987 Doug Raymond stepped down as GSL, having reached retirement age, although he continued to be a strong supporter of the Group until he was 'called home' in 2002. Mr Tony Brown took over as GSL having been the Group Treasurer for a few years before. The Group was fortunate to have

[262] Hill Road Pack Camping Permit Form 6/37 24/07/45

[263] 1945 Winscombe Annual Camp Log p. 3

a number of committed leaders in addition to Doug, including Stephen Coombes, Peter Harris, Judith Sinclair, as well as Tony Brown, who remained with the Group for many years.

The Pack was always on the look out for more helpers, having had assistance from Mr Paul Austin of 1st Uphill Group and Mr John Hall of 3rd Weston (St Paul's) Group during a patch of leader shortage in the 1970s.

The Cub section was led by Mrs Judith Sinclair who ran the Thursday Pack, with help from Mr Keith Underhay. Mrs Caroline Swatton was taking the Wednesday Pack, although with a shortage of leaders it was not long before the two packs, which had being in existence since the mid 1970s, were reduced to a single Pack. Mr Richard Spindler, later to become CSL, had started helping with the Wednesday Pack in the early 1990s. Mr Keith Dudley, currently Locking's SL, joined the Group as an ACSL towards the end of the decade. Mr Spindler succeeded Mrs Sinclair in 1996.

The Group had two attempts at forming a Senior Scout Troop in late 1944 and early 1945 for the older boys. Initial members included D Bailey, P Hoskins, P Harris, C Raymond, D Usher, P Andrews, G Raymond, J Codrington, D Brown, P Burnell, J Charlton, and D Hurley, who had been a member of the 21st Weston Troop, D Baxter and T Gilbert.[264] The Senior Troop continued to meet until 1948 when it disbanded, along with the Troop, with the departure of the founding leaders. Seniors were restarted in 1956 and continued to meet until the implementation of the Advance Report in 1967, with the exception of a gap in the late 1950s. Peter Neathway reformed the Senior Troop serving for two years before moving on when the Seniors closed temporarily. Mr Bull assisted for a short time during the early sixties with the section, however no permanent SSL was appointed for some time.

---

[264] Hill Road Senior Scout Attendance record 1945-48

Mr Teale, who became the VSL, was leading the Seniors during the late 1960s.

1967 saw other changes within the Group as the Advance Report was implemented with the disbanding of Senior Scouts and Rovers to be replaced with Venture Scouts. Hill Road were able to form a Venture Scout Unit which was named '24th Weston-super-Mare Hill Road' and met at 44 Palmer Street. The unit concentrated its efforts on canoeing, making the kayaks from moulds, photography and film making research, with the Ventures assisting Mr Teale in the making of a cine-film of the Mendip Mineral Railway. It would not be until the merger of the 17th and 24th Venture Units into a District Unit in 1975 that the name Smugglers would be used.[265] The Unit during this time had two AVSLs; Mr Coombes who swapped to run the Troop (again) in 1971, being succeeded by Mr Kevin Moore. The Unit merged with the 17th Weston in 1975 to form a District VSU, Smugglers. However in 1990 the Unit returned to the Group, under the leadership of Miss Penny Jeffries who remained with the Unit until her appointment as ADC Ventures in the mid 1990s. Regrettably the Unit closed shortly after.

The Hill Road Group has a keen sense of its own history, having celebrated through its old boys its major centenaries, often with the presentation of new flags to the Group as well as major displays and get togethers for the fortieth and fiftieth celebrations of the Group. These events included a gathering of the leaders present and past, as well as filling their headquarters, the old Church at Hill Road with memorabilia. During the 1960s the Scout Group at Hill Road was joined by their sister organisation when the 23rd Weston Guides were formed which led to the two organisations working together on a number of events. The arrival of Pat and Tony Brown as Guide Leader and GSL in 1987

---

[265] 17th Weston Correspondence 1975 (Gilwell Archive)

marked a much stronger and closer partnership, with joint camps and fundraising activities being organised over the years.

The Beaver Colony at Hill Road was started by Jane Deacon, who was initially assisted by Mrs Wendy Lewis, although two years later Mrs Karen Trevitt had taken a ABSL warrant and remained with the Colony for close to six years. She succeeded Mrs Deacon as BSL upon the latter's appointment as ADC Beavers. The Colony disbanded with Mrs Trevitt's departure just after the Group amalgamated with the 1st Weston to from 1st Ashcombe Scout Group.[266]

The Group was to lose their headquarters when the Hill Road Methodist Church closed in the mid 1990s. The Group was at this point down to a Beaver Colony, Cub Pack and Scout Troop, the latter suffering from a lack of long term leadership. The Group met at several locations during the next five years including St John's Hall (above the Boulevard Post Office) before moving across the road to the United Reformed Church in September 2000 when the 1st and 24th Weston Groups amalgamated to form 1st Ashcombe Group.

25th Weston-Super-Mare (St John's)

Fd:	11/04/44-1947	Reg No. 22930
	06/09/1949-1958	27602

Scarf: Green with mauve edge

St John the Baptist Church formed a Scout Troop in the spring of 1944, led by the curate Rev. A F H Jasper with twelve Scouts in April 1944. Scouting took place at St. John's Church Institute in the Boulevard, the hall being above the shops near the Weston

266 District Directories 1993, 1995, 1998 pp. 30, 9 &9

Mercury offices. As was to happen with several other Church Groups, the Reverend was soon to move on and St John's followed this trend when shortly after the Troop started Rev Jasper moved away and was succeeded by Mr R Case who took over as SM. He remained with the Troop until it folded in 1947.[267]

The Troop reformed two years later under the leadership of another curate at St John's, the Rev. H F Warren, meeting at the Church Institute. The Group had presumably retained its colours. The Church sponsored Troop membership at the time of registration was eighteen boys and one Leader. The first twelve boys were invested at the parish church on Wednesday 20th July.[268] The Group soon expanded when Mr D V F Palmer took out a warrant as an ASM with the Reverend R G Dean becoming SM whilst Reverend Warren took charge of the Group and Miss Barbara Lancaster took charge of the newly formed Cub Pack. The Group met for nine years before disbanding. Miss Lancaster continued her Scouting interest by starting a Cub Pack at her private school in the year that the 25th Weston disbanded.

26th Weston-Super-Mare (Holy Trinity)

Fd: 22/06/44-1948 Reg No. 23043

Scarf: Dark Blue

A Troop, for the local boys who either attended the Church with their families or lived in the locale, was started at Holy Trinity by the Reverend J M Cartwright. The Troop held its weekly meetings at the Parish Hall in Manilla Place.[269] The Troop

[267] Notes from Lapsed Group Logbook (Tanger Scout Centre Archive, Taunton)
[268] Copy of Form C 06/09/49 (Gilwell Archive)
3rd Weston (St Paul's) Logbook 1928-57, p. 209
[269] Copy of Somerset County Directory 1945 p. 21 (Tangier Centre Archive)

continued for four years before disbanding, although no further details have come to light regarding the Troop and its activities.

26th Weston (Salvation Army)

Fd: 23/07/53-31/03/55 Reg No. 30702

The Salvation Army reformed the Pack in the year of the Queen's Coronation, 1953, once again with Miss Violet Floyd as CM to a pack of twelve Wolf Cubs divided into two sixes. The Pack, for its two years of existence, met at the Citadel in Carlton Street.[270] No further efforts to provide Scouting were undertaken after this attempt, perhaps reflecting Miss Floyd moving away from the area. The Salvation Army Citadel was demolished and rebuilt in 2003/04 on the same site.

27th Weston–Super-Mare (Salvation Army)

Fd: 23/09/1948-1953 Reg No. 26592

The first recorded document for a 27th is for a Wolf Cub Pack meeting at the Salvation Army Citadel formed in September 1948. The Salvation Army sponsored Group had ten Wolf Cubs and Miss Floyd as the sole warranted Leader. The Pack had disbanded by 1953, although it was to reform that year as the 26th Weston. Little information regarding this Pack has come to light.

27th Weston (St Andrew's & Birnbeck)

Fd: 13/06/56-01/04/67 Reg No. 32646
25/06/67-31/04/82 38312

[270] Notes from Lapsed Group Logbook (Tangier Scout Centre Archive, Taunton)

The second 27th Weston (St Andrew's Church of England) met on the Bourneville estate on the southern end of the town and was registered on June 13th 1956. The Reverend John Stevens Waller held the post of GSM, with Miss Joyce Elizabeth Maisey as CM and Mr Ronald George Codman, who ran a fish and chip shop, as SM. The Group was meeting at St Andrew's Church hall. During the early years they held at least one gang show at which several other Groups, including the 3rd Weston, sent their representatives along to. Although little information has come to light regarding the Group it appeared to have been an active Group operating into 1967, when the Group merged with the 28th Weston and although keeping the title of 27th Weston on registration it changed its name from (St Andrew's) to (Birnbeck) in recognition of the members from the 28th (Holy Trinity) Anglican Church near Birnbeck pier amalgamating with the Group. At the time of the amalgamation Mrs Helen Bailey was Akela and ran the Pack with the assistance of Mrs Jean Thorne who held an ACM warrant. The long serving Mr A Cook held the position of SL being assisted by Mr Anthony Mounsden as ASL, while Mr E Morris oversaw the Group as GSL. At the same time the Group changed from being a Church sponsored to an open Group.[271] The Group continued to operate until 1982 when the Cub section disbanded due to the usual problem of having no new leaders to take over the reins. The Troop had disbanded two years earlier falling victim to the same problem.

28th Weston-Super-Mare (Lancaster House & Holy Trinity)

Fd: 01/09/1958-01/04/67 Reg No. 33680.

Scarf: Red and blue halved

[271] Copy of Forms C & C2 01/04/67 (Gilwell Archives)

Miss Barbara Lancaster decided to form a Cub Pack and Scout Troop for pupils of her independent day school in Greenfield place, although the Group was registered as an open Group which formed at the start of the 1958 school term with nineteen Wolf Cubs and three Boy Scouts. Miss Lancaster held the position of GSM and recruited Mr Alexander McPhee Maxwell as SM. The Group changed sponsor on May 26th 1961 moving to Holy Trinity Church on the seaward northern slopes of Worlebury Hill and being renamed Holy Trinity. The Group was to remain at the Church until their amalgamation with the 27th Weston in April 1967. The Group's Wolf Cub Flag survives as a memento of the Group.

29th Weston-super-Mare (St Peter's)

Fd: 16/04/64-11/07/99 Reg No. 36899

Scarf: Yellow with blue edge

The start of Scouting at St Peter's Church can be traced to the efforts of two gentlemen, Mr Delwyn Cox, who had moved to the town in November 1962 to teach at Weston Technical College and was a member at St Peter's Church[272] and the Rev William Tuckey, then curate in charge of St Peter's Church. Reverend Tuckey wished to "see a [Wolf] Cub Pack formed at the Church" and Mr Cox agreed to start a Pack and in addition requested that a Scout Troop also be formed, as he felt that "the heart and soul of a Scout Group was the Troop."[273] The first chairman of the Parents Committee was Mr Peter Townsend, Headmaster at Milton Junior School with Mr Ken Ayliffe holding the post of Treasurer.[274]

---

[272] Interview with Mr D Cox Spring 2002 (Biddulph Archive)
[273] Interview with Mr D Cox Spring 2002 (Biddulph Archive)
[274] Interview with Mr D Cox Spring 2002 (Biddulph Archive)
Recollections of Mrs Ayliffe, Dunstone & Sparkes June 2001 (Biddulph Archive)

Shortly afterwards in May 1963 the Group met for the first time, with the first invested young member of the Group being Michael Sparkes, the son of the SM, Mr Peter Sparkes.[275] The Group drew much of its membership from children whose parents were members of the Church. [276] However the Group did not register until April 16th 1964 at which point the Group comprised of twelve Cubs, Four Scouts and one Leader (Mr Cox), the other two leaders were in the process of applying for their warrants.[277] The Troop's first summer camp was taken by Mr Sparkes and Mr Cox in July 1964 on a farm near Seaton and Sidmouth. Mr Cox recalls that the pack comprised of around twenty boys and the Troop had a dozen Scouts. [278]

The Group necker (scarf) of yellow with a blue border was the colours of Mr Cox's former Group the 64th Cardiff Scout Group and was adopted as the 29th's colours. The addition the badge of St. Peters, (four fishes in a net) was believed to have been designed by Mr John Underhay, the SL from 1977 who collected badges, possibly as part of the jubilee celebration.

Cubs and Scouts met in the Church on a Thursday night and preparations for the use of the Church began after Sunday evensong with the clearing away of the chairs ready for Scouts. Following the Troop meeting the process was reversed ready for the Sunday services.[279]. Many of the boys came from church families and well attended Church parades were held monthly reflecting the close relations between the Scouts and Church.[280] In case you are wondering, the original church was the Green hut, the current church being under construction between1964/65.

---

[275] Interview with Mr D Cox Spring 2002 (Biddulph Archive)
[276] Interview with Mr D Cox Spring 2002 (Biddulph Archive)
[277] Copy of Registration Form C 16/04/64 (Gilwell Archive)
[278] Interview with Mr D Cox Spring 2002 (Biddulph Archive)
[279] Interview with Mr D Cox Spring 2002 (Biddulph Archive)
[280] Interview with Mr D Cox Spring 2002 (Biddulph Archive)

Mr Cox held the joint warrants of CSM and GSM, and was assisted by Miss Pam Hammon, (later Mrs Tonkin). The Troop was led by Mr Sparkes with assistance from Mr Ron Dunstone. Mr Dunstone took over from Mr Cox as GSL in 1967 until he was called to higher service in 1973[281]. Mr Cox concentrated his efforts on running the Pack until 1968 when he stood down to concentrate his efforts as District Secretary. He moved to Nailsea in 1971 and joined the 1st Nailsea Scout Group. Mr Nick Christian succeeded Mr Cox in 1968 remaining with the Pack until literally moving up the road to become CSL at the 19th Weston Cub Pack. Mrs Tonkin took over for a spell from 1970 to 1971 before handing over the Pack to Miss Violet Baker. The Pack also had the services of Mr Heard from 1969 and Mrs Payne from 1970. However in 1971 both Mr Heard and Mrs Payne no longer seem to be actively involved with the Pack. Mr Peter Holmes, whose son was of an age to join the Pack, took out a Helper Certificate in order to help Miss Baker who was the sole leader to a Pack of twenty-four Cubs, and stop it closing. Four years later in October 1975, Mr Holmes took over as Akela with his wife Mrs Margaret Holmes and Miss Baker as ACSLs.[282] The Group's monthly Church parades carried on until 1974, when the new incumbent Rev. Derek Taylor arrived and quarterly parades that including Mothering and Remembrance Sunday's were instigated.[283]

Sadly with the passing of Mr Dunstone in 1973 the Troop disbanded and Cubs transferred to the 19th Scout Troop (literally just up the road in Drysdale Close). The Troop reopened in 1975 under Mr John Underhay (who transferred from 27th Weston to became SL), which started with ten boys from the 19th Weston Group and met on Thursday evenings[284]. He was assisted by Mr Chris Horn who had a son in the Troop. Under Mr Underhay, the Troop held their annual summer camps in farmer's fields running

281 Copy of Warrants sheet 1963-75 (Gilwell Archive)
282 Interview with Mr P Holmes Summer 2002 (Biddulph Archive)
283 Interview with Rev D Taylor 24/04/03 (Biddulph Archive)
284 Interview with Mr J Underhay 20/02/03 (Biddulph Archive)

a back to basics style of camping which was very successful, with all the cooking done over an open fire and Skip taught the boys survival skills. Camps were held at such places as Totnes which included a trip to Buckland Abbey, where the Scouts having missed their appointed train hiked to the Abbey from Staverton station.[285]

The Pack was very popular, with a long waiting list so on September 3rd 1977 a second Pack was formed under the leadership of Mrs Eileen Underhay, on loan from the 27th Weston Scout Group.[286] The planting of the Oak and Ash trees in the Church grounds by members of Oak and Ash Cub Packs commemorates the event and later in the year the Group held a camp at Gilwell.[287] With two Packs feeding the Troop, it soon expanded to thirty-six needing to divide into two meetings in 1978. With such a large Group the services of a GSL were required, with Mr Ken Vinnicombe, a member of the Church coming forward to become the GSL[288]. Changes in the leadership of the Cub Pack occurred in the late 1970s when Mr and Mrs Holmes were appointed as ADC and DCSL respectively and moved on from the Pack[289], handing over to Mrs Babs Atherton who had transferred from the 24th (Hill Road) Scout Group. Mrs Atherton was assisted by her husband, and they both served as leaders until 1981 when Mr Atherton passed away. Mrs Atherton handed over the Pack to Mrs D Townsend. The same year the second Pack merged back into the original pack. Further changes in personnel occurred in the early 1980s with the departure of the SLs, Mr Underhay and Mr Horn.

When the author joined the Pack as a Cub in 1985 it was being led by Paul (Akela) and Mandy Seaton (Kaa) who in turn handed

---

285 Interview with Mr J Underhay 20/02/03 (Biddulph Archive)
286 Interview with Mrs B Atherton Summer 2003 (Biddulph Archive)
287 Interview with Mrs B Atherton Summer 2003 (Biddulph Archive)
288 Interview with Mr P Holmes Summer 2002 (Biddulph Archive)
289 Interview with Mr P Holmes Summer 2002 (Biddulph Archive)

over to Mrs Michaela Kattana, (now Mrs Heath and DC since 2005). The Pack also had the services of several parents some of whom like Mr Rod Pegler, Mr Peter Grant and Mrs Renita Griffiths took out warrants and Helper certificates. The Troop had acquired the services of Mr Ian Baird who swapped from ASL at 24th Hill Road Troop with Mr Ian Williams then SL at the 29th Weston around 1988/89. Other leaders in the late 1980s in the Troop included Mr Jason Taylor and Mr Andrew Hurst, whose father Ken Hurst, held the post of Chairman of the Executive Committee for a number of years. Mrs Pat Robbins (who had two boys in the Group) became Group Chairman after Mr Hurst. Other long serving members of the Group Executive included Mr Doug Biddulph, Mrs Yvonne Parrot, Mrs Sue Hogarth and Mrs Babs Atherton who retained her link with the Group.[290].

Troop Summer camps between 1988-93 included a joint 24th-29th Camp at Nine Ashes near Bodmin in 1988[291]. The Troop also camped at Waddacar which was to prove a very wet camp by the river, Beaudesert and Belchamps also featured during these years.[292]

Some time in 1990 Mr Terry Scoble joined the Troop, two years later he had become SL following Ian Baird's departure[293]. Under him and a team of four ASLs, Mr A Hurst, Mr J Taylor, Mr S Townsend and Mr A Bradley, the Troop expanded reaching, by 1995, over fifty Scouts[294]. However numbers dropped in January the following year when Mr T Scoble, Mr J Taylor and Mrs M Harris (formerly Mrs M Kattana) left the Group and moved to 1st Kewstoke Scout Group. Mr Scoble, a charismatic leader, started the Troop with a number of Scouts from the 29th Weston as well

[290] 1993 District Directory p. 32 (Biddulph Archive)
Recollections of Mr D L Biddulph 24/09/05 (Biddulph Archive)
[291] Copy of 1988 Nine Ashes Summer Camp programme (Biddulph Archive)
[292] Recollections of Mr D R Biddulph (Biddulph Archive)
[293] Personal Scouting History of Mr T Scoble 14/01/03 Axe District website (Biddulph Archive
[294] 1993 District Directory pp. 32-33 (Biddulph Archive)

as boys from the Kewstoke Pack. The 29th Scout Troop was subsequently led by Mr Andrew Bradley and Mr Sean Townsend, (a son of former CSL Mrs Diane Townsend), for a few years before Mr Grant took over as SL in 1998, having done a spell running the Pack from 1996. The Troop in 1998 had the services of three ASLs and members of Saracen's V.S.U. Mr Neil Osborn, Mr Stuart Cox and Mr David Biddulph under the leadership of Mr Grant. Over the years the Group were fortunate in that a number of leaders were home grown, which helped with providing stable leadership.[295] The Pack was led by Miss Sarah Glen who had assistance from Kevin Chisholm, Michael Mead and Barrie Robbins, the latter another home grown leader who, along with Kevin Chisholm and Sarah Glen, is still active in the 1st Milton Scout Group.

A Beaver Colony was opened in 1995 under the leadership of Julia Shaw (BSL) and Barbara Hase (ABSL) alongside Beavers James Hogarth, Leigh Burge, Ben Morris, Daniel Wiseman, Ian Williams, Kevin Atkinson, Ryan Lanning, Tom Gray, Darren Hines and Robert Summers being invested at a ceremony attended by ADC Beavers Eileen Nock.[296] The leadership of the Colony was to change several times during the intervening years with Sue Hogarth and then Alana Nuttycombe taking charge of the Colony. Mrs Sue Hogarth had a son in the Colony and an older boy, Philip, in the Cubs. Another parent who took an active part in the Colony was Chris Wiseman whose son Daniel had been one of the first Beavers and still remains with the 1st Milton Group as a Colony Helper Over the years the Colony had assistance from a number of Venture Scouts who helped out as part of their training. Some remained with the Colony, such as Gemma Stacey and Amy Brokenshire, who later took warrants with the 1st Milton Scout Group.

---

295 1998/99 District Directory p. 10 (Biddulph Archive)

296 Weston Mercury 1995

Efforts were being made in 1992 to start a Venture Unit at the Group, the initial meeting was held in November 1992 with ASL Andy Hurst swapping roles to take a VSL warrant with Saracen's VSU. Jeremy Puttnam was elected as the first Chairman which comprised of around ten members.[297] Over the intervening years the Saracens expanded considerably and a regular supply of Scouts from the Troop continued to keep membership high until the Group merged with the 19th Weston in 1999. A very challenging year for the Unit was 1995 with the tragic death of Emma Heath, Saracens Chairperson, in a road accident. Mr Hurst handed over to Mr Townsend and Miss Blackman. In 1997 Miss Jo Freeman became the Saracen's Leader.

On July 11th 1999 the 29th Weston (St Peter's) and 19th Weston (Milton and Worle) Scout Group's merged to form 1st Milton Scout Group, retaining the 19th's Dark Blue and Yellow scarf and the 29th St Peter's scarf badge. The Group relocated to Drysdale Close, home of the 19th for forty years and Scouting at St. Peter's Church came to a close. 1st Milton Scout Group has since that time operated with two Beaver colonies, Two Cub Packs and a well supported Scout Troop, with several of the former 29th leaders remaining at the Group to this day.

30th Weston-Super-Mare (Wadham Street Baptist Church)

Fd: 16/06/1965 Reg No. 37397
Fld: 1970 Form E

The Baptist Church in Wadham Street formed a Cub Pack in the mid 1960s which although sponsored by the Church was an open Pack being led by Miss Barbara Green as CSL with assistance from Miss Jennifer Willett. The Pack disbanded in 1970.

[297] Recollections of the Author

31st Weston-Super-Mare (Church of the Latter Day Saints)

Fd: 04/11/1969 Reg No. 39531
Fld 1971

Attempts were made by the Church of the Latter Day Saints to form a Scout Group in 1969 with Mr Kenneth William Fulfit as GSL and Mr Andrew G Peterken as SL, being assisted by Mr Layton G Gwilliam. The Troop never got going and in 1971 the Group was disbanded.

32nd Weston-Super-Mare (Oldmixon)

Fd: 15/01/1971 Reg No. 40047
Mgr 1984

Scarf: Sky blue with maroon border

In 1971 a Scout Group was formed at Oldmixon Primary School to cater for the children from the Oldmixon housing estate. The founding leaders were Mr Roy Dexter as the GSL, Mrs Devina Dexter, CSL 'A' Pack, and Mrs Cathleen Green, CSL 'B' Pack, with Mrs Silvia Dyke and Mrs Janet Mereweather as ACSLs. Mr Ronald Walters took on the warrant of SL, being assisted by Mr Patrick Green (ASL). The Group opened with fifty-eight Cubs and seven Scouts. The Group operated three Packs until 1972 when the satellite Pack meeting at the British Legion headquarters in Hutton became 1st Hutton.

By 1979 the Group was down to three Leaders, Mr Andy Skillen being the SL and Scouter-in-Charge, with his wife Mrs Helen

Skillen holding an ACSL warrant, the Pack was run by Mrs P Moulton. In 1981 Mr Alex Harries was appointed by the DC Mr Mike Bell to try and turn the ailing Group round. Evidently this venture was not successful as by 1984 the Group closed and the Cub Pack which was now being led by Mrs Helen Skillen, joined the 17th Weston Scout Group.

33rd Weston-Super-Mare (1st Worle)

Fd: 28/02/72 Reg No. 40426
11/07/78 (Changed name to 1st Worle)
01/11/86 (Changed name to 1st North Worle, moves to Wansborough Rd)

Scarf: Purple with white trim

This Group was original formed as a satellite Cub pack when the 19th Weston (Milton & Worle) Scout Group formed a second Cub Pack meeting in Worle. The inaugural meeting was held on 9th September at Worle Church Hall.[298] By the end of September the Pack had started meeting under the helm of Mrs Pansy Langley as Akela, her husband Mr Peter Langley held an ACSL warrant. The Group was detached from the 19th Weston to become known as 33rd Weston (1st Worle) registering on February 28th 1972.[299] Mr Langley had become GSL the following year when Mrs Julie Kattana joined the Group as a member of the Group Executive, as well as helping at Pack meetings where her son, Ali, was a Cub Scout. Mrs Kattana recalled that around this time the Langleys ran the Pack with help from their daughter Paula Allen, their son in law who was an ASL along with Messrs Mike Ralph, David Biggs and M Wallington, with Mr Ron Macklin as SL.[300]

---

[298] 19th Weston-S-Mare (Milton & Worle) committee meeting minutes of 03/09/70
[299] Copy of Form C 28/02/72 (Gilwell Archive)
[300] Copy of Form C 28/02/72 (Gilwell Archive)

Julia Kattana took a warrant in 1978 alongside Mrs Sue Collard with the departure of Mrs Langley in September 1978. Shortly afterwards Mrs Collard departed and Mrs Kattana was running the Pack, becoming CSL and remaining with the Pack until handing over to the husband and wife team of Malcolm and Heather Gale. Mrs Eileen Nock and (briefly) Mrs Pat Page worked alongside Mrs Kattana[301], as well as Mrs Anne Rayband who moved on from the Pack in 1980 to briefly serve as CSL at 1st St George's Pack, before moving on to 2nd Worle Cub Pack.

The Pack held a sausage sizzler day at Sand Bay which proved to be a big hit with the boys, Later that year Steven Wright, Nick Dutton, Chris Cowd and Mark Watler attended the Axe District Sixer's and Seconders weekend held at Huish Woods in September, highlights of which included sedan chair racing, as well as the boys winning the award for best kept site and the Sixers were presented with their stripes by ADC Cub Scouts Mr Peter Holmes. 1980 found the Pack having another active year with entries in the Axe District Olympics held at Hutton Scout Group HQ, St George's Day and Remembrance Day parades, the Bristol Heritage Walk in October, joining in with the Worle Carnival and another sausage sizzler evening at Sand Bay. Cubs in the Pack around this time included; Gavin Gillham, Jeff Bevan, Chris Cowd, Richard Hession, Xenos Cottam, Nick Dutton, Jamie Allen, David Lunt, Anthony Page, Mark English, Steven Jenkins, Stuart Hayes, Douglas Johnston, Dean Smith, Adrian Cole, Steven Wright, Mark and Lee Watler [302]

The Pack camped at Glenny Woods for their annual Summer Camp in 1981 in addition to participating in the District fun day based on a medieval theme at Cheddar. Other highlights of the year included a trip on the Bristol Packet and ice skating on April

[301] Notes from Interview with Mrs J Kattana 01/02/06

[302] Interview with Mrs J Kattana & 1st Worle Pack photo album 01/02/06

12th and a joint meeting with 1st Bleadon Cubs to gain their Entertainers badge in November. 1982 found the Pack out and about with bird watching at Sand Point on February 14th, participating in World Conservation Day near Charterhouse, taking a walk through Velvet Bottom followed in May by the District Adventure Day on a maritime theme and another day on the beach entitled "pre-bronze beachcombers day". Once again the Sixer and Seconders were shipped off to the District Sixers and Seconders weekend in June, oddly enough the Cubs are again seen eating, a well known Cub pastime![303]

On July 11th 1978 the Group changed its name from 33rd Weston (1st Worle) to 1st Worle Scout Group.

Some time in the 1970s Mr Roger Fox took over from Mr Macklin as SL, remaining with the Troop until handing over to Mr Anthony Wild and Mr David Heathcock in 1981. Mr Paul Elliot took out a Troop Helper certificate in the early 1980s, later becoming GSL, working with Mr Wild to draw up the plans for the building of the Scout HQ on Wansborough Road. By the autumn of 1982 the Troop had grown and a fourth patrol was created, with the patrols being named after birds of prey, the Troop's patrol were; Eagles Falcons, Owls and Kestrels.[304]

The Group moved around several times during its life time, initially meeting in the Church Hall, now where the doctor's surgery stands behind the High Street in Worle, then moved to Lawrence Road Community Centre (the old Methodist Church). Around this time the Scouts started meeting at Priory School. The Pack moved in the 1980s and were meeting at Hillside Infants school, then due to a caretakers strike, the Pack met for a few months on Friday nights at the 29th Weston (St Peter's) Group HQ

[303] Interview with Mrs J Kattana & 1st Worle Pack photo album 01/02/06
[304] Notes from 1st Worle Troop Scoutabout Winter 1982 (Courtesy of Weston Library)

before moving into the old section of Mendip Green School in Mendip Avenue.

The first Scout to gain his Chief Scout Award in the Troop was Ali Kattana. In the autumn of 1982 four Chief Scout Awards were presented to Senior Patrol Leaders Jeremy Harris and Paul Macklin, Patrol Leader David Skidmore and Assistant Patrol Leader Richard Hayman by the DC.[305] The Troop Summer camp in 1982 was held at Gilwell and highlights of the camp reported in the Troop newsletter included a visit to London taking in a tour of BP House and a shopping trip to Harrods. Evenings were spent joining in with the other campers onsite, including a Troop of American Scouts playing football in 'the lid' (a large barn) and campfires. Oddly the "lost property from the camp consisted of one brown shoe!"[306]

Woodhouse Park in September was the venue for the Troop Camp, which included in the itinerary a trip to Bristol Industrial Museum and a tour of the deep sea survey ship HMS Hecla, just back from the southern Pacific.[307] In November nine Scouts undertook their expedition badge hiking from Sidcot to Priddy, where they camped overnight in Shepton Mallet Caving Club's hut, before pushing on the following day to Wookey after completing a compass course".[308] The Troop enjoyed a winter disco held at St Martin's Church Hall on Friday 3rd December with 3rd Worle Guides who outnumbered the Scouts two to one. Not that this seemed to faze the Troop.[309]

---

[305] Notes from 1st Worle's Scoutabout Autumn 1982 (Courtesy of Weston Library Archive)
[306] Notes from 1st Worle's Scoutabout Autumn 1982 (Courtesy of Weston Library Archive)
[307] Notes from 1st Worle's Scoutabout Winter 1982 (Courtesy of Weston Library Archive)
[308] Notes from 1st Worle's Scoutabout Autumn 1982 (Courtesy of Weston Library Archive)
[309] Notes from 1st Worle's Scoutabout Autumn 1982 (Courtesy of Weston Library Archive)

1983 saw the Troop camping at Huish Woods for an activity weekend from April 1st to 4th, followed a week later with the PLs and APLs camping at Woodhouse Park and camping at Burrington as part of the District camp. Summer Camp was arranged to be held at Butcher's Coppice at Bear Cross just outside Bournemouth.[310] The Group Annual report from 1983 records that Akela, Malcolm Gale, had twenty seven boys in the Pack. Highlights of the year included twenty Cubs passing their Communicators badge leading Akela to comment that the "whole pack now talks in secret code". The Annual Pack holiday was held at Cheddar as well as attending the District Cub Day on July 9th.[311] The Troop camped at Churchill in July with seventeen Scouts in camp, the main activities included swimming at Churchill baths and games.[312]

The Group changed its name and re-registered as 1st North Worle Scout Group in November 1986. (See 1st North Worle and 1st Worle Village entries).

1st North Worle

Scarf:	Purple with light blue border	(1986-2001
	Royal blue with emerald green border	(from 2001)

In 1986 the 1st Worle Scout Group changed its name to 1st North Worle and at the same time changed the Group colours too. A Scout Group called 1st Worle Village would remain in the old area of Worle (near the High street) which was officially registered by the District Secretary in a letter to the County.

[310] Notes from 1st Worle's Scoutabout Spring 1983 (Courtesy of Weston Library Archive)
[311] Notes from 1st Worle's Scoutabout, Spring 1983 (Courtesy of Weston Library Archive)
[312] Notes from 1st Worle's Scoutabout Spring 1983 (Courtesy of Weston Library Archive)

The GSL was Mr Paul Elliott who alongside Chris Cirkaldy was running the Pack in 1986. The Group started fundraising for a new headquarters next to Priory School on Wansborough Road in the mid 1980s although this was to take a further seven years before the hut was officially opened in 1991. In the early 1980s the Group comprised of roundabout fifty members with a Cub Pack and a Scout Troop. However, as further housing development took place the need for a second pack arose which was duly started in 1983. Two years later the Group had seventy-four Cubs which were meeting as two packs known as Village and Priory Packs. The Village Pack had taken in members of the nearby St Georges Scout Group which had recently disbanded. Pack Leaders towards the end of the 1980s and into the early 1990s included Ann Neill, Anne Churchill, Judy Willetts, Mrs Sutton and Michaela Heath, the current DC. Anne Churchill passed the leadership of her Pack to Graham Miekle. The two Packs had gone back into a single Pack by 1993 and it would be over a decade before a second pack reformed.

1986 saw a change in the GSL with Khalil Kattana being appointed and Richard Knowles beginning his long service to the Group as Group Chairman, a position he still holds at the Group making him the longest serving member of the Group. Khalil Kattana stood down some time in 1994 and the following year Tony Cooksley is recorded as being GSL. The Group would have a number of short-term GSLs with Simon Dutton leading the Group in 1998 before handing over to Sally Tabrett who was succeeded by Carol Pepper, the current GSL.

The Group started a Beaver Scout Colony in 1992 under the leadership of Sue Congram whose sons were members of the Group and Sally Tabrett, later to become GSL. The Colony started with thirteen Beavers and soon expanded to a full twenty-four. Sue Congram and Sally Tabrett ran the Beavers until circa 1996 when a wholesale change of leaders occurred with three ladies Rebecca Wood, Helen Skillen and Sue Bishop all holding

ABSL warrants. A further change in leaders occurred a few years later with the arrival of Carol Pepper as BSL and Wendy Pearson alongside the long-serving Helen Skillen.

The Scout Troop during the later 1980s was taken by Paul Elliott and Dave Heathcock. Following Mr Elliott's departure, Mr Cooksley ran the Troop prior to his appointment as GSL with assistance from Neil Congram who held a Troop Helper certificate and two years later became SL with assistance from Mr D Mountford as ASL. The leadership of the Troop again changed with Richard Hall as SL, Monty Saunders, Phil Geffery and Steve Postma taking ASL roles. Mr Saunders took over the leadership of the Troop when Mr Hall left due to work reasons. Under Mr Saunders the Troop numbers expanded to close to thirty Scouts, which was an improvement on the early part of the decade which saw Troop numbers drop down to a dozen. Mr Saunders moved on from the Troop roundabout 2004 when he was appointed as DSL. Whilst a search for new leaders was taking place, the Troop met under the guidance of the GSL, Carol Pepper. The Troop had a leadership team of Ian Stone, Richard Dunstone and Andrew Beaton who served around eighteen months. Once again the Troop was leaderless with Carol Pepper again holding the fort.

The Group formed a short-lived Venture Unit called Barbarians which met between 1985 to 1990 under the leadership of Martin Tillman. Little more information is known to the author about this unit, apart from Dave Snook being one of its members.

34th Weston (Baytree)

Fd: 02/04/1987-1993 Reg No. 44891

A Scout Group was founded Baytree School, a school for children with special needs in 1987 by Mike Wilkinson who at the time of the Troop's formation had seven Scouts and one Instructor, Mrs

Mary Wilkinson, in addition to himself. Unfortunately not a large amount of information has come to light regarding the Group which folded in 1993.

1st Worle

Fd: 1938--WWII Reg No. 20394

The Gilwell archive records the registration of a Boy Scout Troop being formed in 1938 under the leadership of Mr E K Rake, who was the village chemist with assistance from Mr S Lavell. The Troop's headquarters was at Worle Primary School (now Hillside Infants School) opposite the Parish Church of Worle, St. Martin's. At the time of registration the Troop strength was at eighteen boys.[313] The Troop was to have a short existence, being forced to disband during the Second World War as the Group Leaders undertook wartime service.

1st Worle Village

Fd: 01/11/86-07/11/01 Reg No. 44852

Scarf: Purple with a white trim

The Worle Village Scout Group was started in order to provide Scouting in the old Worle area following the 1st Worle Scout Group's relocation to their headquarters at Wansborough Road. The new Group retained the colours of the former Group. The Cub section was led by the long serving husband and wife team of Malcolm and Heather Gale, with twenty four boys in the Pack. The Gale's handed over to Mrs J Hill in the late 1990s. The Group was to relocate their meeting place several times during

[313] Copy of Form C (Gilwell Archive)

their existence; starting out at Hillside Infants School on Church Road, Worle before moving to meet at the Worle Community Centre in Lawrence Road and, for a brief spell, shared the 29th Weston (St Peters) Headquarters as a temporary measure until moving to St Mark's Church. The Troop lasted for a decade before disbanding being led for a number of years by J R Fox who was assisted by Mr M Bennett. Troop numbers were generally stable ranging from between fifteen to eighteen Scouts who were divided into three patrols. A Beaver Colony was formed in the mid 1990s by Sally Tabrett with help from Mrs P Devereux. However by the end of the Millennium the Group was struggling for leaders and amalgamated with 1st North Worle in November 2001.

2nd Worle (Meadvale)

Fd: 17/09/79 Reg No.43251

Scarf: Lemon with red border

The Group was formed to cater for the Meadvale estate and has met for all of its life at the Community Centre. The founding leaders were Barbara Cousins as CSL with Gillian Taylor and Linda Bell taking ACSL warrants. Within a year the Cub Pack had grown with a Troop being started under the leadership of Richard Swift in March 1980. David Luck provided support as an ASL. A year later the Group appointed John Uttery as GSL. The Group's first chairman was Mr K Andrews. Linda recruited her husband to lend a hand with the Troop and Tim took out an ASL warrant in 1981. A year later Tim was promoted to SL. His wife had succeeded Barbara Cousins the previous year as CSL and the Bells' alongside the Lucks were to provide considerable commitment to the Group until the end of the decade. Tim did a brief stint as GSL. The Group had to wait a year until Dennis

Johnson took the helm as GSL, a post he held for five years, making him one the Group's longest serving GSLs.

Changes in the Pack and Troop leadership also occurred in the later 1980s with Anne Rayband moving from 1st Worle to take the Pack as CSL. Richard Bebb joined the Troop taking the SL warrant. He was assisted by Marko Oblystuck and David Briggs. Marko moved on to open the Hobos VSU, which met for a fifteen month spell between 1986-88. Michael Rayband followed Mr Bebb as SL, and was in turn succeeded by Mrs Judith Vincent. During this period the Troop expanded rapidly and a second Troop was started and would reform a Venture Unit aptly named Phoenix VSU. The Unit was started by Stuart Adams in 1994 to cater for the large number of older Scouts in the Group's two Troops. He switched roles to AVSL before handing over to Ali Kattana, who led Phoenix until it disbanded in 2001, by which time Ali Kattana had been appointed as ADC Ventures. Former members of Phoenix include Sarah Langley–Wheeler, currently the ADC Cubs, Claire Sawyer, Beth Adams, Cheryl and Brett Parker.

The 2nd Worle Troop was the first troop in the District to accept girls into the section following changes to the movement's rules in 1991. This undoubtedly helped the rapid expansion of the Group.

The Troop leadership passed to the husband and wife team of Judith and Kevin Vincent as SL and ASL respectively, in 1993, who remained with the Group for around four years. Mrs Vincent briefly held the role of GSL between 1997-98. She was succeeded by Mr David Hillcock who held a variety of roles since joining the Group including AGSL and GSL, he also worked with the Troop and Ventures. His wife, Marion, joined the Group as a ABSL, later switching sections to lead the Pack, a role she has held for over a decade now. The Pack was led in the early 1990s by Kevin Peters with Paul Barnett, Paul Falloon and Shirley

Hawkes providing warranted assistance as ACSLs. Paul Falloon succeeded Mr Peters as CSL, before handing over to Mrs Hillcock. Shirley Hawkes moved on to lead one of the Troops[314] Another stalwart of the group was Mr Andrew Skillen, who held various roles within the Group, within the Troop and Cub sections.

However the Troop went into a decline in late 2001, at which point it was down to a single Troop which, following Ms Hawkes departure in early 2001, shortly afterwards disbanded and remained dormant for a few years until it was reinvigorated by a new leadership team comprising of SL Richard Boobyer, Strone March and Michelle Kendall.

The Colony was formed in early 1991 by Mrs Johnson with Mrs Hillcock taking an ABSL warrant. The leadership passed to Mrs Hillock in the mid 1990s, before she handed over to Mrs Carol Barnes, who was assisted by Lyn Thomas and Mrs Gillian Savage. These two ladies have continued to run the Colony jointly following Carol Barnes' departure.

The Group has enjoyed a good level of parental support with Sue and Dave Dibbens serving as Chairman and Vice chair in the early 1990s before handing the baton on to Dave Culliford. Mr Paul Savage has served as Group Chairman for a fair few years now, supporting his wife's commitment to the Group.

[314] District Directories 1993, 1995 & 1998 pp. 36, 23 & 23

Hill Road Scouts and Guides

24th Weston (Hill Road)

1st Worle Scout Group 1983

2nd Worle Beaves Opening

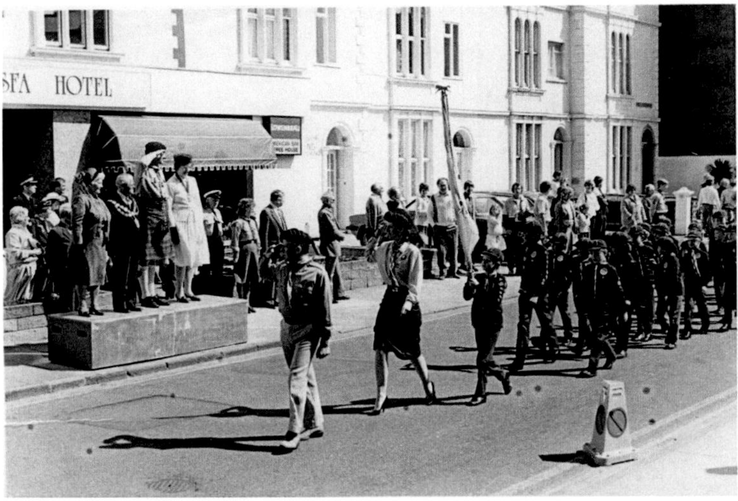

St George's Day Parade c. 1990

1st Axbridge

Fd:	29/11/1930-1934	Reg No. 12092
	28/03/69-1993	Reg No. 39266

The earliest record of Scouting in Axbridge dates from 1930 when Mr O H Thomas started a Boy Scout Troop comprising of eighteen Scouts and meeting at the Town Hall[315]. The Troop was transferred into Mendip District in September 1932. The Troop was unable to continue to meet and amalgamated with Scout Group Registration number 13916[316]. The author is unsure which Group this amalgamation was with.

Scouting restarted in Axbridge with the opening of a Cub Pack under the leadership of Mr Kenneth Griffiths as CSL, with Mrs Olive Woods and Mrs Anne Cannon as Assistant Cub Leaders. The Pack had sixteen Cubs in 1969. Mr Kevin Peters joined the Group as its Chairman in the late 1970s when Joan Flavell ran the Pack. The decision to start a Scout Troop was mooted and carried forward. As the Pack had several boys who were approaching Scout age and the nearest Troops were at either Cheddar or Shipham, it was felt that the boys would not travel to either Group, so a Scout Troop was formed by GSL Kevin Peters in 1977 with twelve Scouts, and assistance from a parent who later took a warrant. The Troop held their initial meetings at the Old Court House near the Town Hall in Axbridge before moving to the Baptist Chapel and in a final move jointly sharing the Old Station premises with the Youth Club in 1985. When the Cub Leader, Mrs Flavell, retired in 1986 an unsuccessful effort was made to find leaders before the Pack disbanded. The Troop continued to meet until 1993 when SL Mike Sartain moved to

[315] Copy of Form C 29/11/30 (Gilwell Archive)
[316] Copy of From C2 (Gilwell Archive)

Shropshire with the Troop suffering the same fate as the Cub Pack [317]

The year after the Troop restarted the first summer camp was undertaken at Cow Castle, being well remembered by former leaders for the fact that a huge storm in the night flooded the campers out. The boys were absolutely soaked, two tents were blown away and a tractor was needed to pull the Group minibus out of the waterlogged valley, with the comment being passed "a good start!".[318] Other camps and activities in the seventy-fifth anniversary year of Scouting included the Group eating a seventy-five yard sausage made by butcher John Burroughs in the Furlong. Membership of the Troop expanded, with four Patrols established, with a wide variety of camps and activities being undertaken in these golden years of the Troop's life. The following year the Group camped at Biblins in the Wye valley, being principally a canoeing camp with timed races including a trip over Swallow Falls. One bright lad paddled too close to the fall with near disastrous results with the leaders having to dash into the current to save the Scout. Nick Richards, who was a keen yachtsman, joined the Troop as SL in 1984 with the Annual Camp being held at Brayford on Exmoor. The move to the Old Railway Station the next year gave the Scouts an opportunity to undertake some DIY and decoration of their new premises. The Troop returned to Exmoor for their summer camp the following summer. Their flare for publicity resulted in the Group mounting a very successful Gang Show at the Town Hall in 1986. The following year the Troop decided to have a change of scenery, camping in Shropshire. With the use of a sailing craft under the guidance of Nick Richards all the boys gained sailing experience. The Troop travelled to Lower Breddy near Dorchester for the 1988 summer camp. One recollection of this camp was the boys piling out the back of the minibus as they arrived on camp and

[317] Recollections of Mr K Peters 11/10/07
Recollections of Mr M Bass 13/09/07
[318] Recollections of Mr M Bass 13/09/07

rolly-pollying down the field. This had an unfortunate result as the field had just been vacated by a herd of cows... the results were dire!

The Group participated in the Axbridge Blackberry Carnival entering a float entitled 'One Giant Step' in 1989. Summer camp that year was held at Creswell Key near Tenby where the Troop went puffin watching on Skoma Island. Mr Bass was appointed as GSL of the Group during the year. The following year saw a return to the Troop's old haunt, Exmoor, as well as appearing on ITV's Lost Lines programme about disused railways, as the headquarters was the former Axbridge railway station which formed part of the old Strawberry Line, running from Yatton to Wells. The programme focussed on the different uses of the old stations of the Strawberry Line which Mr Bass recalls being "completely caught out when I was put in front of the cameras totally unprepared and asked to give a short history of the station's use. It took four takes; 1- an initial run, 2- a 'take' but missed out an item, 3- a 'take' but the crew forgot the film and 4- final bag of nerves 'take'. In November Mr Bass was awarded his Wood Badge by the DC Mr Don Hurrell.[319] Michael Sartain joined the Troop in 1991 as SL, which at that time had four Patrols, camping that year included a 'dads and lads' camp at Pinkney Pond on Exmoor, notable for the game whereby volunteer Scouts pulled pound coins from a shallow stream with their teeth, needless to say this proved very popular and somewhat expensive. The Troop held Summer Camp at Challaborough near Salcombe in Devon, participating in climbing and abseiling sessions at Chudliegh, a trip round the naval fleet at Plymouth and a hike to Burgh Island. The following year's summer camp was held at Ferny Crofts where the Scouts visited the Montague Motor Museum. The Group held another Gang Show, again a great success, and which turned out to be farewell evening to Mr Bass who was retiring with the local press and old

[319] Recollections Mr M Bass 13/09/07 p.2

SLs attending to say farewell, all of which came as great surprise to Mr Bass.[320]

The Group were keen supporters of, and were in turn supported by, the local community, regularly involved with local fetes, garden parties, the Axbridge Blackberry carnival and fundraising endeavours. The main Group fundraiser was the fortnightly paper collection which was stored in a lockable shed. On one occasion the Scouts on returning from a camp caught a local youth attempting to set fire to a pile of papers left outside the store for collection, needless to say the fire was quickly extinguished without causing any damage. The Group benefited from a very supportive Parents Committee and several adults regularly helped with events. Activities within the Group included sailing under Nick Reynolds, with the Troop looking after a small sailing boat kept on the reservoir. Other activities included caving on the Mendips and participation in the District events, one year the Troop won the football competition.

Badgworth and Biddisham

Fd: 1924-26 Reg No. Not known

A Scout Troop comprising of eleven Boy Scouts was formed in 1924 in Axbridge District Association. The Troop headquarters was the Parish Hall in Biddisham under the leadership of SM Mr Mildary Hall. The Troop had the services of an ASM Mr Reginald Read. Beyond these basic details very little information is known about this early Troop and its activities. It was to have a short existence disbanding two years later.[321].

---

[320] Recollections Mr M Bass 13/09/07 pp. 2-3
[321] Copy of Form C 10/06/24 (Gilwell Archive)

1st Banwell

Fd:	1914-1926	
	20/11/31-1933	Reg No. 13357
	10/06/1947-31/03/52	25391
	18/06/1954-1966	31398
	31/03/1969	39273

Scouting in Banwell dates from just prior to the First World War, the exact date of formation is unknown. Despite the lack of leaders, who were on active service, the Troop continued to meet during the Great War. Banwell is mentioned again in 1920 when Mr H H Pruen is recorded as the warranted leader, alongside his wife as lady ASM and Miss C J Clothier who took out an ACM warrant.[322] It is unclear whether the Troop had been restarted following the war, or that the arrival of the Pruen's marked a period of stable leadership. The Troop and Pack had their flags dedicated at the church, which were a gift from a well-wisher. Mr Pruen was promoted to District SM in June 1925[323]. The following year Mrs Pruen stepped down as ASM along with ACM Miss Clothier[324]. It appears that the sections had disbanded around this time and there is no mention of 1st Banwell Scouts or Cubs in the registration of Scout Groups which took place in 1928.

The Troop was briefly reformed during the early 1930s by Messrs C E Welbourne and P H Marshall, warranted as SM and ASM respectively, with a membership of eighteen Scouts. However during 1933 the Troop folded, a reference mentions that the Group folded into Group No. 4237, the 12th Weston (Boulevard

[322] Mr R Ivens' North Somerset Scouting Notes p. 2 (2002)
Early Somerset Warrants 1908-30 (Gilwell archives)
[323] Misc Notes North Somerset compiled by Mr R Ivens 25/10/04 p. 5
[324] Misc Notes North Somerset compiled by Mr R Ivens 25/10/04 p. 5

Congregationalist Church), which seems a very odd Group to amalgamate with, being based in Weston town centre.[325]

Scouting returned to the village following the Second World War when the veteran Bristol Leader and Silver Wolf Award holder and the recently appointed vicar of Banwell, Rev. Edward Courtney Dawson, restarted the Group comprising of twelve Wolf Cubs and eighteen Scouts with himself as the sole leader.[326] The Group met at the Old School Room in the village[327]. More leaders were soon attracted to the Group with Troop meetings taken by SM, Mr R J Cousin, whilst the Pack was ran by Mr J Sanderson, who lived on the RAF base at Locking.[328] Despite this promising start the Group disbanded in 1952 as a result of that old problem of a lack of warranted leaders. The Group reformed two years later due to the activities and encouragement of the Rev John Bromwich, vicar of Banwell and GSM, with Miss Joyce Johnston holding a warrant as CM to a Pack of eight boys and Mr William Henry Blackmore being SM to a Troop of sixteen boys, meetings were held in the same place as the previous Group had met. However by 1960 the Reverend Bromwich was the sole leader[329] who kept the Group going until an influx of new leaders arrived in 1963 including Mr G W Barron as GSM and the Acting CM, Mr G Parsons.[330] The following year Mr D R Yarde took out a SM warrant, although the Pack appeared to have closed as Mr Parsons was not registered with the Group. The Troop continued to meet until 1966 when the Group was again to disband.[331]

<u>Scarf:</u> <u>Red with a white trim</u>

---

[325] Copy of Registration Form C 20/11/1931 (Gilwell Archive)
[326] Notes from Mr R Ivens (Avon Scout County Archivist)
[327] Copy of Registration Form C 10/06/1947 (Gilwell Archive)
[328] Notes from Lapsed Scout Groups (Tangier Scout Centre Archives, Taunton)
[329] Copy of Somerset County Directory 1960 p.12 (Tangier Centre Archive)
[330] Copy of Somerset County Directory 1963 p.14 (Tangier Centre Archive)
[331] Copy of Somerset County Directory 1964 p.15 (Tangier Centre Archive)
Copy of Registration Form C 18/06/1954 (Gilwell Archive)

The current Group was reformed at the end of March 1969 with the formation of a Cub Pack founded by Mrs Sheila M Reynheart as CSL and ACSL Mrs Devina Dexter. The Pack was off to a good start with twenty-one boys, who met at the Methodist Church Hall in the village[332]. The following year the Troop was restarted under the leadership of Mr G H Reynheart, who handed over the running of the Troop to Mr Maurice W Wooley when he and his wife left the Group in July 1971.[333] In 1993 Mr David Colbourne was running the Troop, his wife Alisa held the position of the BSL. The Troop had the services of Mr George Rice as a Troop helper with an average of fifteen boys in the Troop throughout the 1980s. From 1998 Mr A Oakley ran the Troop. After his departure the Troop was run by the author and Mr David Poole 'leaders on loan' from 1st Ashcombe Troop in conjunction with GSL Mr Khalil Kattana and Mr Michael Griffin who held an ASL warrant in the Troop. Mr Poole took over the leadership of the Troop in January 2005 until stepping down in September 2007. A new team of leaders came forward including Mr Roger Houghton, Mrs Jane Gomm, Scott and Jo Macleod taking ASL warrants, who all had children in the various sections of the Group.[334]

The Cubs were led by Mr Colin Bawden, one of the Pack's longest serving leaders who served for over a decade. The challenge of finding another leader resulted in Mrs Julia Kattana taking over as Akela, as well as serving as ADC Leader Training, following her retirement in 2004 handing over to Miss Sarah Langley-Wheeler, who remained with the Pack until work commitments led to her being unable to attend regularly. The reins were handed over to Mrs Fran Ford, who held an ACSL warrant and juggled operating the Pack with running a farm and looking after a young family. Another search for leaders was

[332] Copy of Registration Form C 31/03/1969 (Gilwell Archive)
[333] Group Data Document 1969-1982 p. 2
[334] Group AGM reports 2004-07
Recollections of the D R Biddulph

undertaken to assist Mrs Ford. Sue Watts joined becoming a regular Helper being followed shortly after by two ACSLs, Miss Clare Sawyer and later Mr Stuart Dolman, whose son had joined the Pack. The leadership team of Raksha, Bagheera, Hathi and Chill currently share the responsibility for leadership between themselves. Despite leadership challenges the Pack has camped several times recently with two boys joining the Ashcombe Cubs camp in 2007 and previous camps at Huish Woods and Glennywood campsites.

The Beaver Colony was started in 1986 by Mrs Colbourne and was the first Beaver Colony in the District. Mrs Calbourne later handed over to Denise Leighton Price. The Colony briefly disbanded in 2005, a year that witnessed three leaders come and go before Mrs Barbie Bradbury, who had previously been a Beaver Leader in another District, took the reins with a team of Helpers. Her husband was appointed GSL following the retirement due to ill health of Mr Mick Harley, who had succeeded Mr Khalil Kattana who had retired in 2004. The Banwell Group had struggled for long-term leaders but the Group now stands on a much better footing with an increased number of adults and young people joining the Group.

1st Blagdon

Fd:	05/04/1933-1935	Reg No. 15110
	1994	45756

The first record of Boy Scouts meeting in Blagdon dates from April 5th 1933 with a Scout Group comprising of fifteen Wolf Cubs, fifteen Boy Scouts and two Warranted Leaders. The Group belonged to Mendip District. Mr Charles Haddon was recorded as the SM, with Mr Alfred James as ASM, the Group's temporary meeting place was "Four Winds" the home of the two leaders.

The Group was an open Group, and had a brief lifespan disbanding in 1935.[335]

After a period of nearly sixty years Scouting returned to Blagdon with the opening of a Troop catering for the boys of the village by leaders Colin and Pip Riley and Mr and Mrs St Ledger-Harris. Mrs Riley took the helm as SL following the departure of Simon St Ledger Harris.[336] Sadly, Mr Riley, who was the AGSL, passed away in 2002. The Group formed a Cub Pack in the summer of 2003 under the leadership of Mr Jenkins of Rhodyate Farm, although they struggled for additional leaders. Following the emigration of their CSL, the Pack was seeking a new Akela, whereupon Mr Harper came forward. The Group's meeting place is the Methodist Church in the village.[337]

1st Bleadon

Fd: 01/04/80-01/05/03 Reg No. 43758

Scarf: Blue and orange halved

The Group was founded in 1981 at the behest of some of the members of the District Sub Appointments Committee who felt that the village of Bleadon needed a Scout Group. The Group opened with a Cub Pack under the leadership of CSL Mrs Gillian Taylor with Claude Simpson as GSL. Other leaders included Miss Penny Jefferies who held an ACSL Warrant. Mrs Betty Paterson succeeded Mrs Taylor, with assistance from ACSL Mr Howard Fisher and Mrs Jones, Mrs S Matthews, Mrs Phillips and Mr C Blatchford, the latter being Pack Helpers. Mrs Paterson handed over to Mrs Stevie Rhodes who remained as Akela until standing

[335] Copy of Registration Form C 05/04/33 (Gilwell Archive)
[336] Axe District Directory 1998 p. 12
[337] Axe District Directory 2003

down in April 2003 when the Pack folded due to no new leaders coming forward.

The Troop was originally led by Mr David Boley who stood down as SL in April 1983 He was assisted by Mr R Brown who held a Troop Helper warrant. Ms Lesley Hunt took over as SL. During her time the Scouts camped at Woodhouse Park, Braggers Wood in Christchurch and in the following year an overseas camp at Belgium from August 10th -17th costing £120, travelling by public transport to Ramsgate and crossing the channel to the campsite, each Scout was allowed one rucksack for all of his kit. Following the departure of Mr Hunt, Mrs Heather Grant briefly ran the Troop before handing over to Mr Huw Boyce who had two daughters in the Group. In 2000 the Troop began holding their annual weekend winter camp at Blackpool staying at Waddacar Scout campsite, the highlight of the weekend was the trip to Blackpool's famous Golden Mile and the Pleasure Beach with Scouts and Leaders, numbering thirty-one in all, enjoying a traditional tea in the resort. The Troop numbered around twelve to twenty four Scouts during its lifetime with at least two patrols in existence, the Cobras and Panthers.

Summer camps were also held at Horner Wood, Braggers Wood in 2000, which was Mr Boyce's last camp as leader in charge, handing over to Mr David Biddulph who was the Troop's last leader. The final summer camp mounted by the Troop was to the Northamptonshire Jamboree; Nailer 2001; camp held at Towcester racecourse between Saturday 28th July to August 4th, with activities ranging from climbing, kayaking and a day trip to Alton Towers. Two other Groups attended the camp from Axe District, 1st Kewstoke who had their own sub camp with eighty nine Scouts attending and the 3rd Weston (St Paul's) Saints VSU. All three groups came together for a Christmas meal during the camp which was hosted by the Kewstoke SLs.[338] The Troop

[338] Group papers 1st Bleadon 1995-2002

occasionally mounted weekend camps at Woodhouse Park, They regularly participated in Church services attending Mothering Sunday, Harvest, patronal festival, St George's Day and Remembrance Day services.

The Group was suspended in April 2003 after the Cub Leader Mrs Stevie Rhodes stepped down and no replacement came forward. The Scout Troop had closed due to a lack of leaders with the departure of Mr David S Biddulph who had only three Scouts remaining in the new age range for Scouts in August 2002. Mr Huw Boyce attempted to keep the Troop going whilst a search was made for new leaders. This was unsuccessful and the Troop disbanded by the spring of 2003.

The Group opened a Beaver Colony in the late 1990s which by 1998 was being led by ABSLs Jane Steele and Nicola Hulin. However following their departure the section folded in September 2001 as no new leaders came forward.

1st Brent Knoll

04/08/43-1958 Form E	Reg No. 22316
22/10/68-	Reg No. 39028

Major E Abbott started a Scout Troop with eight boys, which belonged to North District (the predecessor of Axe District), in the Burnham, Highbridge and District Local Association, meeting at Park Farm. Little more is known about the Troop, other than it had folded in 1958.[339]

The Group was reformed a decade later by CSL Mr David Marwood and ACSL Mr Norman Trenner. The Pack's meeting place was the village hall in Brent Knoll with a Pack of twenty-

Recollections of Mr D S & Mr D R Biddulph

339 Copy of Registration Form C 04/08/43 (Gilwell Archive)

three Boys and two Scouters.[340] By 1971 Mr Marwood had started a Scout Troop with Mr Trenner moving up to take the Cubs. Six years later this Group was transferred to the newly formed Sedgemoor District following local government changes in county boundaries.

1st Burrington

Fd: Unknown but active in 1918
Fd: 30/11/61 Reg No. 35833

The Weston-Super-Mare Directory of 1918 has an entry for a Scout Troop at Burrington in 1918, although the SM was on active service[341]. It is unclear as to how long the Troop continued after the Great War.

Scarf: Red

A Wolf Cub Pack opened in Burrington, meeting at the village school under Malcolm Parsons as CM and James Yeats as an ACM with twelve Cubs.[342] The following year the Group was transferred to Keynsham & Chew Valley District[343] before being transferred the following year to North East Somerset. The Group was returned to Axe a few years later[344]. The Group opened a Scout Troop in 1962/63 under the leadership of Mr Malcolm Parsons. The Group was flourishing. By 1966 Mr Yeats was being assisted as CM by Assistants Miss J Hilsen and Miss J Sherer, with Mr P F Endicott assisting with the running of the Troop alongside SM Parsons.[345]

---

340 Copy of Registration Form C 22/10/68 (Gilwell Archive)
341 1918 Weston-Super-Mare Directory p. 51
342 Copy of Form C 30/11/61 (Gilwell Archives London)
343 Copy of Form C-2 07/03/62 (Gilwell Archive, London)
344 Copy of Letter from Mr D Wells, of Scout HQ 19/12/67 (Gilwell Archives)
345 Copy of District Directory 1966 (Tangier Scout Centre Archive, Taunton)

The Group moved from the village school to the Parish Hall, until 1968 when the Group brought and moved into the former Methodist Church in Wrington, purchased at the cost of £1200. The Group had earlier been seeking to put up a wooden headquarters on the recreation ground for £600, the building would have been provided for free, with the costs coming for moving and siting the building.[346] The Group changed its name when they moved to the new headquarters to become 1st Burrington and Wrington Scout Group. However the new headquarters required considerable work to make it suitable for the Group and was officially opened in 1970.[347]

By 1968 Mr Endicott had succeeded Mr Parsons as SL and Mr Yeats had left the Pack which was now being taken by Mrs Cushworth. Three years later the Group had obtained the services of Mr D Hustwick as GSL whilst Cubbing proved to be popular in the village resulting in the formation of a second Pack, the Packs were referred to as Yeo and Wring, after two local rivers. The Packs were led by Messrs W R Lord and D F Davey. Later on Mr Bearman took over the role of GSL whilst Mr M Hunt took out a CSL warrant of the Yeo Pack and the leadership of the Wring Pack passed to Mr C Ball. During the mid 1970s Mr Endicott was able to recruit new ASLs with Mr Yeoman and Mrs Davis joining the Troop's leadership team. Mr Endicott was appointed as GSL in 1980 remaining in post until the mid 1990s when he took on the role of Group Chairman, passing over the baton of leadership to Mike Hunt, who had joined the Group in the 1970s as a Cub Scouter. By 1993 the Troop was being lead by a team of ASLs including Sue Bendall, Steve Ball, Andy Hutchings and Troop Helper Marshall Tucker, who later took an ASL warrant. Sue Bendall took responsibility for the Troop for a short duration, handing over to Tony Harden in 1997 and resumed

[346] Interview with Mr Malcolm Parsons 01/03/05

[347] Interview with Mr Peter Endicott 01/03/05

her role as an ASL. The Troop was a very active and successful Troop during these years and was well placed within the District events. A prime factor in the Troop's success lay in the support provided by the band of ASLs and Helpers, who included Robert Masding, Gary Clements, Matthew Attwell and Mr and Mrs Christie, who had sons in the Troop and took out Helper certificates within the section. Following the formation of the Explorer Units in 2002, Tony Harden stood down as SL in order to lead the 'Yeo' Explorer cell. Leadership of the Troop passed to Marshall Tucker and David Thorneyoak, the latter continues to lead the Troop, though the Troop has struggled to attract more adult help.[348]

Mr Alan Dors was appointed as CSL of Yeo Pack following Mr Hunt's promotion, whilst the Wring Pack was led by Mr Patrick Brown. A team of ACSLs provided support for the two leaders with Miss D Evans at Yeo Pack, and Messrs John Cook, Roy Clarke and David Ellis with the Wring Pack. Further help was provided by Pack Helpers the husband and wife team of Tony and Sally Harden and Miss Emma Weissei. Mr D Jenkins took out an ACSL warrant, he succeeded Mr Ellis as Akela of the Wring Pack with assistance from Mr Andrew Whiting. Mr Dors continued to lead the Yeo Pack with Mr Marshall Tucker taking an ACSL warrant. The section had three regular Helpers Mr Paul Benwell, Mrs Monica Duthie and Mrs Janet Willems. Several Group Helpers who were able to work within all three sections are recorded in the later 1990s, these being Mrs Harden, Mrs Dors and Messrs Forward, Fryer and Martin.[349] The two Packs met on Tuesday and Thursday evenings, whilst the Troop met on a Friday evening, as it has done for most of its existence.

---

[348] 0702/95 Axe District Directory p.13
1998 Axe District Directory, p. 14
2007 Axe District Directory

[349] 1998 Axe District Directory p. 14

The Group started a Beaver Colony in 1989 under the leadership of Mrs Libby Cook as BSL,[350] within four years a second Colony was operational under Mrs Brenda Cheeseman's care. The two Colonies were named Mendip and Prestow. The Colonies had the services of Mrs Karen Dors and Mrs Elaine Mills who both held ABSL warrants with Miss Paula Clarke held a Helper certificate. The Colonies were meeting on Thursdays and Fridays. However by the close of the Millennium the Colonies were struggling for leaders and it would not be long before the Prestow Colony was to disband. The Colony leaders changed in the early 21st century with Jonathon Rata and Alastair Cruse taking out ABSL warrants.

In 1997 the Scout and Guide Groups joined together officially to form 1st Burrington and Wrington Scout & Guide Group.[351] The Packs closed in 2002 with the departure of the Cub Leaders, remaining dormant until being re-opened in 2004, although the section has struggled to recruit enough leaders and of late, the GSL, Paul Badman, has been helping out.

1st Cheddar

1st Founding

Fd:	August 1910-By 1928	
Fd:	08/09/30-1947(BST)	Reg No. 11747
Fd:	27/10/49	27723

The earliest record of Scouting in Cheddar village dates from the summer of 1910 with the registration of a Boy Scout Troop in August with Mr F M Paull being warranted as ASM from May

---

350 1993 Axe District Directory p. 11
0702/95 Axe District Directory p.13
1998 Axe District Directory, p. 14

351 Copy of registration Form C2 01/06/1997 (Gilwell Archive)

10th 1910.[352] It is recorded in the oral history and recollections of the Troop that Mr Paull joined up in the First World War and the Troop was, quite unusually, run by a lady Scoutmistress, Mrs Scamp, during the war. After the War the Rev. G Schofield was appointed as SM, remaining with the Troop until January 1921. He was assisted by ASMs R Chinn and J Brice (Junior) who joined the Troop in December 1920. In 1922 Daryl Robertson joined as an ASM and later became SM in September 1930. The next vicar of Cheddar, the Rev. H F Palmer, joined the Troop in 1923 having an interest in the Troop and took out a SM warrant. He became GSM in 1928, departing three years later. During the inter-war years the Troop probably met in the Parish Room next to Daryl Robertson's chemist and newsagents near the cross. The Group appears to have disbanded some time in 1928 for a brief period, before re-starting the following autumn under the leadership of SM Robertson. At the time of registration the Troop comprised of seven boys belonging to the Mid-Somerset District. The Troop meeting place was again at the Parish Room in the village.[353] In November of 1932 the Troop was transferred from Mid-Somerset to Mendip District.[354] The Troop disbanded in 1947 and remained dormant for a year before being reinvigorated by Mr Tyson of Cheddar County School.[355] Mr Tyson, the Headmaster and SM, approached one of his fellow teachers, Mr Walter Reed, who started the Pack in October 1949 and which also met at Cheddar County School.[356]

During the mid 1950's the troop was seeking a new SM and Mr Tony Dyer was approached by the scouts to become their leader. He had previously been a scout in Taunton at Taunton school and also participated in 1st Yatton Group's camps and activities during

---

[352] Copy of 'Extracts from Headquarters Gazette 1909-12' Registration of new Troops, Somerset
(Gilwell Archive)

[353] Copy of registration Form C, 08/09/1930 (Gilwell Archive)

[354] Copy of Form C2, 22/11/1932 (Gilwell Archive)

[355] Notes from Lapsed Group Logbook (Tangier Scout Centre Archive, Taunton)

[356] Copy of registration Form C, 27/10/1949 (Gilwell Archive)

the holidays. He remained with the troop until 1961 when he moved away from Cheddar with his job in the bank. Mr Dyer's daughter, Jane Gomm, has followed in the family tradition taking ASL warrant at 1st Banwell Scout Group.

Mrs Eve Mills, who became involved after dropping off the sandwiches her son had left behind whilst at Pack meeting at the school, started out as an ACM, with the Pack name of Bagheera, before taking on the role of CM following the departure of Mr Reed and, within a year, when he moved away from the area with a new teaching post, Mrs Mills took over as "Akela". She approached Mrs Helen Hill (a parent whose son wished to join the Pack) to become an ACM resulting in a partnership that lasted many years. Mrs Mills served with the Pack for close to twenty-three years during which time she was assisted by Mrs Jean Westby, Mrs Kathleen Anwick and Mrs Marion Saye.

During her time with the Cheddar Cubs the Pack regularly attended the annual District Pack rallies held in Grove Park, Weston-Super-Mare, some being organised by Miss Gwen Francis (CM of the 4th Weston-Super-Mare, St Saviour's Pack), which was followed by Cub tests and quizzes, 1st Cheddar took home the District Cub Shield three times. The Pack travelled to the Royal Albert Hall, London to see "Boy Scout", a production put on by Ralph Reader, who after the performance agreed to meet the Pack backstage (much to the boys delight). Mrs Mills recalled that he was very good with the boys, being keen to hear what they had been doing at Pack meetings. After meeting Mr Reader and the Pack had tea at the Scout shop on Buckingham Palace Road.

The Jubilee year, 1966, included a service held at Wells Cathedral, attended by the Pack where they, along with the other Groups, paraded their standards. Other elements of the Jubilee national programme included doing a good turn, for which the Pack gave a tea party as well as providing entertainment for the residents of a sheltered housing estate in the village. Cheddar Cubs attended the big rally held on the beach lawns Weston, which included a rocket creation competition. As part of the national celebrations all Packs in the country had been sent the words and music for a special jubilee song “half a ton up” and the Cheddar boys were the sole pack who knew the words on the day of the rally!

For a number of years the Cubs camped at Porlock Methodist Church Hall, which had a large room and several other smaller rooms, with a well equipped kitchen. From this base the Pack enjoyed trips to Exmoor, Minehead and Dunster Castle. During summer months each six built and cooked on open fires, as the Group headquarters was located close to the hill, known as “fry up evenings” where Cubs, armed with bacon eggs and frying pans, proceeded to cook their supper. Akela recalls that the activity was much enjoyed by they boys and “what gastronomic horrors they produced, sausages burnt black, eggs half cooked all mixed up with bits of grass, but they ate it as although it was the mayor’s banquet!”[357]

For her long service to 1st Cheddar Cub Pack, Mrs Mills was awarded Long Service Award and also Medal of Merit by the Chief Scout in 1969. In 1974 the Group transferred to Sedgemoor District due to a change in District boundaries. The Group continues to offer a varied and exciting programme for the local young people, although they are, at the time of writing, seeking a new SL. The headquarters is a popular venue for Scout Groups from all other the country who use it as a base for their camps in the Mendip hills.

Churchill Troop

Fd: Not known

---

[357] Correspondence Mrs E Mills 01/04/04

Fd: 15/02/30-1932 Reg No. 10157

This Troop is known to have been in existence during 1918 under the leadership of Mr W A Bell. No date of formation has been located at this time and very little being known about this Troop, other than having disbanded by 1920.

Scouting did not return to Churchill until 1930 when the 1st Langford Troop changed their name to 1st Churchill. The GSM was Mr C Young who had yet to be issued a Scouter's warrant. The Troop folded in 1932 into Scout Group 4234, the 4th Weston (St Saviour's)[358].

1st Compton Bishop

Fd: 16/02/34-1936 Form E Reg No. 16032
Fd: 15/07/38-31/03/49 Form E Reg No. 19666

A Wolf Cub Pack opened in the village, meeting at Cross schoolroom under the leadership of Miss Mildred M Stark as CM and Mr John Gazzard, the latter being warranted as an ACM with the Pack strength at the time of formation standing at seven Wolf Cubs. The Pack gradually expanded to around a dozen during its two years of operation. During their time as the Pack's leaders Miss Stark and Mr Gazzard tied the knot.

A short break ensued until the Pack was reformed in the village, meeting at the Children's Home and Open Road School under the leadership of Miss V A Gunton who held the warrant of GSM. Little is known of the Group, although it continued to operate until the close of the decade, having gone through the Second World War without apparently ceasing to operate.

[358] Copy of Form C 24/02/30 (Courtesy of Mr R F Faraghar)

1st Congresbury

Fd:	Pre-WWI	
	03/11/1924-1937	Reg No.13068
		1928 Reg No. 4207
	07/04/64 (WCP)	Reg No. 36886

The first documentary reference to Scouting in Congresbury dates from the final year of the Great War when a Boy Scout Troop was meeting in 1918, without a leader as he was on active service. It is very likely that the Troop had been in existence for a few years, perhaps predating the outbreak of war. Like so many other Troops the Congresbury Troop struggled to find adult leaders during the war years and had gone out of existence by 1920.

The Scout Troop was reformed in the mid 1920s, registering in the Axbridge Local Association, under the leadership of Mr Wallace A Walter as SM and Mr Leonard Curtis as ASM. The Troop strength stood at seven Scouts, with meetings being held at the Mill in the village. The Troop was registered as a Scout Group four years later, whereupon Mr Walter took on the warrant of GSM. The Group was assigned a new registration number, 4207. The Troop had expanded to thirteen Scouts and four Rovers in the Group. The following year the Group was transferred from Axbridge Local Association to Axbridge District on October 31st.[359]

Mr Walter left the Group, being promoted to District SM and the following year to District Rover SL[360] whilst Mr L Curtis took over the Troop. The section folded in 1937, presumably due to a lack of leaders[361] and Scouting within the village was not resumed until twenty-seven years later.

---

[359] Copy of Form C2 Transfer of District 22/12/04 (Gilwell Archive)
[360] The Scouter Nov 16th – Dec 15th 1933
[361] Notes from District Warrant records, The Scouter

Scarf: Green with white trim

Following the call for the Group to be reopened in the 1946 North West District review Scouting got going again in the village in 1964, meeting at the village Memorial Hall with Mrs Phyllis Muston as CM forming a Cub Pack with twelve Cubs at the time of registration. Alan Tuckfield took out a warrant as an ACM at the same time.[362] In the February of the following year Mr Ken Hill was recruited by ADC Mr John Rewse to open a Troop, which started out with sixteen boys[363] and met in the Memorial Hall. Boys wishing to go to Scouts had previously been going to the Troop at Cleeve. The Group moved from the Memorial Hall to the Methodist School room. Mr Mike Bell was appointed as an ASL and later became VSL at Yeo Trogs before rising to be DC of the District. 1965 saw the Group gain the services of Bob Grainger as GSL.

[364]. The Guides approached the Group in 1966 with a request to start a fundraising project to purchase a Scout and Guide Headquarters. The headquarters at Mill Leg was built on land donated by Mr Wallace A Walter, who had been a Leader of the pre-war Scout Group. The same year the Troop held their first Summer camp at Eype in Dorset with Mr Grainger at the helm.[365] Mr Hill took on the role of GSL in 1970 taking over from Mr Grainger as he and his family were leaving the Group due to moving to another part of the country, having played a great part in the fundraising efforts for the new headquarters, which was officially opened in 1970 by Mr Gervas and Mrs Betty Clay (BP's daughter). The opening parade was led by the 234th Bristol (North

[362] Copy of Group registration Form C 22/12/04
Notes from Somerset records held at Gilwell Park Archives Dept 22/12/04
[363] Correspondence, DHP form P. 1 (Mr K Hill) 09/12/04
[364] Correspondence, DHP form P. 2 (Mr K Hill) 09/12/04
[365] Correspondence, DHP form P. 2 (Mr K Hill) 09/12/04

Winds) Scout Group Band[366]. With Mr Hill appointed as GSL, David Collier took over as SL. In 1978 Dr Ian Penny joined the Troop as an ASL and later on succeeded David Collier in leading the Troop.[367]

Troop camps during the period included camping near Ben Nevis, as well as in South Wales, the Black Forest and Exmoor. Woodhouse Park, the Bristol Scouts site at Almondsbury, was a regular haunt for camping by the Group. The Group took off and over the years expanded out to include two Packs, two Troops and a Venture Scout Unit, Warlocks V.S.U. Congresbury started two Beaver Colonies in 1988, although by 1999 they were down to one Colony and that Colony disbanded by the turn of the Millennium.

In 1994 the Group celebrated its thirtieth birthday and a new badge was designed and worn on the apex of the Group scarf.[368] They have recently celebrated their fortieth birthday and after a period of struggling to locate leaders, the Group is on a more sure footing under the leadership of long term leader and recently appointed GSL, Alex Ballard, with Geoffrey Bailey and Andrew Purdy taking the Scouts. Scouts and Cubs recently attended the very wet and windy Centenary camp held at Woodhouse Park, alongside four thousand other campers as part of the Ton of Fun camp.

The Harptree Scout Groups

1st East Harptree Scout Group

Fd: 1956-67 Reg No. Not known

---

366 Photograph 1970 234th Bristol, Mr K Hill, 09/12/04
367 Correspondence, DHP form P. 2 (Mr K Hill) 09/12/04
368 Correspondence, DHP form P. 2 (Mr K Hill) 09/12/04

The formation of the Group occurred in 1956 when word went around the village that any boys who wished to form a Scout Troop should turn up at the home of Mr Mayo, at the bottom of High Street in East Harptree. Quite a few boys turned up and the room was very crowded. The potential Troop was formed with two leaders 'ready to go', Mr Wilf Beer as 'Skip' (SM) and Mr Graham Rowe known as 'Cobber' as an ASM. Mr 'Pop' Mayo became GSM for a while, having a son in the Troop. Over the years Mr Mayo remained involved with the Troop in a variety of ways not least as the Chairman of the Parents Committee. Later on Mr Tony Pow, the local policeman, served as Group Chairman.

The Troop drew boys from both East and West Harptree as well as surrounding hamlets such as Hinton Blewitt. The Troop met for a time at the school room belonging to the East Harptree Methodist Church before acquiring their own clubroom over the village theatre, (now the village club), in a room that had been used as a snooker room. The table had disappeared though a pile of slates remained in the corner of the room for a number of years. The room was reached by an outside wooden staircase with the room more or less L shaped. The Group made use of the theatre below from time to time for fundraising efforts.

The Scouts tested their camping skills by camping locally at Shrowel for two nights, in four fourteen foot ridge tents, (some of which came from the disbanded 1st West Harptree Scout Group), and a bell tent donated from a person in the forces. The site was about a mile away from the Troop headquarters. The first Summer camp in 1958 at Castle Dyke (between Teignbridge and Dulverton), was to be a memorable camp as the Troop elected to camp inside the earthworks of the Celtic hill fort. The coach carrying the Troop encountering heavy traffic at Telegraph Hill, becoming stuck in the ensuing traffic jam whilst the Scouts sat on the side of the road and asked Skip for a brew up whilst waiting.

The request was denied and the Scouts eventually arrived at their drop off point with kit having to be transported two miles on a two wheeled trek cart to the site, with the nearest water supply being a mile away at a nearby cottage. Whilst in camp heavy rain coupled with the siting of the camp resulted in Scouts taking to the high ground of the tables in the stores tent and playing games when the water rose. Eventually the camp had to be abandoned as a result of the weather. Though a 'baptism of fire' (or rather water) for the Troop on its first summer camp it did not put the Troop off camping.

Whitsun saw the Troop at camp at Blagdon for the weekend. Further summer camps were held at West Quantoxhead between 1959 and 1960 at the Gibbon's family farm in a paddock which grew a huge amount of mushrooms. Scouts merely had to lean outside their tent for a bountiful supply of mushrooms for breakfast! Activities revolved around hiking in the Quantocks, which would later serve the Troop well in the Quantock Follies challenge, as well as days out to Minehead. The Troop also held their summer camp near Ham, halfway between Seaton and Sidmouth in 1961 and 1962 and then at Exford for two years, (presumably) 1963 and 1964. It was whilst looking for potential camp sites around the area that Skip and the PLs had a chance meeting with two SLs from Bristol who advised the Troop not to camp on their intended site at the head of the Doone valley as previously they had camped there in the disastrous flooding of Lynton and Lynmouth in 1952 and had been forced to abandon the camp due to the heavy flooding. They claimed that their patrol box was washed away and found in Lynmouth harbour. One member, David Lions, was selected to attend the World Scout Jamboree in Greece in 1963 as part of the Somerset contingent.

The Quantock Follies, was (and still is), a navigation event run by Somerset County for older Scouts. Teams of Scouts were dropped of in the middle of nowhere on the Quantock hills, then had to navigate their way to set bases. In the case of the Harptree Scouts team they had to navigate their way to 3rd Taunton, Bishop's Lydeard Scout headquarters for an early breakfast before going on to Crowcombe youth hostel. Sundays concluded with a church service for those attending, usually at Bicknoller church.

Mr Lions took up canoeing whilst with the Scouts and joined in a Bristol youth cruise, run by Mr Byron Monday. The training for which included learning to canoe in November in an open air pool, where Mr Lions, attending in Scout uniform recalls "nearly freezing to death", the water being somewhat cold. The evening do which followed the course was for Scouters in uniform, needless to say Mr Lion's uniform was soaked so he attended in borrowed clothes. Other training trips included a paddle on the Kennet and Avon canal from Freshford to Devizes, the canal was derelict in those days and posed not a few challenges to the canoeist, such as pushing canoes through mud where the canal had silted up. Further training included sea canoeing and surfing in Cornwall and training at Simonsbath.

In 1966 the Group was being led by Mr Wilf Beer GSM and SM, with the mother and daughter team of Mrs R N Downer and Miss W J Downer taking the Cubs. Mr R D Downer held an ASM position with the Troop alongside Mr R S Edwards and Mr M Ryley, who also was acting as SSL.[369] However by 1969 the Group was down to the Downers as the sole leaders of the Cubs and Scouts.[370]

1st West Harptree Scout Group

Fd:	08/02/39	Reg No. 20018
Fd:	26/08/48	Reg No. 26538

[369] Copy of 1966 District Directory (Tangier Scout Centre Archive Taunton)
[370] Copy of 1969 District Directory (Tangier Scout Centre Archive Taunton)

Little is known of this Troop beyond the registration form. The Troop was led by the Reverend H F C Higgs, who had previously been a Leader with the 3rd Weston (St Paul's) and 18th Weston (Church of the Good Shepherd) Scout Groups and in the late 1930s became vicar at West Harptree and soon started Scouting in the village, being assisted by Mr Maurice Symes with a Troop of ten to twelve Scouts. The headquarters is given as the Scout Den in the village although the author is not sure as to where this was. The Group presumably ceased to operate during the Second World War.[371] An effort was made by Reverend Higgs to reform the Troop in 1948 with himself as the sole leader to a Troop of eleven Scouts. The Troop was again meeting at the Scout Den in the village[372]. The Troop disbanded in the early 1950s. Some of their equipment was given to the East Harptree Scouts in the mid 1950s.

1st Axbridge Scout Troop in Camp

[371] Copy of Group registration Form C 08/02/38 (Courtesy of the Gilwell Archive)
[372] Copy of Group registration Form C 26/08/48 (Courtesy of the Gilwell Archive)

1st Cheddar Cubs with the District Trophy c. 1950

1st East Harptree Scout Troop c. 1958

Hutton Beavers on HMS Beaver

Hewish Troop

A Troop at Hewish was meeting during the Great War, being one of a handful of Troops in 1918 to have a leader, Mr W A Bell. No further information has come to light on this Troop, it had disbanded by 1920 as it not mentioned on the Local Association report for the year.

1st Hutton

Fd:	01/08/39	Reg No. 20469
Fd:	27/10/49-31/03/54	Reg No. 27724
Fd:	05/10/72-01/10/01	Reg No. 40650

-

A Scout Group was started by Reverend J M Scutt, which numbered fifteen Wolf Cubs and ten Boy Scouts and Mr Scutt was the sole Leader and met at the Legion hut in the village. Not much more is known about this Scout Group.[373] Presumably the Start of the Second World War the following month led to the closure of the Group.

A second attempt at operating Scouting in the village lasted for five years with a Scout Troop forming in October 1949 under the leadership of Mr V Denne as GSM and SM as a one man band with eight Scouts at the time of formation. He soon recruited other villagers to assist: Mr J B Haress took out a SM warrant shortly afterwards, and Wolf Cubs were formed under the leadership of Miss L Pike who was assisted by Miss J Parleth. The Group folded in 1954 (probably) due to a lack of leaders.[374]

---

[373] Copy of Form C 01/08/39 (Gilwell Archive)

[374] Notes from Lapsed Scout Groups (Tangier Scout Centre Archive, Taunton)

Scarf Green with a yellow border

The Group started as a satellite pack of 32nd Weston (Oldmixon) and in 1972 became 1st Hutton and at the time of registration the Group had four Leaders, two Instructors, twenty eight Cubs and sixteen Scouts[375]. The Troop continued to meet until a lack of leaders led to its closure in the late 1990s.

With the expansion of numbers a Venture Unit was opened in 1983, called Vikings, under the leadership of Mr Tim Sutton and Mr David J Cardwell, though a decade later the Unit was not active. The remaining section, Cubs, was suspended in October 2001 as a result of insufficient leaders, the remaining six Cubs moved to 1st Locking Scout Group.

Langford Troop

Fd: Not known
Fd: 24/09/29-1930 Reg No. 10157

This Troop was operational before World War 1 although in 1918 their leader was on active service. The Troop seems to have disbanded shortly afterwards.

Efforts to get Scouting going again occurred at the end of the 1920s with Mr H R Kirk opening the Troop in September 1929 as 1st Langford Scout Troop meeting in Churchill near Wrington, being off to a good start with sixteen Boys in the Troop. Mr Charles Wright was recorded as the GSM although his name had been crossed out on the registration form. The Troop changes its name some months later to 1st Churchill Scout Troop.[376]

375 Notes taken from Form C 21/12/04
376 Copy of Form C 24/09/29 9 (Courtesy of Mr R F Faraghar)

1st Kewstoke

Fd:	17/02/30-1931 Form E	Reg No. 10901
Fd:	26/05/88	Reg No. 45054

Scarf: Yellow with Green border

Scouting briefly ran in Kewstoke from 1930-31, with a Scout Troop of nine boys meeting in the Parish Hall. The Troop's leaders were Eric Armstrong who held the warrant of GSM and J S Anderson as the ASM. The Rev. J H H Doober was the Troop's Chaplain.[377] The Troop soon disbanded, although the reason for this has gone unrecorded.

Scouting restarted in the village over fifty years later when at a meeting in the newly built Village Community Centre, villagers were asked to decide what they wished to have in the village, with some one suggesting the formation of a Cub Pack and Scout Troop. Mr and Mrs Langley were identified as former leaders, being founders of the 1st Worle Pack in the 1970s, before moving away to Egypt, then returning and settling in Kewstoke in the mid 1980s, and were approached to help. Mrs Langley was asked if she would form a Cub Pack for the village boys. She agreed to do and had the assistance of Martin White, a former Scout from the 1st Weston (YMCA) Troop who lived at Culme farm, and Katy Topham, as well as Mr Langley. The Pack opened in the spring of 1988. [378] Mrs Langley recalls that there were around sixteen to twenty boys at the start of the Pack. The following year, the Pack were undertaking a sponsored shoe shine as part of the 'bob a job' week, and having polished the mayor's shoes, spotted the late

---

377 Copy of Form C 17/02/30 (Gilwell Archive)

378 Copy of Group registration Form C (Axe District Archive)
Interview with Mrs P Langley 06/03/06

Leslie Crowther approaching and offered to shine his shoes, unfortunately Mr Crowther was wearing (blue?) suede shoes.[379] The Pack were regular attendees at District events joining in with the cross country, chess and handicraft competitions, Seconder Day and Sixers Weekends as well as Christmas Capers and the adventure day held at Sidcot School. The Pack were presented with a Union flag, donated by the local Royal Navy National Reserve, and from funds brought a Pack flag. The Pack's last camp with Mrs Langley as Akela was at Bishops Lydeard near Taunton in 1993. Mrs Langley remained with the Group serving as Group Chairman for a few years before handing over in 1996. Martin White succeeded Mrs Langley as Akela at Kewstoke, with Miss D Scott holding an ACSL warrant in 1995. Martin had run the Pack for two years as the sole warranted leader with help from parent helpers, which included Mr R Brown in 1993[380] and Martin Price in 1995.[381]

In 1995 the Group opened a Beaver Colony under the leadership of Nina Price and Sue Tuchy (Grey Beaver). The Colony started with eight Beavers meeting on a Monday evening at the village hall and expanded quickly with three lodges being created. The Colony adopted a North American Indian theme with the teams of Beavers, known as Lodges, being named Apache, Cherokee and Sioux lodges.[382] Nina Price continued to lead the Colony which had a number of Helpers by 1998 including Jane Cross, Karen Rackham, Charlotte Plaister and the husband and wife team of Mike and Annette Doble.[383]

The Group's fortunes improved during 1996, which saw the opening of a Scout Troop in the village, started by Terry Scoble and Jason Taylor, formerly of the 29th Weston (St. Peter's) Troop

---

[379] Recollections of Mr M White 10/10/07
[380] Notes from District Directory 1993. p. 17
[381] Notes from District Directory 1995. p. 17
[382] Notes from District Directory 1995. p. 17
[383] 1998 Axe District Directory p. 17

with help from Neil Mocklin and Kevin Trevitt. A new influx of leaders joined the Pack with Michaela Harris taking the role of CSL with assistance from Julie Fraser and Martin White, while Matthew Robinson took out a Pack Helper certificate. The Pack expanded to two Packs around this time, although it was to revert to a single Pack at the end of the decade. During 1996 the Group held a summer camp at Watcombe (Torbay) which stood out as a very wet camp with rain and a gale blowing down a Cub Tent in addition to Martin White's and the SLs tents also proving incapable of keeping the weather out.[384]

During the next few years the Group were to move from the village. The Scout Troop under Mr Scoble grew in size and became in 2001 the largest Troop in the Country with one hundred and eleven Scouts! The large Troop moved to St. Martin's school gymnasium in order to have sufficient room to carry on meeting. In 1999 the Group formed a Venture Scout Unit called 'Renegades' to cater for boys moving up from the Troop, which was led by Ian Halliday[385]. The Unit continued to meet until 2002. Mr Scoble was appointed to the position of ADC Scouts in 2001 handing over the running of the Troop to Mr Jason Taylor, while Miss Lewis moved from 1st Milton to become CSL with the Pack. The Troop continued to be successful although numbers had declined they still had a membership of over-thirty six Scouts and the Pack and Colony have continued to prove popular with locals from the village, as well as Worle.

---

[384] Notes from District Directory 1999. p. 17

[385] Venture Scout report 1999 District AGM 2001 Report p.

1st Locking (RAF)

28/06/39	Reg No. 20395
03/07/1953-31/03/60	30719
09/01/1961	35390

Scarf: Black with yellow trim

The earliest known recorded founding of Scouting in Locking is dated from June 1939 when a Rover Scout Crew formed at the RAF base. The Crew was a controlled Group sponsored by the Air Ministry and was presumably set up for the apprentices who were undergoing training at the base. The Rover Crew started out with ten members and was led by the Rev. J M Scutt who was also the camp's Chaplain. The Crew had a short existence, disbanding due to the pressures of the Second World War, which started three months later.

Towards the latter period of the Second World War the District expressed a desire to see the Rover Crew reformed at RAF Locking, yet it was to take a further eight years before a Scout Group was restarted at RAF Locking with the Group being registered by Tim Mowforth in the summer of 1953. The Group comprised of a Wolf Cub Pack, Boy Scout Troop and Rover Crew, which catered for boys from the village and base. The sections met at the RAF Base which provided a headquarters as well as the space and skills to provide occasional skills instructors, as well as warranted leaders. Stephen Vigurs took out an ACM warrant, with nineteen Wolf Cubs in the Pack, while the four Boy Scouts were supervised by SM Richard W Kirkham, and the largest section, the Rovers, led by Mr Elijah P Schofield, numbered thirty members.[386] However due to life in the forces with personnel moving from base to base on a regular pattern the Group was to have a high turnover in leaders as well as boys. In

[386] Copy of Registration Form C from 03/07/1953

the mid 1950s the Rovers are recorded helping with 19th Weston (St Jude's) by running the occasional Troop night[387], no doubt this was repeated by the Rovers at other Troops in the District.[388] Other leaders within the Group included Miss J Fletcher as CM and Mrs M O Brownhill holding an ACM warrant.[389] Mr A F Taylor took the Troop, later succeeded by Mr Kevin Hibberd, who had assisted with the 19th Weston (St Jude's) Troop beforehand, whilst Rover Leaders included P A Cricraft.[390] However the Group went into a decline and disbanded in March 1960, having only four leaders, Squadron Leader W G Russell as GSM, L Lines as CM with P Cricraft still at the helm of the Rovers with L Walters as acting ARSL for the final two years of the Crew's existence[391]

The Group remained closed for nine months before reforming, again based at the RAF station. [392] Elijah Schofield, the founding Rover Leader in the previous Group, took responsibility for the Group as GSM. The Pack was led by Ronald Cox, with assistance from Christopher Stone with Trevor Beach taking the Scouts and Leslie Patterson providing leadership to the Senior Scout Troop, with assistance from Peter Davis. With the exception of Mr Cox who resided at Elborough all the leaders were living on the base and in the forces and as the life of a member of the forces they would move on to another posting.[393] The Group operated a Senior Scout section from 1961 to 1965. The Rover Crew continued right up until 1967 and the implementation of the Advance Report[394] when the older two sections, Senior Scouts and Rover Crews, were disbanded to be replaced with Venture Scout Units. A Venture Unit operated at the Group from 1967 to

---

[387] 19th Weston-s-Mare (St Jude's) Scout Troop logbook 2 Troop meeting of 1954
[388] 19th Weston-S-Mare (St Jude's) Troop Log 1 1954-64 (courtesy of Mr R E Cooke)
[389] Copy of Lapsed Group records 31/03/60 (Tangier Centre, Taunton Scout Archives)
[390] Copy of Lapsed Group records 31/03/60 (Tangier Centre, Taunton Scout Archives)
[391] Copy of Registration Form C from 03/07/1953
[392] Copy of Registration Form C from 09/01/1961
[393] Copy of Registration Form C from 09/01/1961
[394] Copy of Group Census datasheet 1953-1983

1972 before going dormant for eleven years. The Venture Unit "Musketeers" was reformed in 1983 lasting for around a decade, when numbers had fallen from around fifteen to three.

The Cub Pack expanded from one to two Packs between 1966-79. G Monger led the Pack between 1964-68, before handing over to the long serving Hilda Titchard, and met at the camp. Other leaders included Mrs Lewis who took the village Pack with John Curd and Graham Maggs holding ACSL warrants. Kevin Bunting joined the Group taking the second Pack, which he ran for a decade before serving a short period as ADC Cubs. Graham succeeded Kevin as Akela. In 1993 the Group had sufficient Leaders and Cubs to reopen the second Cub Pack and met in the village hall and later on in the Church hall, being led by Albert Nowlan. In 1989 the Group opened a Beaver Colony which has met since that time with a continuity of long serving leaders.

Following the departure of the Troop's previous SL, Bob Tonkin, who served in the RAF, at short notice in 1976, the Troop were seeking a new SL, which was no easy task. By the spring of 1977 the Troop was still struggling to recruit Leaders, resulting in appeals being made through the village newsletter. This approach resulted in William 'Bill' Belshaw offering his services as SL, with assistance from Alan Fields who, like Bill, had previous Scouting experience and took out an ASL warrant. The GSL at the time was Keith Joblin who was an officer on the base and later that year was posted away, resulting in Bill Belshaw temporarily acting as 'Scouter in Charge' until a parent of a Scout and a retired squadron leader, Mr Stan Norman, was appointed GSL.

The Troop was meeting in a timber hut on the eastern end of the camp, which was put up in 1939 as hospital accommodation and now served as their headquarters. They moved into permanent buildings in the 1980s.

Being a RAF Sponsored Group led to the Group being reviewed by the camp Commanding Officer, as well as attending anniversary events such as the Battle of Britain and Remembrance Sunday services held in September and November respectively, as well as parading with the rest of the District on St George's Day through the resort.

The Troop membership comprised of a mixture of camp and village boys, with the Patrol Leaders tending to be village boys, as those boys who lived on the camps often moved on as the forces families were posted elsewhere after a few years and as Bill Belshaw recalls "although frustrating, the constant through put of 'camp' scouts did bring many new games and ideas into the Troop."[395]

One significant highlight for the Troop was the 1979 'Bob-a-job week', which saw the Scouts cleaning a Canberra bomber which was acting as a gate guardian at the entrance of the base. This generated a lot of local publicity, with a member of the Troop being interviewed on Radio Bristol, articles in the Weston Mercury and the Bristol Evening Post and a copy being reproduced in Scouting magazine. In May of the following year Bill Belshaw was awarded the Medal of Merit for his services to Scouting.

A test camp held at Loxton in 1977 revealed that the Troop members were not experienced campers and a weekend camp was held at the hut over the Easter weekend the following year when a complete patrol campsite was built alongside the headquarters. Subsequently the Troop held a successful camp at Llangorse, near Brecon in Wales that summer. Other Summer Camps included Llangorse (1979), Cheshire County site near Sandbatch (1980), Bickley near Plymouth, (1981), Bala in Wales, (1982), Stogoursey near Cannington, (1983) back to Llangorse in 1984

---

[395] Mr Belshaw's recollections

and Littlebredy near Weymouth in 1985 and at Penlee near Plymouth at the South West International Jamboree in 1986. In 1985 Mr Belshaw attended the 15th World Jamboree held in Canada as part of the Avon contingent as an Assistant Leader to Mr Mike Bell who was the Contingent Leader, along with Karim Ladu from the Troop. That year's Summer Camp was taken by the 'Musketeer' Venture Scout Unit under the leadership of Ralph Newey, VSL. In April 1985 Mr Belshaw was appointed ACC Scouts and remained as SL at Locking until after the Troop's annual summer camp in August. Due to a career change Mr Belshaw moved away from the area in August 1986 and resigned his warrants, he did manage one night with the Troop on their Summer Camp to say goodbye.

The leadership of the Troop fluctuated for a short while until Richard Lewis, who had been a Scout in the Troop during Bill Belshaw's tenure as SL, was appointed SL at the Troop, a post he held for eighteen years, making him probably the longest serving leader of the Troop. During this time the Troop expanded reaching around forty Scouts and additional leaders were recruited including Malcolm Lloyd, another long serving leader. Other ASLs who served within the Troop include Mark Lake, Anthony Oakley and later Steve Postma. With the disbanding of the Hutton Troop in 2000, the Locking Troop took boys form Hutton Cub Pack and allowed the boys to retain their Scarves. The Troop relocated to the Hutton Scout and Guide HQ as they were struggling to find a suitable meeting place in the village after the RAF Station closed in 1997. A wholesale change of leaders occurred within the Troop in 2004 alongside a rapid decline in Scout numbers, dropping to half a dozen Scouts. The Group's recently appointed GSL, Paul Thomas, who became involved with the Group as an ACSL when his son Michael joined the Pack, took the Troop until being joined by Keith Dudley from 1st Ashcombe Troop, along with a number of Scouts from that Troop in 2006. Over the past year the Troop has rebuilt itself with twenty-four Scouts in the Troop, many having fed through from the Pack. This period of change also saw a new Executive Committee being appointed.

The Beaver Colony opened in 1989 with Carol Draper as the BSL, Mrs Alison Greaney (nee Venn) as ABSL along with Mrs Cherry Sheppard. Some of the Beavers who started with the newly opened Colony were Mark Cogan, Ian Glendenning, Richard Purcell, Gareth Sutherwood, Aron Walters, Michael Wilson, whose mother, Mrs Celia Wilson took out a Colony Helper's certificate, Paul Walken and Jonathon Boldick.[396] A decade later the two leaders were joined by Miss Kirsten Kimpson, Ian Almer, Andrew Childs and Mr Carl Rylance as Colony Helpers. Mrs Greaney took over as BSL following the departure of Mrs Draper. Alison remained with the Colony until stepping down in 2006 after fifteen years service with the Group. She was succeeded by ABSL Sheena Thomas, whose husband Paul is the GSL. [397]

Recent camping events have included participating in the 2006 Axejam and the following year attending the Ton of Fun Avon County Jamboree which had close to four thousand in Cubs, Scouts, Explorers, Network Scouts and Leaders in camp over Whitsun weekend.

[396] Weston Mercury (ref 243589/14) Courtesy of the Weston Mercury & Mrs E Nock
[397] Axe District Directories 1993, 1995 & 1998

1st Redhill

Fd:	26/04/1926-Not known	Reg No. 14942
	04/05/39-31/03/47 Form E	20270
	05/05/53-31/03/59 Form E	20601

Mr A C O Mann started a Troop at Redhill near Wrington for boys from the village, which had at the time of registration ten Scouts meeting at the parsonage in the village. The Troop was in the Axbridge Local Association in North West District. The Troop had closed by 1939 when the name was reassigned.[398] Mr Ashman recalls being a member of the Troop and attending the Birkenhead Jamboree in 1929.[399]

Scarf: Standard Green

The second reforming of the Redhill Troop dates from just before the outbreak of World War II with a Troop of ten Scouts meeting at the village hall and two warranted leaders, Mr Robert Buxton as SM and Mr Percy Brean as his Assistant. Mr E N Goodenough took over as SM when Messrs Buxton and Brean left the Troop, presumably called up for the forces with the Troop meeting on Tuesday nights in the Hall in Redhill.[400]The Troop folded in 1947, presumably with the departure of Mr Goodenough[401].

The Wrington SLs, Tom Collins and Malcolm Parsons, started a Cub Pack in Redhill for boys who wished to go to Cubs, Mr Collins was the GSM, while Mr Parsons took a warrant as CM with an old Scout from the original Troop, Mr Ashman taking an ACM warrant. The village Pack started out with nine Cubs

[398] Copy of Form C 26/04/26 (Gilwell Archive)
[399] Interview with Mr H Ashman 01/03/05
[400] Copy of Somerset County Directory 1945 p. 21 (Tangier Scout Centre Archive, Taunton)
[401] Notes from the Lapsed Groups Logbook (Tangier Scout Centre Archive, Taunton)

meeting at Redhill School and expanded shortly afterwards.[402] The Pack folded on March 31st 1959, along with the closure of 1st Wrington Scout Troop.

1st Sandford

Fd: 23/01/78-2001 Reg No. 42626

Scarf: Brown with a light Blue trim

A Scout Group initially comprising of a Cub Pack was started up in the village under the leadership of Mr Wilfred Ainsworth as CSL, with Mr Derek Blay and Mr Anthony Carr taking ACSL warrants for a Pack of twelve Cubs.[403] The following year the Group had gained the services of Mr J Jenkis as GSL. Mrs Sandra Lund took over from Mr Jenkis in the early 1990s, serving for most of the decade.[404] The Cub Pack leadership had changed by the early part of the 1990s with the Pack now being run by ACSLs Mr Steve Threaser, who a year later took the CSL warrant, and Mrs Christine Leaney, with assistance from Pack Helper Mrs Pauline Cornish.[405] Between 1994-97 Miss Wendy Hebbum took an ACSL warrant. the leadership of the Pack was to change again at the end of the decade with a team of Mrs Sharon Laws, Mrs Kathleen Burgess and Mr Bob Hoy-Green taking the Pack, the ladies held ACSL warrants whilst Mr Hoy-Green took out a Pack Helper certificate. Following their departure the Pack disbanded sometime in 2000.[406]

---

[402] Copy of Form C 05/05/53 (Gilwell Archive)
[403] Form C 23/01/78 (Mrs A Coombes, (Axe District Archive)
[404] Axe District Directory 1979 p.22
[405] Axe District Directory 1993 pp.21-22
[406] Axe District Directory 1993 p. 22
Axe District Directory 07/02/95 p. 21
Axe District Directory 1999 p. 20

The Troop was opened in the early 1980s with eighteen Scouts in 1983, the Troop would fluctuate between fourteen to twenty Scouts for the rest of the decade before slowly rising to around twenty four Scouts by the mid 1990s. By 1985 the Troop was seeking a new SL. In the eventuality Mr David Perriman transferred from the 1st Weston (YMCA) Scout Troop to take over as SL, alongside Mr Perriman the Troop had support from Mrs Judy Morrison, as an ASL, with Mr Tony Wyatt, Mr Graham Murdoch and Mr Andrew Moon who were Troop Helpers. Mr Perriman remained with the Troop until 1993 when he moved to the 3rd Weston (St Paul's) Troop. The Troop was not to have a SL for the remainder of its existence.[407]

Within two years a fresh set of leaders was in place with Mr Laurence Johnston and Mr David Leary being appointed as ASLs. Continuing support was provided by Graham Murdoch. David Leary was later joined by his wife, Kim, who took out a Troop helpers certificate as the decade drew to a close, although by this time they were the only leaders with the section, and remained with the Troop until 2001. With the disbanding of the Pack in 2000 the Scout section was the sole operating section in the Group, with the Leary's departure, as they were moving abroad, the Group closed.

The Group had opened a Beaver Colony in 1993 under the leadership of Mrs Joyce Moore and her daughter Miss Kelly Moore which started with fifteen boys. Although two years later the leadership had changed with Mrs K Appleton being appointed as BSL and Mrs Mary Green holding an ABSL warrant. In 1998, when these ladies stood down the Colony was forced to close as no new leaders could be located.

---

[407] Axe District Directory 1993 p. 22
Axe District Directory 07/02/95 p. 21
Axe District Directory 1999 p. 20
Recollections of Mr D Perriman

1st Shipham

Fd: 11/05/1944-31/03/47 Reg No. 22005
28/02/57-1961 Form E
1965-1986
1987-

Scarf: Brown

Shipham Scouts started with twelve recruits[408] in 1944 under the leadership of Mr Frederick Alan Cresswell and was registered in the North District, Somerset. Troop meetings were held at the Chapel Hall, Shipham. The following year Mr A O Perkins was Scouter in Charge of the Group as well as SM. He soon recruited Mr J E Elliott who took an ASM warrant.[409] However despite a promising start the Troop went out of existence three years later. Scouting in the village remained dormant for a decade until in early 1957 Mr James Leslie Frost was appointed SM and restarted the Troop with six Scouts. The numbers expanded to around a dozen boys although by 1960 the Troop was struggling to find a permanent SM. Troop meetings were being taken by Acting ASM Mr P J Morris, an ASM at the 1st Cheddar Scout Group.[410] The following year, as a result of not being able to find a regular leader the Troop folded into 1st Cheddar Scout Group.[411]

Scarf Maroon

The Group reopened in 1965 with the formation of a Cub Pack led by Mrs Pat Hoyland, who had moved into the village the previous year from Kent where she had been a CM with 1st Hayes.[412] Shipham was full of lots of young boys of Cub age and

---

[408] Copy of Registration Form C, 11/05/1944 (Gilwell Archive)
[409] Notes from the Lapsed Groups Logbook (Tangier Scout Centre Archive, Taunton)
[410] Copy of Somerset County Directory 1960 p. 12 (Tangier Centre Archive)
[411] Notes from the Lapsed Groups Logbook (Tangier Scout Centre Archive, Taunton)
[412] Mrs P Hoyland Memoirs 20/03/08

Mrs Hoyland agreed to start a Pack, The Pack started with four sixes, with a membership of twenty four boys and a waiting list. Besides Mrs Hoyland as Akela, the Pack had two other warranted leaders, Elsie Hemmings as Bagheera and Carol Sawtell as Baloo. The Pack first met in the games room of Mrs Lucas' Penscot Guest House. The Pack soon outgrew these premises and moved up the road to the Women Institute hall.[413]

During Mrs Hoyland's time as Akela the Pack were involved in District activities, including swimming galas, five-a-side football competitions and Sixer weekends held at Highbury Hotel and a County Sixers weekend just outside Yeovil, Seconder days, fun days, some of which were held at Kelstons farm in Wedmore, home of the ADC Cubs (rural) Mrs Banwell. The Pack held a number of camps during this time with venues ranging from Charterhouse to Ramscombe on the Quantocks. Joint meetings with other Packs took place with the Shipham Cubs joining up with Olive Woods and the Axbridge Cubs, as well as Mrs Maureen Faraghar, CSL of 1st Winscombe and Mrs Mills at the Cheddar Pack.[414] Mrs Hoyland passed over the leadership in 1976[415] to Mrs J Pinder who was assisted by Mrs C Bryant, who stood down in December 1986 at which point the Pack briefly disbanded as they could find no new leaders to continue the section.[416]

The Group had a very strong parents committee which helped in a large effort to fundraise sufficient money to erect their own headquarters on the corner of the football field. Fundraising activities included barbecues, fairs, and fireworks displays on the village football field.[417] With the closure of the Group in the early

[413] Mrs P Hoyland's memoirs 20/03/08
[414] Interview with Mrs P Hoyland 09/03/08
[415] Mrs P Hoyland's memoirs 20/03/08
[416] Copy of Sedgemoor District Directory 1985-86 p. 3. (Biddulph Archive)
[417] Mrs Hoyland's memoirs 20/03/08

1980s the headquarters fell into disrepair and was pulled down to make way for the new village hall.

With Cubs coming up to Scout age a Troop was formed in the village in 1970 under the leadership of Mr Fred Ward, who became the GSL. By the early 1980s the Troop was being taken by Mr B Kew who was assisted by Mr J Bailey. When both men stepped down in 1986 the Troop disbanded.[418]

New Leaders arrived with husband and wife partnership of David and Pam Rogers who restarted the Pack in 1987. Mr Rogers was collecting his Scouting magazine and was wearing his uniform in the village newsagents when he was approached about restarting the Pack, which he agreed to do with assistance from his wife who took an ACSL warrant. During their tenure there were three sixes with numbers of around sixteen to twenty boys. The Rogers handed over to a team of three ACSLs, Mrs Sue Ovenden and Messrs John Moorhouse and Paul Redfearn. Mrs Ovenden took on the CSL warrant shortly afterwards. Highlights of the Pack's activities during this time include making a patchwork flag by all the members of the Pack, who each had a square to design their idea on. Designs ranged from pictures of the village Church and War Memorial through to daffodils and sheep, reflecting various aspects of the village community and environment. These squares were sewn together to form a flag which the Pack and their leaders took underground on a trip to the Singing River mine, under the leadership of caver (and later ASL Andrew Newton), that lies beneath the village. As far as the Shipham Cubs are aware, they were the sole Pack in the country to go underground during the celebrations. This experience initiated an interest in caving by the Cubs and helped with the recruitment for the Troop. The Pack held several Church parades each year, with Mothering and Remembrance Sundays seeing the Group attend the Church, whilst St George's day they joined the rest of the District on

418 Copy of Sedgemoor District Directory 1985-86 p. 3. (Biddulph Archive)

parade. The Pack Sixers and Seconds would travel to visit the Troop on their annual Summer Camp and take up fresh meat supplies from the local butcher, Nick Hansford, in addition to their own camps. Mrs Ovenden's final camp was held at Huish Woods, where she recalls nearly setting fire to the Tone Cabin kitchen, having left the Cubs' clay models in the oven for too long, and came back in to the kitchen to find it filled with smoke. Sue Ovenden continues to support Scouting and is currently a member of the County team. The Pack was then taken by John Moorhouse. During the life of the Pack membership numbers varied depending upon how many boys of Cub age were in the village. The Pack could be down to six members one year and could rise to twenty plus within a short period of time.

An effort to restart the Troop was undertaken in 1990 with Jimmy Miller being appointed SL the following year, as the village again had sufficient boys of the age to form a Troop. With the disbanding of the Axbridge Troop in the mid 1990s a small influx of Axbridge boys arrived at the Shipham Troop.[419] However history was to repeat itself again and the Troop went out of existence in 2000. The Group is currently led by GSL Helen Ingleby. The Group had not formed a Beaver Colony.

1st St George's

Fd: 29/06/81-1986 Reg No. 43833

Scarf: White with a red border

A Cub Pack was formed in the village in June 1981 to cater for local children and met at the old village hall which was demolished in 1985 as it had become unsafe for use. During the Group's short existence it was led by GSL Ray Beckingham, who

[419] Copy of Sedgemoor District Directory 1993 (Biddulph Archive)

was the local village policeman, whilst the Pack was run by Akela, Pauline Morr. The Pack opened with sixteen boys and within a few years a Scout Troop opened briefly, run by Mr Derek Claridge as SL with assistance from the late Andy Skillen who took an ASL warrant. Mr Skillen later ran the troop with Mr David Luck. However the Troop folded in 1985 reducing the Group to a Pack which merged with 1st North Worle Group the following year. This connection is perhaps the reason behind the title of village Pack in the North Worle twin Packs. However within the past few years the area has witnessed large scale housing development a new community centre and school now provides facilities for the village. It remains to be seen if a new Group will emerge in this community.

1st Uphill

Fd: 27/12/1951 Reg No. 29461

Scarf: Black with white trim

There would be a gap of almost thirty years before Uphill saw the return of Scouting to the village, with the formation of 1st Uphill in December 1951 under GSM Rev John Carpenter of St. Nicholas Church, Uphill. The Group comprised of a Wolf Cub Pack and Boy Scout Troop. The Pack Leaders were Miss Vera Winifred Hillman who was CM and Mrs Joan Flavell as an ACM, later moving on to take charge of the section. The Troop was under the guidance of SM Mr Douglas Heathershaw. Their first meeting was held on January 18th 1952 in the Church hall, with the Group Committee's inaugural meeting held on November 21st.[420] Changes within the leadership team arose in the winter of 1953 when Miss Hillman resigned in October handing over to Mrs Flavell whilst Mr Heathershaw left the Group the following

[420] Group History Notes 1951-2004 Mr C Hart (1st Uphill Group Archive) p. 1

month[421]. The Rev'd Carpenter announced his departure from Uphill in January 1954 leaving the Group without a GSM. Despite these changes in personnel the Group had been successful in fundraising which had included a Scout fete held in June in the Rectory garden, as the PCC notes record that the Group had applied for an extension to the shed to store their kit. The recently appointed Rev. Birch became the Group's Chairman. Around this time Mr Albert (Bert) Collings took over as SM. Other new faces in the Group included Rex Lay who initially took an ASM warrant, helping Mr Collings to run the Troop alongside Alan Marshall, who was a civilian instructor from RAF Locking. Mr Marshall would later serve as a leader with the 4th Weston (St Saviour's) and 24th Weston (Hill Road) Scout Groups. Mr Collings was a painter and decorator by trade and was appointed as GSM the same year. During 1958 the Group purchased four drums and four bugles, which reflected the Group's effort to form a Scout band, this was to be a short lived affair and the instruments were sold within a couple of years.

With the departure of Mrs Flavell in 1959, Mr Lay swapped sections to take over the leadership of the Pack, where he was assisted by his wife, Brenda. The Group purchased new colours in 1959, which were dedicated the following March at a ceremony in St Nicholas Church. The same year saw the formation of the Senior Scout Troop with five boys joining to form the Sir Richard Grenville Patrol.[422] After a gap in having a SM, the Troop having been taken by the GSM, Mr Collings, the Group Committee met Mr Hamilton, the prospective new SM on Dec 1st 1961. The same meeting recorded that the decision was taken to sell the band instruments.[423]

[421] Group History Notes 1951-2004 Mr C Hart(1st Uphill Group Archive) p. 1

[422] Group History Notes 1951-2004 Mr C Hart(1st Uphill Group Archive) p. 1
Recollections of Mr R Lay 1957-68 (Biddulph Archive) 06/09/07

[423] Group History Notes 1951-2004 Mr C Hart(1st Uphill Group Archive) p. 1

Tragically Mr Collings was killed in an accident in the summer of 1966. Following the Group's sad loss, Mr Lay was appointed GSM, his wife, Brenda, moved from an ACM to CM running the Pack with assistance from Paul Austin.[424] The numbers in the sections fluctuated during the period with Pack numbers ranging from nine Cubs one year to thirty the following resulting in the formation of a second Pack.

The Group began seeking a plot of land to build their own headquarters in November 1963. The following year the Troop attended the County Jamboree at Amersham over Whitsun weekend where the Troop performed very well and gained sixth place overall in the County flag competition.[425] Mr Teale joined the Troop as SM although he had to take a backstep in 1964 due to ill health. Mr Hawley assisted the Troop. The Scouts were to enjoy a very successful Summer Camp at Leamington Spa in 1965. Mr Teale stepped down from the Troop in the winter of 1965. The Senior Troop disbanded in 1965 with the Group taking over the maintenance of the Grenville hut. Another hut was owned by the Group in the same location, known as the Farley hut, which was later sold off. Paul Austin is mentioned as helping with the Pack in the Committee Meeting Minutes for June. The Group were once again seeking to appoint a new SM and the following year Mr Grove was appointed taking over as SM in February 1966 with Mr Hawley handing over in summer. Ken Foulkes joined the committee in 1967. Later he took on the responsibility of running the Troop before moving on to lead the Group as GSL. In 1967 the Group's long standing Treasurer, Mrs Teale, stood down. The Group sold the Grenville hut for £15 to Bleadon Guides in September of that year and another hut measuring 40 by 18ft was purchased from Mr Bartlett as part of the Group's efforts to have their own headquarters. It was located next to the Church hall and was erected in 1967, although it had

[424] Recollections of Mr R Lay 1957-68 (Biddulph Archive) 06/09/07
[425] Group History Notes 1951-2004 Mr C Hart(1st Uphill Group Archive) p. 3

no heating, no running water and no toilet. The Group had met until this time in the Church hall.

The Group changed their name in 1963 from 1st Uphill to 7th Weston (1st Uphill) so as to get nearer to the front of the District parade which was led by the 3rd Weston (St Paul's) Band.[426] The Group reverted to 1st Uphill on July 11th 1985 when they relocated to their current location in Windwhistle Lane.[427] On April 12th 1990 the Group held a grand opening of their current headquarters which cost £17,000 to purchase. The ceremony was conducted by the Lord Lieutenant of Avon, Sir John Wills, the GSL at the time was Mr Cyril Hart. In 2007 the Group won the Weston Mercury newspaper vote which awarded £8000 for renovations to the headquarters.[428]

The early 1970s saw the Troop again seeking a new SL. In the spring of 1974 Mr Ray Alford, an ASL with the 19th Weston (Milton & Worle), moved over to lead the Troop, a post he held for two years before moving away from Weston. [429] Mr David Perriman, another leader from the 19th Weston, then took the reins for two years until 1978. History was to repeat itself with the Group again on the lookout for a new SL. A successful result was obtained when in 1980 Mr Ian Williams took the SL warrant and remained with the Troop for three years. His departure sent the Group back on a search for another new SL. Mr John Hall took over as SL in 1984 until October 1987, when he was succeeded by a team of ASLs including Peter Harvey, who served as Acting SL, Daniel Carver, Steven Southwell, Paul Austin and Mark Matthews, whose son was a member of the Group and his daughter took a Helpers certificate. The Matthews family were keen supporters of the Group over a long period of time with Mrs

---

426 Recollections of Mr R Lay 1957-68 (Biddulph Archive) 06/09/07
Copy of Form C2 13/11/63 (Gilwell Archive)

427 Copy of From C2 11/07/85(Gilwell Archive)

428 Notes from Scout file (Courtesy of Weston Library)

429 From the 19th Weston-Super-Mare Scout Group Records (Courtesy of Mr R Cooke)

Kay Matthews assisting with the Pack.[430] The Troop had from its earliest days struggled to find a long term leader, the average length of service undertaken by leaders was between three to four years.

From 1987 Ian Morton, ADC Scouts, ran the Troop for twelve months until a new leader, Tim Morgan, came forward, with assistance from the long serving Paul Austin and Mr Dave Bird. Tim Morgan handed over to David Bird and Zara Case who ran the Troop for three years. Towards the end of their time they were travelling from Swindon to keep the Troop going before standing down in 2001 resulting in the Troop again being led by the ADC Scouts, Terry Scoble. A search for a new leader proved successful (albeit temporarily) with Miss Rachel Stafford, an ASL with 1st Kewstoke Troop, joining the Troop and remaining until 2004. As no new leader came forward the CSL, Richard Spindler, took both Troop and Pack meetings whilst a search for new leaders was conducted. Happily this resulted in the appointment of several new leaders including Mark Whitehouse and Mark Wilfan who were both former leaders at the 29th Weston (St Peter's) and later 1st Milton Scout Troops, who still lead the expanding Troop.[431]

In comparison to the Scout section, the Cub pack was to enjoy relative stability with their leaders. The original leader, Mrs Hillman, resigned after eighteen months and her Assistant, Mrs Flavell, took the helm, remaining with the pack until 1959. Mr Lay, who had started with the Troop as an ASM, changed sections to become Akela. His wife, Brenda, joined him as an ACM, and upon Mr Lay's promotion took charge of the Pack. During the Lays time with the Cubs, the Pack undertook two successful Camps, the first at Porlock in 1966 and Weymouth two

[430] Axe District Directory 1993, p.24
Axe District Directory 07/02/95, p.21

[431] Group History Notes 1951-2004 Mr C Hart (1st Uphill Group Archive) p. 2
Axe District Directory and archives entries 1950-2006 (Mrs A Coombes)

years later. The Troop mounted a summer camp in 1968 at Beer. Weekend camps included sites ranging from Keynsham to Bishop's Lydeard and the Troop also participated in District camps and competitions. The Group also attended the Uphill and Cheddar County Jamborees. Mr Lay recalled that the Uphill Jamboree site was not a very good site due to the shallow earth on the site which barely held a tent peg and very shallow grease pits. The Cheddar camp in comparison was much better though the weather was terrible, raining all day Friday and into Saturday. Despite this a good time was had by those who attended.[432]

The Group's longest serving leader, Paul Austin, whose older brother John was a leader with the 17th Weston Troop, began helping out with the Pack in 1965 and remained with the Cub section for close to twenty years before moving up to help with the Troop. Mr Austin served under Cub leaders; Mr Rex Lay, Mrs Jane Platt and Mrs Hodgin. Following Mrs Lay's departure in 1974, the Pack leadership passed to Jane Platt who remained for several years.

With Cubbing proving popular the Pack almost doubled in size going from nineteen to thirty six Cubs in 1975.[433] Over the next few years the Group remained on a strong footing with thirty two Scouts in the Troop by 1978 and the Pack continuing to be popular. Mrs Ann Hodgin joined the Group as a Helper in 1974, known as Chill, before acting as the Group Secretary in 1977, moving back to lead the Pack for eighteen years from 1981.[434] Other leaders with the Pack include Mrs K Matthews and Mrs A Bull who worked alongside Mrs Hodgin. Following the retirement of the Cub Leadership team in 1999, the Pack was run for a short period by Mr C Boyce before the Pack disbanded. Mr Richard Spindler restarted the Pack, moving from 1st Ashcombe Cub Pack, with assistance from Shaun Dobson and Caroline

---

[432] Recollections of Mr R Lay 1957-68 (Biddulph Archive) 06/09/07
[433] Group History Notes 1951-2004 Mr C Hart (1st Uphill Group Archive) p. 2
[434] Group History Notes 1951-2004 Mr C Hart (1st Uphill Group Archive) p. 2

Bartlett. Shaun took the helm following the departure of Richard Spindler in 2005.

Mr Foulkes stood down in 1978 as GSL handing the baton to Mr Munn who remaining in post for a year. The period of regular changes in the GSL role ceased in 1979 when Mr Cyril Hart, a former Scouter from the Hill Road Group, who had been actively involved in Scouting throughout his life in various parts of the country, took over and began his long tenure as GSL at the Group until 1999, then serving as Group Chairman for three years afterwards.

The Group started a Beaver colony in February 1994 with Anthea Tyler leading the new section. She remained with the Colony until 1998 when she married and moved away from the town. Emma Warburton took over the reins until standing down in July 2000. Due to the old problem of a lack of leaders rearing its head the Colony disbanded. A gap of four years ensued until the Colony was reformed by Mrs Debbie Astbury, whose son was a member of the Troop. She was succeeded by Jon Aucott before he moved on to run the Explorers within the District and Miss Yvonne Matthews took the reins.

2nd Uphill (St Barnabas) Reg No. 34423

03/04/59-71 Form E

The Group started out with a Scout Troop, formed by St Barnabas Church, on the housing estate on the northern edge of the village and which met at Uphill Secondary School. Rev. Henry Birch started the Group and held the warrant of GSM with the Rev. T Fullern as SM and D White holding an ASM warrant.[435] Shortly after a Cub Pack was started although the Troop disbanded in the

[435] Copy of From C 03/04/57 (Gilwell Archive)

mid 1960s. In 1969 Mrs Morris was recorded as being ACSL, the following year she stepped up to CSL and evidently resigned shortly thereafter as Mrs Devina Dexter took over in 1970. The Pack at that time had 12 Cubs and 2 Pack Scouters, a CSL and a GSL. By the following year the Group had closed.

1st Wedmore

01/10/19-WWII	Reg No.	4158
	(1928)	4208
18/08/47-1958 Form E		25534
14/10/65-1992 Form E		37522
01/05/93		45667

The first record of Scouting in Wedmore dates back to October 1919 when the Reverend A Chisholm started a Scout Troop in the Axbridge Local Association area. At the time of registration he had twenty Scouts under his leadership.[436] Probably the highlight of the life of the Troop was summer camp five years later, see report below. The Troop was fortunate to have in the Rev Chisholm a long serving leader, which undoubtedly provided stability and continuity for the village Troop. In addition, several Rovers took an active part in the leadership of the Troop, the prime example being Geoffrey Pavey.

Diary notes of the French Camp 1924 Monday 11th August – Wednesday 27th August[437]

The Scouts mounted an overseas expedition in the summer of 1924 to France, under the guidance of their SM, Rev. Chisholm. The Wedmore Rovers and Scouts who participated were; Rovers

[436] Copy of Troop Registration Form (Gilwell Archive)
[437] Notes taken from Troop logbook 1924, Ref D/P/Wed on 02/05/05 (Somerset Archive)

A Collins, R Curtins and G Pavey. Scouts; PLs F A Curtin and H Redman, PS J Hicke and E Norman, Scouts V Curtin, brothers C A and H D Burroughs, D Fear, A Merriman, J Morgan, L Redman, J Scammell and L E Walsh. During their camp the Troop visited Salisbury, Southampton, Le Havre, Paris, Versailles, Honfluer, Vascouy, Deauville Trouville, Caen and Rouen.

The Troop left Wedmore at 8am being taken by friends and family to Cheddar station and by 9am they were standing on Wells station platform waiting for a train to Westhay then on to Salisbury, reaching the city around midday. Confusion with the luggage led to Rover Scouts Geoff Pavey and Bert Collins travelling on with the luggage to Southampton, whilst the rest of the Troop took a tour of Salisbury. The Troop took their packed lunch on Cathedral Green and whilst having lunch they met an American Scoutmaster who took some pictures of the Troop. The Troop then travelled onto Southampton arriving at 7:30pm and were "greeted with joy" by Geoff and Bert before the Troop boarded the SS Hautonia at 8:20pm with a calm crossing to Le Havre. Most of the boys could not sleep and stayed on deck throughout the night. Arriving at 7am on Tuesday 12th August the Troop were met at the quayside by ADC M Delaware and two French Scouts who set off at a fast pace keen to get their guests to breakfast of delicious coffee and rolls. However during the rush three Wedmore Scouts were lost and rejoined the Troop later at 9:45 when they steamed out of Le Havre heading for Paris on the train. In Paris the Troop was met by two Englishmen, Fred Bayliss and an ASM. Fred was to act as the Troop's tour guide whilst in Paris. The Troop then headed off to their accommodation, Mr Denny's school at 12 Rue de Sevres. Six boys made use of a Patrol tent loaned by Major Golding whilst the rest of the Troop slept indoors, they had the better deal as it poured with rain all night.

Whilst in Paris between August 12th and 15th, the Troop undertook a sight seeing tour taking in the Eiffel Tower, the Palace of Versailles, including the famous hall of Mirrors and the room where the Peace Treaty was signed and the Place de Concord, as well as Notre Dome and the Louvre. On their penultimate day in Paris the Troop visited the tomb of Napoleon, which they voted one of the best things they had seen. At the tomb the Scouts met a Troop of Jamaican Scouts who were visiting Paris.

August 16th was an early start for the Troop as they travelled from Paris to Le Havre and by boat onto Honfluer carrying on to Vascouy, where a campsite bordered by woods and the sea was to be the Troop's residence for next week. The Troop's arrival was welcomed enthusiastically by thirty French Scouts in camp. The Troop visited Deauville for bathing on Wednesday 20th and the following day rose early to travel to Caen travelling via Lisieux seeing its beautiful cathedral. In Caen the Troop visited a number of churches including St Etienne and St. Pierre. The boys were greeted by a lovely morning on Friday 22nd, which was a rest day with some Scouts going in to Honfluer for supplies and visited St. Leonard's church, whilst others sunbathed or sported in the sea. For their evening meal the Troop tucked into sausages, sardines and potatoes, followed by a fine camp fire with the French Scouts.

Tuesday 26th saw the Troop striking camp with Bert and Arthur Collins travelling with the kit in a motorcar. The Troop sailed from Honfluer at 10am arriving at Le Havre at 10:45 and headed for the docks, where they had a guided tour around an American warship 'the Pittsburgh' in harbour followed by a game of football against a French Troop.

The Troop sailed in the afternoon arriving the next day at 6:45am in Southampton and began the long journey home arriving at Cheddar station at 5:30pm to be greeted by parents and supporters.

The Troop re-registered in the 1928 census with a strength of fourteen Scouts, two Assistant Scoutmasters, Mr H Brown and Mr George Pavey and Reverend Chisholm, the SM.[438] A transfer document from 1932 refers to 1st Wedmore with the Group transferring Districts from Mid Somerset to Mendip District.[439] The Group is mentioned in the Local Association returns in 1932 as having 16 Scouts, two Rover Scouts and two Leaders.[440] A Wolf Cub Pack was opened by Colonel Onmanney who lived at the Manor house in 1936 with Mr Alan Banwell being one of the first Sixers in the Pack and, many years later to his wife's surprise, the first name on the Pack record book.[441]

In 1935 Mr Pavey stood down an ASM in July and the following May was appointed as RSL. The following year saw a change in the leaders within the Troop with the departure of Mr L J Redman in April and the appointment of Mr F C Porter as an ASM. The Troop retained the services of Mr C Curtis and the Reverend Chisholm as GSM. The Vicar left the parish in 1937 and resigned his warrant, the new incumbent the Reverend H C T Morgan took the role on briefly in March before handing over to Colonel C H Omnanney the following year[442]. In February 1938 two new ASM warrants were presented to Mr K G Bailey and Mr G E Curtin, the latter having come through the ranks being one of the early Scouts.[443] The following year, on the eve of the outbreak of the Second World War, Colonel Omnanney switched warrants from GSM to SM within the Group. The Reverend Morgan returned as GSM.[444] During the war the Group appears to have been dormant.

Along with many other Scout Groups, Scouting in Wedmore was reformed shortly after the war on August 18th 1947 in the Mendip

[438] Copy of Group Re-registration Form F from 1928 (Gilwell Archive)
[439] Copy of Change of Group Registration From C2 1932 (Gilwell Archive)
[440] Taken from Mr W Belshaw's Notes 14/10/05
[441] Interview with Mrs V Banwell 20/01/05
[442] Taken from The Scouter 1935-37 (Gilwell Archive)
[443] The Scouter Vol. May-June 1938 (Gilwell Archive)
[444] Taken from The Scouter 1939 (Gilwell Archive)

Local Association, a part of the Mid Somerset District. The prime mover for the Group's re-emergence was the Reverend H C T Morgan, who reprised his position of GSM with Mr D A Kennewell taking out a SM warrant. Twelve Scouts were present at the time of the Group's restart.[445] At some point in the Troop's life Mr Pavey returned to the Troop, succeeding Mr Kennewell as SM though he had left by the time of the Group's closure some time in 1958.

Scarf: Red
Yellow

Despite a reforming of the Scout Troop in the post war period, village boys who wished to join Wolf Cubs had to wait until the autumn of 1965 when the Group was reformed under the leadership of Mrs Vera Banwell, who had been a leader with 1st Cheddar Cub Pack run by Mrs Eve Mills. Mrs Banwell's twin sons were the first members of the new Pack being experienced Sixers, who were soon joined by eight other boys. The original colour of the Group scarf was plain red, but this had to be changed as it was already a colour of 1st Burrington Scout Group in the District who had registered prior to 1st Wedmore Pack. So the scarf was changed to plain yellow.[446] Mrs Banwell's leadership team consisted of herself and a Queen's Guide, Gillian Brown, later being joined by Judith Hunter who became an ACSL at the Pack until sadly she passed away with cancer. Mrs Beryl Higgs from Mark took out a warrant and she would bring in her car a number of boys from Mark to the Pack meetings.[447] The Pack met in the village hall until moving on to the Scout Headquarters located just outside the village. The Scouts had been meeting there for some time, although the headquarters at that stage had no running water or a toilet, hence the Pack staying

---

[445] Copy of Group Registration From C 1947 (Gilwell Archive)
[446] Interview with Mr & Mrs Banwell 21/01/05
[447] Interview with Mr & Mrs Banwell 21/01/05

at the village hall for a considerable time.[448] The Pack had great assistance from Scouts in the Troop who were undertaking their Duke of Edinburgh Award, who came down and helped the Cub leaders run the Pack for a three to six month period.

On June 5th 1969 Mrs Banwell was appointed ADC Cub Scouts (Village).[449] When Mrs Banwell stepped down from being ADC Cubs and Akela at 1st Wedmore in 1984 she was given a 'Grand Howl' by the massed Packs at the District day on Brean beach, a somewhat loud send off! In her tenure as ADC Cubs Mrs Banwell, along with Mrs Emsley, ADC Cubs (Town), had held Sixer weekends at Kelston farm, the family home, with Cubs camping in the nearby fields. Cub days were also held at Weston beach and Wraxall (in wet weather), which included a visit from Captain Bird's Eye, much to the delight of the Cubs. Sixer's Training days were held at Highbury Hotel where Mrs Emsley was the manageress. The first Pack holiday was held at Woodspring Priory at Sandbay and was taken by two Guiders, Kathleen Mapstone and Kath Cottrell, as Mrs Banwell was in the process of applying for her camping permit. Further camps over the years were held at such places as Porlock Methodist Church with Mrs Mills and 1st Cheddar Cubs, at Greatwood campsite at Overstowey, as well as the County Cub Camp at B. P. House.[450] Following Mrs Banwell as Akela was Roger Reynolds, with ACSLs Kate Hicks (Kaa) and Ann Robinson (Bagheera). The Pack in 1984 comprised of; Andrew Duckett, Peter Nichols, Robert Lloyd, Robert Owen, James Mottram, Simon Prentice, Jamie Avis, Darren Hendry, Damien Rousell, Nicholas Windridge, Adrian Hutchinson, James Fraser, Michael Cawer, Greg Leale, Raymond Bennett, Rupert Lock, Neil Harris, Stuart Hall, Daniel Morrison, James Badman and Richard Banwell.[451]

---

[448] Interview with Mr & Mrs Banwell 21/01/05
[449] District Annual Report 1970/71 p. 6
[450] Interview with Mr & Mrs Banwell 21/01/05
[451] Pack Register 1984 (Wedmore Group Archive)

The Group started a Beaver Colony some time in 1987, which rapidly became successful with twenty boys, led by BSL Jean Windridge and Sue Eadie, the latter holding an ABSL warrant. The Pack under the charge of Akela Sue Munnay numbered twenty two Cubs, divided into red, blue, white and tawny sixes, including Adam Girling, Nicholas Evans, Grant Garge, Charlie Rose, James Hendry, Kerry Davies, Matthew Wood, Ross Arden, Richard Stacey, Dominic Ripon, Justin Fear, Stephen Peakall, Christian Miller, Ian Williams, George Scotland, Duncan Holliman, Ian Long, Alan Archer, Gordon Lloyd, Mark Grice, David Richardson and Thomas Drew.[452]

The Scout Troop was opened in 1970 under the leadership of a local teacher, Mr Godfrey Daine, and Mr D Johnson, who had a son on the waiting list for the Cub Pack. Mr Daine served as ASL until 1975 when Mr Johnson took on the warrant of SL remaining in post until 1982 and standing down due to a lack of adult helpers. The Troop struggled on with a number of adults taking the Scouts until the leadership team settled down with Pete Westrick as GSL and John North and Jeremy Morse holding ASL warrants. The Scouts were operating an active programme during this period with climbing and abseiling at Burrington Combe, caving, hiking, with a particularly keen interest in night hiking, perhaps in preparation for the Somerset Scout County run Quantock Follies challenge, as well as working parties at the headquarters and Chief Scout Training exercises taking place.[453] Membership of the Troop grew during this period with at least three patrols existing, including Eagles and Buffaloes. Members of the Troop in the mid to late 1980s included; Raymond Bennett, Stuart Hall, Neil Harris, John Amesbury, Phillip Bennett, Adrian Biggs, Ben Frost, Ian Harris, Oliver Hatch, Giles Hicks, Simon Ellis, Graeme Kite, Timothy Morse, Harvey Rook, whose father served as the Group Treasurer, James Stacey, Ken Wotton, Mark

---

[452] Pack Register 1987 (Wedmore Group Archive)

[453] Troop programmes 1984-89 (Wedmore Group Archive)

Wilde and Martin Westrick, who was the son of the GSL.[454] The Group Secretary, Charlie Hicks, had a son in the Troop and Colin Wilde held an Instructor's Certificate with the Troop alongside Ken Redman the Group's Caving Instructor.[455] The Troop's strength in 1989 stood at fifteen Scouts, including; Nicholas Armitage, Richard Banwell, Adrian Biggs, Rhodric Davies, Nicholas Ellis, Darren Faulkener, Benjamin Frost, Thomas Gillibrand, Stuart Hall, Neil Harris, Damien Holt, James Stacey, James Wilde, Kenneth Wotton and Chris Rousell, led by Mr Peter Westrick.[456] The following year saw a slight rise in the Group's membership with twenty three Cubs and nineteen Scouts, by this point in time the Colony had closed.[457] However in 1992 the Group was to disband due to a lack of leaders.

The Group was re-established in May 1993 by Mr William Belshaw as GSL, who had recently moved into the village, and had been a former Scouter. The Group was reformed initially with the opening of a Beaver Colony, led by Mr Clive Palmer (BSL) and Cliff Besley (ABSL)[458]. Messrs Palmer and Besley departed in 1996. The search for new leaders began, although this took three years, during which time Mr Belshaw's wife, Mrs Norah Belshaw, a former primary school teacher, took the Beavers as well as the Cubs. In 1999 two adults, Mrs Katherine Perry and Mrs Launa Howell, offered to take over the leadership of the section, although they moved up to Cubs when the Colony had low numbers and the Cub section was struggling to recruit new leaders.

The Cubs were re-started in 1994, as the older Beavers progressed. The new Pack was run by Mrs Belshaw as CSL and

---

[454] Partial Troop Register 1984-86 (Wedmore Group Archive)
[455] 1987 Group census (Wedmore Group Archive)
[456] Pack Register c.1987 (Wedmore Group Archive)
Correspondence Mr P Nicholson CSL c. 1987 (Wedmore Group Archive)
[457] Group census 1988 (Wedmore Group Archive)
[458] Mr W Belshaw Notes 14/10/05

Mrs Jean Tincknell as ACSL until 1999, when Mrs Jackie Chalmers, who moved into the area from Hampshire, took over as CSL. Due to the shortage of help with the Cubs, the Beaver Leaders Mrs Katherine Perry and Mrs Launa Howell moved up to help run the Cubs in the autumn of 2000. However, these ladies subsequently departed in 2002 and with Mrs Chalmers resigned at Easter 2005, which has left the Cubs leaderless for some while. A search for leaders was conducted by the Group, with new leaders coming forward in 2007.

The Troop was started again in 1996, again, as boys became too old for the Cubs. The Troop was run by Mr Martin Davey, who had previously been a SL in Hampshire, until he stood down after eight years with the Troop. He still works with the Group as a caving instructor. Mr Belshaw has acted as ASL for the Troop since 1996 and been acting SL since Mr Davey left. The current Troop has a love of the Welsh countryside having held camp five times in nine years in the principality, other camping sites have included Winsford on Exmoor, Dorset, Huish Woods and Tincknell's orchard in the village[459] Despite the challenges of finding leaders the Troop and Pack continue to meet and offer an active programme for the young people of Wedmore.

459 Mr W Belshaw's Notes 14/10/05

Wedmore Scout Troop camps 1970-2007		
Year	Event	Location
1972	Summer camp	Eype, Dorset
1973	Summer camp	Cwmcynwyn, Brecon
1974	Summer camp	Rydal
1975	Summer camp	Chudleigh
1976	Summer camp	Monmouth
1977	Summer camp	Torr Down
1987	Summer camp	Tewkesbury, Gloucestershire
1979	Summer camp	Llandetty Hall
1980	Summer camp	Cleavel Point
1981	Summer camp	Leeford Farm, Brendon
1996	Spring camp	Tincknell's orchard, Wedmore
1996	Summer camp	Y Gaer, Brecon
1997	Spring camp	Tincknell's orchard, Wedmore
1997	Summer camp	Y Gaer, Brecon
1998	Summer camp	Dorset County Camp Site
1999	Eclipse Summer camp	Winsford, Exmoor, West Somerset
2000	Millennium Summer camp	Severnvale, Chepstow
2001	Summer camp	Severnvale, Chepstow
2002	Summer camp	Digistow, Nr Monmouth
2003	Summer camp	Y Gaer, Brecon
2004	Sedgemoor District Camp	Taunton
2004	Summer camp	Lyme Regis, Dorset
2005	Summer camp	Winsford, Exmoor, West Somerset

Kewstoke Cubs Grand Howl 1

Kewstoke Cubs Grand Howl 2

1st Wedmore 'Brew up', Weymouth Camp 1923

1st Wedmore Dawlish 'Boyhood Raleigh' 1934

County Jamboree – Glastonbury – Camp Fire – 1935

1st Wedmore Cubs and DC 1965

1st Winscombe

Fd:	1913-24		
	16/06/24-37 (BST)	Troop Reg. No. 12662	
	23/11/25 (WCP)		
		'28 Reg.	4210
	22/03/38-WWII	Reg No.	19306
	11/01/66	Reg No.	37636

The earliest records for Scouting in the village dates back to 1913 when Mr Harold Weeks was appointed as SM.[460]Mr Weeks appears to have been the sole leader throughout the Great War and is mentioned in the 1918 Local Directory as SM of the Troop, continuing until 1924, at which point the Troop disbanded.

Scouting was soon restarted in the village with the formation of a Boy Scout Troop, registered in Axbridge District Local Association, North West District, under the leadership of Mr George Hutchinson, who taught at Sidcot School. The Troop's headquarters is recorded as the Haynes in Sandford Road, perhaps someone's home?[461] The following year in November Miss Hilda Clothier, formerly an ACM at 1st Banwell, opened a Wolf Cub Pack, although the Pack did not operate for long having disbanded by 1928[462]. The '28 census reveals that the Troop comprised of eleven Scouts, an SM (Mr Hutchinson) and an ASM Mr Geoffrey Baker and was now in the Weston-Super-Mare Local Association.[463] Mr Pruen joined the Troop in 1931 as an ASM with the departure of Mr Hutchinson to start 2nd Winscombe Scout Troop at Sidcot School.[464] Mr Brown was appointed as GSM during the early 1930s and was attending Somerset County

460 Misc Notes from Mr Richard Ivens (Biddulph Archive)
461 Copy of Boy Scout Troop Registration Form (Gilwell Archives)
462
463 Copy of Form F 14/11/28 (Gilwell Archives)
464 Copy of Form C (Gilwell Archives)

Scouter's meetings in 1933. The Troop was still active, perhaps with Mr Pruen running the Troop, although it had ceased to meet within four years.[465]

The Troop quickly reformed with the registration of a Troop in spring 1938. The initial impetus included fourteen Scouts under the leadership of GSM Mr G W Thomas and ASM Mr W Salter, meeting at the Recreation field in the village. The following year only Mr Thomas remained with the Troop[466] and by 1944 the Troop had folded, probably as a result of a shortage of leaders coming forward during the Second World War.[467]

Scarf: Red with black trim

There would be a long period, over twenty-one years, until Scouting returned to the village, although during this time Scouting continued at Sidcot School with 2nd Winscombe. The 1st Winscombe Scout Group reformed in January 1966. The early meeting place of the Group was the Lynch Union Chapel where Mrs Maureen Faraghar ran the Cub Pack and SM Mr Malcolm J Fowler took the Troop meetings. The GSM was Mr Michael W Mason-Smith. At the time of registration the Group started out with eight Wolf Cubs and Six Boy Scouts, although numbers soon grew, necessitating extra adult leaders, for example, Mrs Fowler took out an ACSL warrant the following year. Mrs Mary Wilkinson followed Mrs Faraghar as CSL who stepped down after eight years as Akela. Mrs Wilkinson joined the Group in April 1971 and took charge of the second Pack which had been started to cater for the long waiting list for the Pack, the second Pack existed for approximately three years. Under the leadership of Sandie John the Cubs camped at London. Highlights of the camp included a trip to Downing Street, and watching the royal

465 Somerset Boy Scouts County meetings Attendance book, from 05/08/33 (Tangier Scout Centre Archive, Taunton).
466 1939 Somerset County Directory p. 29 (Tangier Centre Somerset County Archives)
467 1945 County Directory p. 21 (Tangier Centre Somerset County Archives)

tournament. Mrs Pat Evans took over the helm in 1980, receiving her warrant alongside SL Roger Starr. Tim Mogg, a former ASL of the Troop, received his five years certificate at the same presentation evening.

In 1987 Winscombe Cubs raised £50 for the 34th Weston (Baytree School) Cub Pack which had been started by a former Winscombe Cub, Mike Wilkinson. Other fundraising efforts undertaken over the years included Christmas bazaars, sponsored hikes, taking part in the second West Mendip Way Walk in 1984, as well as two horse racing nights organised by Richard Evans, where footage of horse racing was shown at the Winscombe Club whilst supporters betted on individual horses. Each race was sponsored by local companies including Bass and Ushers brewers, this different approach to fundraising raised over £500 for the Group.[468]

The Group moved from the Lynch Chapel to the current Group headquarters in 1969, with the official opening on September 19th, with the Somerset County Commissioner Gervas Clay and his wife the Hon Betty Clay, daughter of Baden-Powell and Deputy Chief Commissioner for the Girl Guides, presiding. Even at this early stage Mr Clay mentioned that a Venture Scout Unit was the next step for the flourishing Scout Group, although this concept took seventeen years to germinate. Following the official opening the Cubs and Scouts put on displays for their guests demonstrating what skills they had learned.[469] The Group's headquarters, refurbished by the Scouts efforts through fundraising, which was leased for seven years initially, continues to this day to be the base for Scouting activities within the village. Prior to the Scouts lease of the hall it had been the village men's club.

---

[468] Recollections of Mrs P Evans Spring 2007

[469] Weston Mercury 19/09/69 (Courtesy of Mrs P Evans)

The Group had a strong base of support from parents, many of whom served on the Group Committee. Previous chairmen of the Committee have included Mr Gordon Hutchings, the village solicitor whose son took a warrant with the neighbouring 1st Burrington and Wrington Scout Group. Mr Neville Brenchley, whose sons went through the sections at Winscombe, with William Brenchley becoming Senior Patrol Leader during Mr Starr's time as SL and achieving his Chief Scout Award. Mr Brenchley served for fourteen years before handing over to Mr Parslow, although he remains active in the Scout District, currently serving as District Chairman. Mr Roberts served a spell as Group Chairman at Winscombe, prior to taking roles within the District as Chairman of the Appointments Committee. Another Winscombe Chairman was Mr G Johnstone whose sons Lawrence and Steven were Cubs, Scouts and later Venture Scouts.

The Group started a Venture Scout Unit, the Anglo Saxons, in the autumn of 1986 to cater for boys within the Troop who preferred to remain in the village rather than travel to nearby Venture Units in Weston or to the Trogs VSU over at Congresbury. The Unit was from its start co-educational with four female members Rachel Cox, Sarah Curtis, Helen Daglass, and Wendy John invested in 1987. In keeping with Venture Scout tradition for investitures in unusual places, Clyve Evans and Steven Johnstone were invested into the Unit on top of St James the Great Church tower in the village.

Chief Scouts' Awards were gained by Steven Johnstone, Duncan Wilson, who represented his Group, District and Country, attending the (1987) World Scout Jamboree held in Australia, Alex Starr and Clyve Evans, the latter two Scouts were sons of the leaders within the Group. The Group achieved national fame in February 1994 when Andy Aston, a member of the Anglo-Saxons VSU and former Scout, walked through the recently completed Channel Tunnel along with the British athlete Daley Thompson, walking thirty-one miles of the channel tunnel on

February 12th 1994. Aiming to raise £1400 for the Children's Society Andy's efforts resulted in a cheque for £3600 being given to the Children's Society. At the half way point of the walk Andy received his Chief Scout's Award from Gareth Morrison, the Chief Scout.[470]

The Troop's founding leader Mr Fowler stood down in 1974 handing over to Messrs Rossiter and Copsey. Within two years, due to the popularity of Scouting within Winscombe, a second Troop was formed in 1975 meeting on a Friday night under the leadership of Peter Copsey,. The second Troop continued to meet until the mid 1980s when Troop numbers had declined resulting in the second Troop merging back into the Tuesday Troop. The Tuesday Troop was led by Peter Rossiter who handed over in 1982 to Martin Hagen, who remained with the Troop for a year. Mr Starr took over the helm from Martin Hagen, having been a parent helper for a few years beforehand. Assistant leaders of the Troop during this time included Les Saker, Dave Lund, who moved on to form the Venture Unit in 1986 and Tim Mogg. With the departure of Mr Starr to the role of ADC Development in 1985 Les Saker ran the Troop until the early 1990s. The Troop struggled to find a leader for a while until Mr Oakley took the helm, remaining at the Troop for several years before moving on. Another search for leaders ensued at the close of the 1990s until the husband and wife team of Mike and Mandy Turner joined in 1999. They remained with the Troop for five years and during this time the Troop numbers expanded to close to forty Scouts who participated in a very active programme including hiking, adventurous activities and a number of trips abroad. Mr Starr assisted with the running of the Troop. Change was again on the cards when the Turners stepped down. Neil Sweet and Kevin Peters kept the Troop ticking over whilst efforts were made to find new leaders, which resulted in success in 2006 when Alex

[470] Recollections of Mr R Starr 14/10/07
Recollections of Mrs P Evans Spring 2007
Weston Mercury Feb 1994 (Courtesy of Mrs P Evans0

Saker took over with continuing support from Messrs Sweet and Peters. Alex Saker's father, Les, had been a SL with the Troop.

The Group were keen supporters of the pedal car races held on Weston seafront. The Group's cars were designed by Scout parent and engineer, Mr Gibson, and success came with Peter Body, of Winscombe Cubs achieving the fastest speed whilst Neville Brenchley took first place in the veteran class race and the Group took the BSM trophy for the highest placed Scout team of the race.

The Group had several GSLs with Mr M W Mason-Smith who led the Group from its inception for two years before handing over to Mr S B Swain for a brief spell. Mr J C Bearman was appointed in April 1970 and resigned his GSL warrant taking out an ASL warrant in 1973. He was followed by Mr Robert Faraghar who is probably the Group's longest serving GSL, a post he held until 1984. He was appointed ADC Venture Scouts in 1983. Following Mr Faraghar's departure the Group ran for some time without a GSL until Mr B S Hawkins was appointed.

Cub Scouting was proving so popular in the village that five years after the Group started a second Cub pack was opened under the leadership of Mrs Mary Wilkinson. Mrs Elvens led the Pack after the departure of Mrs Wilkinson until handing over to Mrs Pat Evans in 1981. Other leaders with the Pack include Russell Sands, Joanna Evans (Mrs Evan's daughter and a Queen's guide now residing in Australia), Laurence Johnston, Alex Lund, Sandy John and Carol Marshal. Mrs Evans was forced to stand down in 2000 due to ill health, she returned to the Pack as Akela in 2002. During the intervening period Mr Kevin Peters ran the Pack, continuing to assist with the Scout Troop. A period of instability and lack of leaders around 2004 saw the founding Beaver Leaders, Sue Read and Jill Lyons moving on to run the Cubs and new Beaver leaders coming forward. Joanna Chidley joined as ABSL shortly after the colony formed, being assisted from 2004 by Mike Martin. Joanna Chidley departed in 2005 and Mr Andrew Dudbridge joined the Beaver leadership team, being joined in 2006 by Mrs Wendy Rees after the departure of Mr Martin.

2nd Winscombe (Sidcot School)

Fd: 01/06/31-1968 Reg No. 12770

Scarf: Dark Blue

Sidcot School, the Quaker founded School, formed a Scout Troop from its pupils on June 1st 1931 with Mr Charles Rowlands as GSM and Mr John N Briscoe as SM with a Troop of six Boy Scouts and the headmaster Mr J G Elliot as controller (sponsor).[471] The following account of the Scouts comes from Ms Christine Godwin's book *Reflections of an Island* which the author gratefully acknowledges the use of.

"Scouting had been popular at Sidcot *since 1931 {Italics mine}* when Mr George Hutchinson who had been SM at 1st Winscombe decided to form another Troop, 2nd Winscombe at Sidcot School. In May 1931 the finance committee agreed to authorise the expenditure of £25 to £30 on a portable hut which was placed in the drying yard. There had been some worry that Scouting would be seen as too militaristic for a Quaker school, but as the order of Woodcraft Chivalry had been successful in the early part of the century, it was understood that activities such as camping, cooking and personal survival were useful and not a threat to pacifist ideals.[472]

[471] Copy of registration Form C, 01/06/1930
[472] C Godwin *Reflections of an Island* p. 58

Certainly the military aspects did not worry the boys as one Scout Kurt Strauss recalls "we all had a uniform with badges, wide brimmed hat, staves and a small wooden Scout hut behind the laundry, where the Troop would meet on Friday afternoon, which was hobby day. To begin with almost all the new boys would join the Scouts, but soon most of them found other, more rewarding hobbies, and by the time we got to the sixth form only three or four of us were still involved, and we naturally became the Patrol Leaders. We had four Patrols, Seagulls, Eagles, Owls and Peewits, and were usually pitted against each other in various competitions, games, etc. The headmaster was also the SM and the head of English his Assistant. So we tended to have privileged treatment when it came to doing things out of School, often on the surrounding seven hills and involved a degree of map reading, path finding and maybe some construction work using whatever materials were to hand. And of course the famous knots which we were all taught to make with our plentiful supply of rope. Proficiency badges were much worked for and sought after and their award was always a matter of some ceremony. We read Scouting for Boys avidly, quite ignorant of the quazi-military implications of our activities".[473]

George Hutchinson was assisted by maths teacher Francis Armitage, nicknamed 'Army Hut', John Briscoe (Bisto) who taught English and later Ivan Gray. During the war, the authorities had to be notified of wide games at night in case the boys were mistaken for paratroopers.

John Thompson recalls his experience of wide games with the Troop as "I remember night wide games on Wavering Down – a special excitement organised by the Headmaster, and I have a fleeting memory of his heavy figure looming ahead of a charge of boys hurtling down the hill towards Shute Shelve. It all ended

[473] Ibid p. 58

with hot cocoa in the kitchens. A sense of officially played truant was particularly delicious".[474]

It was George Hutchinson who developed the single–wheeled trek carts, which were used so successfully by both the Scouts and Guides to carry provisions on camping trips. Michael Stadnage recalled the trek carts as "it was a sort of wheelbarrow fitted with a motorbike tyre. Then, when laden, was pushed and pulled by the patrol. They were used to trek over Exmoor and, in 1936, on a trek around the Ardennes in Belgium. The sleeping bags and groundsheets were made up by us in spare evenings after prep in what was a small room leading into the Nat. Soc. Room. The chicken feathers used for the sleeping bags went everywhere". Other leaders of the Troop have included Mr R Hinton, who taught at the school. The Troop folded in 1968 after providing thirty seven years of Scouting to the students of Sidcot School.

1st Wrington

Fd:	29/09/23-1928 (BST)	Reg No.	11744
	17/01/25-31/03/35(WCP)-		7501
		(1928)	4209
	05/05/41-31/03/57		21969

A Scout Troop was opened by Mr George Bass as SM and Mr William Brown as ASM with a membership of twenty Boy Scouts. The Troop address is given as the Village High Street and was in the Axbridge Local Association.[475] In January 1925 Miss Elizabeth Stuckey opened a Wolf Cub Pack. She was assisted by Mr Bass who took out an ACM warrant. The Pack numbered twelve boys at the time of registration.[476] The 1928 census return for the Group records only the Cub Pack being operational with

---

[474] Ibid p. 59
[475] Copy of registration Form C 29/09/23 (Gilwell Archive)
[476] Copy of registration Form C 17/01/25 (Gilwell Archive)

Miss Stuckey as the sole Leader to a Pack of twelve boys. By 1935 the Group had folded.[477]

The village had a second attempt at Scouting during the Second World War in May 1941, although this may have been premature and ceased to operate, then re-registered in 1946. Three years later the Group was transferred from Mid Somerset District into Clevedon Local Association, part of North District.[478] The SM who restarted the Group was the Rev. Father Dan from Redhill Chapel who was followed by Tom Collins who remained with the Troop until the 1950s, when he was travelling down from Long Ashton to run Troop meetings, which were being held in the John Locke hall in the village on Monday nights.[479] Malcolm Parsons took over the running of the Troop from Tom Collins. However the Troop closed due to a lack of leaders in 1957.[480] Whilst in operation the Group camped at Dawlish with ten Scouts cycling the eighty miles there and back in the late 1940s[481] and in 1950 held a summer camp on a farmer's field near Fowey. The camp was memorable to Mr Parsons when the farmer's wife informed the Troop who had travelled down to the site in a lorry that the site was not for camping on. The arrival of the farmer cleared the matter up, he had not informed his wife that the Troop was camping there and she had had a previous bad experience with a Troop from another part of the country who had left a bad impression. By the end of the week the Scouts had won the farmer's wife round, by their good behaviour and assisting in the milking of the farm cows. Local camping was undertaken nearer to home with regular camps held around the Mendips at Ebbor and Wookey Hole and further north at Glennywood campsite at the top of the Gordano valley.[482]

---

[477] Copy of registration Form F 24/11/28 (Gilwell Archive)
[478] Copy of registration Form C2 30/03/49 (Gilwell Archive)
[479] Copy of Somerset County Directory 1945 p. 21 (Tangier Centre Archive)
[480] Interview with Mr Malcolm Parsons 01/03/05
Copy of lapsed Group Document 31/03/57 (Tangier Scout Centre Archive, Taunton)
[481] Interview with Mr George Martin 01/03/05
[482] Interview with Mr Malcolm Parsons 01/03/05

The Group formed a Wolf Cub Pack under the leadership of the Reverend B J Leigh. Other leaders with the Group included B Chard and R F Gulliver both recorded as being ASMs.[483] The 1st Burrington Group which opened four years later incorporated the title Wrington into their name when they moved into the village a few years later, hence the Group's current title as 1st Burrington and Wrington Scout Group based at the old Methodist chapel in Wrington village.

[483] Copy of lapsed Group Document 31/03/57 (Tangier Scout Centre Archive, Taunton)

The District Venture Scout Units 1968-2002

With the implementation of the Advance Report in 1967/68 a number of the Scout Groups formed their own Venture Scout Units, in addition to District Units being formed. The Yeo Trogs were the only District Unit to run for the duration of the life of Venture Scouting from 1968-2002. The Smugglers and Jabberwocks came a close second and the Saints ran for most of the period. Several other Units opened and closed over the years, as demand occurred. Three Venture Scout Units were registered and operated as District Units during the period, although only the Yeo Trogs were to continuously meet from 1968-2002. The Smugglers were to become a District Unit for a fifteen year spell between 1975-90 after the amalgamation of the 17th and 24th Weston group based Units. During 1990 the Smugglers amalgamated with the 24th Weston (Hill Road) Scout Group. Axe Pathfinders, whose history is somewhat of a mystery, were operating as a District Unit in 1979 meeting at the south end of town and had disbanded before 1983. The Group based Units histories are recorded within the individual Groups histories.

V.S.U. Name	Fd	Fld	Notes
Axe Pathfinders	1975	1983	District Unit
Smugglers	1975	1990	District Unit
Yeo Trogs	1968	Sept 2002	District Unit
1st Weston-S-Mare (YMCA) Jabberwocks	1968 1975	1972 2002	Group Unit Group Unit
3rd Weston-S-Mare Saints	1971 Sept 1999	1989 Sept 2002	Group Unit
17th Weston-S-Mare 'Smugglers'	1968	1975	Group Unit
19th Weston-S-Mare Celts	1968 1983	1969 July 1999	Group Unit Group Unit
24th Weston-S-Mare (Hill Road)	1968	1975	Group Unit

Smugglers	1990	1998	Group Unit
29th Weston-S-Mare Saracens	Nov 1992	July 1999	Group Unit
1st Congresbury Warlocks	1983	1987	Group Unit
1st Hutton Vikings	1983	1995	Group Unit
1st Locking (RAF) Musketeers	1983	1998	Group Unit
1st Milton Inquisitors	July 1999	Sept 2002	Group Unit
1st North Worle Barbarians	1985	1990	Group Unit
1st Winscombe Anglo-Saxons	1986	2001	Group Unit
2nd Worle Hobos Phoenix	 1986 1994	 1988 2001	 Group Unit Group Unit

Yeo Trogs

Fd: 28/05/1968 Reg No. 38826

Scarf: Black

The Yeo V.S.U, later renamed Yeo Trogs due to a VSU called Yeo in existence in Gordano, was registered in May 1968 under the leadership of Mr Michael R Bell. The original Unit comprised of seven Ventures including two from Cheddar and two from Cleeve. Over the years the Unit expanded, with Mike Bell remaining at the helm until being appointed ADC Venture Scouts. Leadership passed to Mr C Maslen. By the 1990s the position of VSL was vacant, although leadership was provided by the Faraghar brothers, John as AVSL and his brother Andrew as a Unit Helper. Paul Barnfield took out a warrant with the Unit, becoming VSL, with Mr John Faraghar continuing to assist. By the close of the 1990s the Unit had three Unit Helpers; Mr Robert Riley, Mr Simon Barnes and Mr Matthew Lee, in addition to Mr

Barnfield.[484] During the life of the Unit they met at several locations over the years, ranging from Kenn Moor to Congresbury and settling at Wrington

Smugglers V.S.U.

1968-75	17th Weston-S-Mare Scout Group (Grammar School)	
1975-1990	District Unit	Reg No. 41525
1990-1999	24th Weston-S-Mare (Hill Road)	

Smugglers D.V.S.U.

The 17th Weston 'Smugglers' were amalgamated with the 24th Weston Unit to form a District Unit called Smugglers V.S.U. in 1975, over the objections of the GSL Mr Anderson and ASL Mr J Austin of the 17th Weston (Broadoak). The 17th Weston had wished to retain the name 'Smugglers' for use in future when they hoped to reform the Unit. The Unit's proposed meeting place was at Broadoak School.[485] Mr Teale took charge of the Unit, which soon developed an interest in photography and cine film on the history of the Mendip mineral railway. The Unit rented a house in Palmer Street, where the Unit built canoes using plastic moulds and stored their equipment, as well as using the venue as a headquarters. Mr Andy Lee joined the Unit as an AVSL having moved to the resort in the early 1980s and took over from Mr Teale when he retired. The Unit continued to be popular drawing its membership from the 29th Weston (St Peter's), 24th Weston (Hill Road) and some boys from the 17th Weston Scout Groups.

---

[484] District Directories 1995 & 1998, pp. 24 & 25

[485] Correspondence with Gilwell (Gilwell Archives)

Axe Pathfinders D.V.S.U. Reg No. 41526

Fd: 1975-83

This District Venture Unit was started to cater for the southern end of town with members predominantly drawn from Hutton, Locking and the Oldmixon area. Aside from a list of warranted leaders for this District Unit little information has come to light about the activities of the Unit. The meeting place is not recorded beyond the illusive reference of meeting at the south end of town. The Unit's founding leader was Paul Cowdrey although within nine months of the April start the leadership passed briefly to Peter Stephenson. The veteran leader Dave Perriman took the reins for an eighteen month stint. Following Mr Perriman was Christopher Wood and later Alan Peake, with assistance from Andy Lee as AVSL. The Unit's final leaders were AVSLs John Singsby, whose father Alan was a leader with the 19th Weston Scout Group, Nick Ryan and Chris Brown. The Unit is recorded as disbanding in July 1983, although less than a year later Venture Scouting was restarted with a Group based Unit meeting at 1st Hutton. The previous year the 1st Locking Scout Group had opened a Unit, Musketeers, after a period of eleven years without a Venture Unit.

District Explorer Scouts

Scarf:		
	Yeo ESU	Black
	Saracens ESU	Blue with yellow trim
	North Worle	Green with scarlet border (District colours)
	Uphill	Green with scarlet border (District colours)

The changes in the national movement's age ranges which were implemented in September 2002 within the District saw the disbanding of Venture Units to be replaced by District Explorer Units. Provision was made for several cells to be located within various parts of the District. Explorer Scouts can attend any Unit meeting within the District and are not necessarily tied to one Unit although most tend to adopt a Unit as a "home unit". Anthony Mounsden briefly held the role of District Explorer Scout Commissioner before stepping down due to work commitments. Since that time the post has remained vacant.

The Yeo Explorer Unit caters for the area surrounding Congresbury, Wrington, Winscombe and Banwell and meet at Burrington & Wrington Scout HQ under the leadership of Tony Harden ESU Leader with assistance from Andy Hutchings AESU Leader, both of whom are former leaders with the Burrington & Wrington Scout Troop.

The Saracens ESU caters for the Milton and Weston area having around a dozen members under the leadership of Pete Grant ESU Leader with Neil Osborne and Christina Pople as AESU Leaders. The Unit draws most of its strength from 1st Milton Scout Group.

The North Worle ESU caters for the Worle and Banwell areas and is based at North Worle Scout HQ. The founding leader Carl Warren stepped down from ESU Leader to AESU Leader alongside Richard Dunstone also AESU Leader.

The most recent ESU is the Uphill Unit which was formed to cater for the southern end of Weston which had not previously been covered. The Unit was opened by ESU Leader Jon Aucott who had previously been an ABSL with 1st Uphill Group before moving on to become ESU Leader at the North Worle Unit. The Uphill Unit has only been operational for about a year.

The Young Leader Unit falls under the remit of the District Explorer Scout Units and is led by Andy Lee as Young Leader Unit Leader. Young Leaders are aged between 14 and 18 and must be members of a Young Leader Unit. Young Leaders are Explorer Scouts who choose to assist in other sections.[486]

[486] www.scoutbase.org.uk Young Leaders' Scheme

The District Scout Band 'The Axemen' 1983-2001

Scarf: White with a red axe on apex of scarf

The impetus for a District Scout band came from the DC Mr Mike Bell who raised the idea with Skipper Anderson (GSL of the 17th Weston Broadoak Scout Group) around Christmas 1983. Skipper Anderson's aim for the District Scout band was that it would offer Scouts the discipline of drumming, bugling and marching. The aim was to ensure that all members were proficient in both instruments, giving boys the option to be either a 'bugler/drummer or a drummer bugler', and to encourage band members to take their skills back to their respective Troops. The structure of the band was based on the patrol system, which allowed for the opportunity of leadership for members. With three 'patrols' the band at full strength would have three of each, drum majors, chief drummer and chief buglers.

Scouts who have been members of the Axemen at some point in its life include; Peter Bolger, Richard Churchill, Neil and Nigel Congram, Andrew George, Andrew and Mark Gale, Jon Godwin, Ian Griffin, Tristan Newey, Peter Tyler, Chris Bartlett, Philip Batten, Andrew Thompson, Phil Stevens, Paul Congram, Edward Thornback, Rick Hobbs, Nathaniel Tabrett, Paul Coomber, Robert Mountfort, Simon Hathaway, Robert Stokes, Tom Riley and David Pepper.

The band had a lack of funds. Skipper Anderson received a quote for £1000 to put 'a Scout band on the road', which would pose a problem for the fledgling band. To this end Skipper Anderson went round the County scrounging equipment and buying good quality old band equipment which included four side drums from the Bristol Ravens band for £150. Equipment was loaned from 3rd Weston (St. Paul's) Scout Group in the form of "four kettle drums, four side drums and one bass drum which needed an overhaul".[487] An appeal for bugles through the local press yielded a response from a Miss Higgs who offered two bugles. A further appeal on Radio Bristol led to the offer of three 'B flat' bugles for the sum of fifteen pounds from a Mr Toomer.[488]

Skipper Anderson devised a drill system of musical scoring that allowed Scouts who had little or no traditional musical training, which he referred to as "its easy when you don't know how"[489].

A venue for practising was required for the band, with the 24th Weston (Hill Road) Group HQ being made available for Saturday morning rehearsals from 9 to 10am. The leaders who assisted were Mr Derek Bendall, an ASL at 3rd Weston (St. Paul's), and a local policeman Mr Lionel Hawkins, as well as the ADC General Duties Mr Norman Underwood who 'looked in from time to time'. On May 15th 1995 the Axemen moved their rehearsals to 1st North Worle headquarters following the closure of the Hill Road Methodist church.

During the Bands existence they attended many events and acted as a great advertisement for Scouting. The band regularly attended the annual Claverham Fete for a run of six years from 1988 and St. Mark's (Worle) Fete. The Axemen provided a marching band for the Worle Remembrance Parade, as well as the Annual St George's Day Parade. One off events included the ceremony of the commemorative tree planting for the 75th birthday of Scouting in Grove Park and attending Kewstoke Fete in 1988. As part of their recruitment the Axemen regularly visited the local Scout Troops to raise their profile and to attract new members. Recruitment was a common theme in the band records with the band being keen to attract more members. In June 1990 members of the Axemen went to the National Band Championships.

---

487 Axemen Log (J A Anderson) p.1
488 Ibid pp. 1 & 2
489 Axemen Archive (J A Anderson)

Despite efforts to recruit members the Axemen's numbers dwindled in the late 1990s. The band was unable to carry on as Skipper Anderson was running the band single-handedly at this time as well as celebrating his eightieth birthday and as there was no increase in membership the decision was taken to wind up the Axemen in 2002.

Appendice A Past and Present Scout Groups

Name of Scout Group	Dates of operation	Registration Number	Scarf Colours
1st Ashcombe (Weston-Super-Mare)	01/04/00	46441	Black and Red halved
1st Milton (Weston-Super-Mare)	18/07/99	46345	Dark blue wth yellow edge
1st Weston-super-Mare (YMCA)	1909-21/10/88 21/10/88-25/08/00	10356 (BST) 4229[490]	Dark blue with light blue edge
2nd Weston-super-Mare (St Saviour's) (Etonhurst School) (Clarence Park Baptist)	15/03/10-28/02/19 28/02/19-1923 24/01/45-1947 10/01/25-1928	Not known, Not known 22514 (Gr) 15328 (BST)	
3rd Weston-super-Mare (YMCA) (St Paul's)	1910-13 21/01/14-Present	Not known BST Not Known 4365 (WCP) 4230	Maroon with gold edge
4th Weston-super-Mare (Etonhurst School) (St Saviour's)	15/03/10-28/02/19 28/02/19-21/06/66	Not known Not known (BST) 6155 (WCP) 4231	Yellow
5th Weston-super-Mare (Worlebury) (Christchurch)	24/10/10-1926 23/03/27-WWII	Not known 16070 (BST) 4232	
6th Weston-super-Mare (Kingsholme School) (Milton) (Brynmelyn School)	29/07/12-1923 19/11/24-1927 11/07/27-1933	Not known 13232 (BST) 16471 (BST) 4233	

490 Rover Crews, Boy Scout Troops and Wolf Cub Packs that were in existence in1928 were re-registered as Scout Groups in 1928 and assigned a new number. For the Groups in the Weston area a four digit number was assigned.

7th Weston-super-Mare (Christchurch) (Uphill) (Ashcombe)	 1914-24 01/06/1926-1932 19/03/34-12/01/38 1963-85	 Not known 15043 (BST) 9195 (WCP) 4234 16129 (SG)	
8th Weston-super-Mare (Worle) (Weston) (Hill Road)	 15/10/14-24 02/10/26-1927 09/08/34-31/02/39	 Not known 15110 (BST) 16528 (SG)	
9th Weston-super-Mare (Victoria Methodist) (Mendip/Emmanuel)	 1914-27 20/04/28-38	 Not known 18253 (RSC) 4235	
10th Weston-super-Mare (St Martin's Worle) (The College)	 1914-24 23/11/26-1930	 Not known 15637 (BST) 4236	
11th Weston-super-Mare	No record	Not known	
12th Weston-super-Mare (Boulevard Congregational)	 06/12/1927-34	 9977 (WCP) 4237	
13th Weston-super-Mare	No record	Not known	
14th Weston-super-Mare (Corpus Christi)	 1919-20 02/12/29-37 20/03/46-31/04/49 20/08/69-1980	 Not known 10516 (SG) 39451 (SG)	 Yellow with White edge
15th Weston-super-Mare (Petergate School)	 05/12/1929-WWII	 15043	
16th Weston-super-Mare	No record	Not known	
17th Weston-super-Mare (County, Grammar & Broadoak School)	 04/11/30-1993	 11558 (SG)	 Maroon & gold halved
18th Weston-super-Mare (Good Shepherd)	 16/10/31-06/01/37	 13225	
19th Weston-super-Mare (St Jude's) (St Jude's & Milton & Worle))	 22/02/32-1943 16/06/48-20/06/99	 13695 (SG) 26263 (SG)	 Dark blue with yellow edge
20th Weston-super-Mare (Moorland Rd) (Milton Methodist)	 02/09/32-1934 19/05/36 -1946	 14377 (SG) 20777 (SG)	

21st Weston-super-Mare (Sunnyside)	19/03/39-1947	20169 (SG) 22723 (SG)	Yellow with a green diamond on the nape
22nd Weston-super-Mare (St Peter's School)	1940-43 16/06/59-71	21971 (SG) 34545 (SG)	
23rd Weston-super-Mare	1943-44	Not Known	Operating in 1943
24th Weston-super-Mare (Hill Road)	15/06/43-25/08/00	21240 (SG)	Mauve and red halved Grey Black and Red halved
25th Weston-super-Mare (St John's)	11/04/44-1947 06/09/1949-1958	22930 (SG) 26702 (SG)	Green with a mauve edge
26th Weston-super-Mare (Holy Trinity) (Salvation Army)	22/06/44-1948 23/07/53-55	23043 (SG) 30702 (SG)	Dark blue
27th Weston-super-Mare (Salvation Army) (St Andrew's Bourneville Birnbeck)	23/09/48-53 13/06/56-1982	26592 (SG) 32646 (SG) 38312 (SG)	
28th Weston-super-Mare (Lancaster House Sch) (Holy Trinity)	09/01/58-26/05/61 26/05/61-01/04/67	33680 33680	Royal blue with a red edge
29th Weston-super-Mare (St Peter's)	21/04/64-25/08/00	36899 (SG)	Yellow with blue edge
30th Weston-super-Mare (Wadham Street)	16/06/65-1970	37397 (SG)	
31st Weston-super-Mare	04/11/69-1971	39531 (SG)	
32nd Weston-super-Mare (Oldmixon)	1970-1984	40047 (SG)	Sky blue with maroon edge

33rd Weston-super-Mare (1st Worle) **1st North Worle**	28/02/72-	40426 (SG)	Purple with white edge Purple with pale blue edge Blue with green edge
34th Weston-super-Mare (Baytree School)	1988-93	44891 (SG)	
1st Worle	05/03/38-WWII	20394 (SG)	
1st Worle Village	01/11/86-2001	44852 (SG)	Purple with white edge
2nd Worle (Meadvale)	1979-Present	43251 (SG)	Lemon with red edge
1st Axbridge	29/11/30-34 28/03/69-1993	12092 (SG) 39266 (SG)	Blue with yellow edge
Badgworth & Biddisham	1924-26	Not known	
1st Banwell	1914-1926 20/11/31-1933 11/06/47- 31/03/52- 18/06/54-1966 31/03/1969-	Not known 13357 (SG) 25391 (SG) 31398 (SG) 39273 (SG)	Red with white edge
1st Blagdon	05/04/33-1935 1994-	15110 (SG) 45756 (SG)	Green
1st Bleadon	01/04/80-01/05/03	43758 (SG)	Orange and blue halved
1st Brent Knoll	04/08/43-1958 22/10/68-	22316 (SG) 39028 (SG)	

1st Burrington	Not known 30/11/61	Not known 35833 (SG)	Red
1st Cheddar	1910-28 08/09/30-1947 27/10/49-	Not known 11747 (SG) 27723 (SG)	Yellow
1st Churchill	Not Known 15/02/30-1932	Not Known 10157 (SG)	
1st Compton Martin	16/02/34-1936 15/07/38-31/03/49	16032 (SG) 19666 (SG)	
1st Congresbury	Not Known 03/11/1924-1937 07/04/64-Present	Not Known 13068 (BST) 4207 36886 (SG)	Green with white edge
1st East Harptree	1956-67		
1st West Harptree	08/02/39 26/08/48	20018 (SG) 26538 (SG)	
Hewish Troop	Not Known	Not Known	
1st Hutton	01/08/39-WWII 27/10/49-31/03/54 05/10/72-01/10/01	20469 (SG) 27724 (SG) 40650 (SG)	Green with yellow edge
1st Langford	Not Known 24/09/29-15/02/30	Not Known 10157 (SG)	
1st Kewstoke	17/02/30-1931 26/05/88-	10901 (SG) 45054 (SG)	Yellow with green edge

1st Locking (RAF)	28/06/39-WWII 03/07/53-31/03/60 09/01/61-	20395 (SG) 30719 (SG) 35390 (SG)	Black with orange edge
1st Redhill	26/04/26-1928 04/05/39-31/03/47 05/05/53-31/03/59	14342 (BST) 20270 (SG) 20601 (SG)	Green
1st Sandford	23/01/78-2001	42626 (SG)	Brown with blue edge
1st Shipham	11/05/44-31/03/47 28/02/57-1961 1965-1983 1985-present	22005 (SG)	Brown Maroon Maroon
1st St George's	29/06/81-1986	43833 (SG)	White with red edge
1st Uphill	27/12/51-Present	29461 (SG)	Black with white edge
2nd Uphill (St Barnabas)	03/04/59-1971	34423 (SG)	
1st Wedmore	01/10/19-WWII 18/08/47-1958 14/10/65-1992 01/05/93-	4158 (BST) 4208 25534 (SG) 37522 (SG) 45667 (SG)	Red, Yellow
1st Winscombe	1913-1924 16/06/24-1937 22/03/38-WWII 11/01/66-	Not known 16612 (BST) 4210 19306 (SG) 37636 (SG)	Red with black edge
2nd Winscombe (Sidcot School)	01/06/31-1970	12770 (SG)	
1st Worle	05/03/38-WWII	20394 (SG)	

1st Wrington	29/09/23-31/03/35 17/01/25-31/03/35 05/05/41-31/03/57	11774 (BST) 7501 (WCP) 4209 21969 (SG)	Green
Yeo Trogs DVSU	1967-2002	38826	Black
Smugglers DVSU	1975-1990	41525	Black and white halved
District Explorer Unit	2002-		Green with scarlet edge
The Axemen	1983-2001		White with a red Axeon the nape

Appendice B District Commissioners 1910-2006

North West District

Colonel H T Daniels		1910-13
Colonel R Brittain D.S.O.		1913-17
Lord Wharton		1918
Colonel H T Daniels		1920-22
Position vacant		1922-27
Lt. Colonel G Flemming	O.B.E. M.C.	1927-28
Mr H V James		1928-33 (37?)
Position vacant		1937-40
Lord Teignmouth		1940
Mr A R N Joseland		1943-44
Lord Teignmouth		1945

Axe District

Colonel H Harvey	1950-63
Mr A J L White	1963-69
Mr F Haynes J.P.	1969-75
Mr E Scarlett	1975-80
Mr M Bell	1980-88
Mr M Fitch	1988-97
Mrs D Townsend	1997-99
Mr B Taylor	1999-2005
Ms M Peatman (now Heath)	2005-present

Appendice C Whitsuntide Somerset Jamborees 1929-38 & 47-73

The following list has been constructed from several Group archives. Although not every Jamboree is recorded, the majority are. The Second World War interrupted the Jamborees which were not held again until after 1945. 1974 has been chosen as the cut off date as that is when most of the District was moved out of Somerset County and became part of the newly created Avon County Council. Traditionally the camp was held over the Whitsun weekend and involved a Patrol camping competition. Avon Jamborees were held at various venues which included the County campsite at Almondsbury, Woodhouse Park, and Tyntesfield, with the permission of the late Lord Wraxall, who was a keen supporter of the Scouting movement. Details of the Avon Jamborees will be covered in a possible History of the Bristol Scouts.

Year	Venue	Year	Venue
1929	Wells	1951	Nettlecombe Court Williton
1930	Weston-super-Mare	1952	Bath
1931		1954	Williton
1932	Corsten	1955	Ammerdown, Bath
1933	Taunton	1957	Yeovil
1935	Glastonbury	1963	Amersham
1938	Bath	1966	Uphill
1947	Ilminster	1970	Taunton
1950	Burnham on Sea (May Day Weekend)	1971	Bath

Miscellaneous

Seven Counties Jamboree Corsten 1933

BP visited the great West Country Jamboree on Monday 16th May which was being held at Corsten and included Scouts and Scouters from seven counties. Amongst those attending were 3rd Weston (St Paul's), 9th Weston (Emmanuel) and 17th Weston (County School) Scout Groups.[491]

[491] 3rd Weston Group (St Paul's) Logbook & 9th Weston (Emmanuel) Troop Archive

Appendice D Axe District Membership statistics 1955-71 & 1983-93[492]

Year	No. of Groups	Beavers	Cubs	Scouts	Seniors (Inc Rovers)	Leaders (Inc Instructors)	Total
1955	12		241	209	52	48	**550**
1956	12		219	213	58	52	**542**
1957	14		257	251	51	53	**612**
1958	14		237	282	51	53	**623**
1959	14		209	277	52	53	**581**
1960	15		228	310	53	58	**649**
1961	15		222	291	45	68	**626**
1962	15		283	261	57	70	**671**
1963	15		316	275	61	64	**716**
1964	15		300	274	65	72	**711**
1965	17		300	299	69	9	**758**
1966	18		351	309	54	88	**804**
1967	17		387	296	65	98	**846**
1968	20		411	311	78	111	**911**
1969	23		506	322	58	115	**1001**
1970	23		507	404	52	139	**1102**
1971	21		584	377	56	146	**1163**
1983	17		499	370	65	126	**1060**
1984	17		474	340	80	123	**1017**
1985	17		508	414	116	133	**1171**
1986	17	18	492	445	120	151	**1226**
1987	18	15	474	378	104	145	**1101**
1988	19	54	498	391	113	149	**1205**
1989	19	92	503	312	115	159	**1181**
1990	19	112	539	365	104	161	**1281**
1991	19	91	502	353	74	173	**1193**
1992	19	121	411	379	57	188	**1153**
1993	19	185	494	399	60	186	**1324**

[492] Axe District AGM Report, Weston-S-Mare, Quantock Press, 1968-69, p.13 & Axe District Statistics 1983-93